Quality
6.95
30-99

W9-BYN-362

THE
50 Funniest Movies of All Time

NO LONGER THE PROPERTY OF
BALDWIN PUBLIC LIBRARY

THE
50 Funniest

A CITADEL PRESS BOOK

Movies of All Time
A CRITIC'S RANKING

Kathryn Bernheimer

BALDWIN PUBLIC LIBRARY

PUBLISHED BY CAROL PUBLISHING GROUP

Copyright © 1999 Kathryn Bernheimer
All rights reserved. No part of this book may be reproduced in any form, except
by a newspaper or magazine reviewer who wishes to quote brief passages in
connection with a review.

A Citadel Press Book
Published by Carol Publishing Group
Citadel Press is a registered trademark of Carol Communications, Inc.

Editorial, sales and distribution, rights and permissions inquiries should be
addressed to Carol Publishing Group, 120 Enterprise Avenue, Secaucus, N.J. 07094

In Canada: Canadian Manda Group, One Atlantic Avenue, Suite 105, Toronto,
Ontario M6K 3E7

Carol Publishing books may be purchased in bulk at special discounts for sales
promotion, fund-raising, or educational purposes. Special editions can be created
to specifications. For details, contact Special Sales Department, 120 Enterprise
Avenue, Secaucus, N.J. 07094.

Manufactured in the United States of America
10 9 8 7 6 5 4 3 2 1

Library of Congress Cataloging-in-Publication Data

Bernheimer, Kathryn.
    The 50 funniest movies of all time : a critic's ranking / Kathryn Bernheimer.
        p.   cm.
    "A Citadel Press book."
    Includes bibliographical references.
    ISBN 0–8065–2091–4 (pbk.)
    1. Comedy films—History and criticism. I. Title. II. Title:
Fifty funniest movies of all time.
PN1995.9.C55B45   1999
791.43′617—dc21   98–53838
                                                                CIP

To Shayna and Naomi, whose laughter lights my life

Contents

Acknowledgments

Almost everyone I spoke with while working on this book told me, in no uncertain terms, that I had better include his or her favorite comedy. All of these invaluable suggestions were taken under advisement and helped spur my enthusiasm for the project, which elicited a surprisingly passionate reaction from fellow movie lovers, who clearly take comedy very seriously.

In particular, I owe heartfelt thanks to Scott Woodland, owner of the Boulder Video Station. Scott not only operates the best video store in the known universe—without which I wouldn't have been able to view many of the lesser-known comedy contenders—but also served as an eminently reliable sounding board. I am also grateful to my former editor and mentor, Jim Ellison, for his unwavering support. I count myself extremely fortunate to have found a knowledgeable and enthusiastic partner in editor Gary Goldstein, with whom it has been a joy to work. It has also been a great pleasure and **privilege to work with Lynn Seligman, my agent and friend in need.**

Introduction

Humor, like so many of life's great pleasures, is highly subjective. Although everyone loves a good laugh, some folks guffaw at slapstick while others chuckle with glee at witty wordplay. Anyone with enough hubris to rank the all-time funniest films has to accept that such an undertaking is bound to evoke strenuous disagreement from anyone whose taste differs one iota from their own, which is every person who draws breath.

Although this ranking of the world's most cherished comedies, created by the cinema's most beloved and brilliant humorists, has been designed to serve as a critical retrospective of a century of screen humor, there's no use trying to deny that personal preference played a part in my selections. In my defense, I must point out that my taste is quite eclectic and far ranging, which I believe is a prerequisite for any film critic. A critic who likes only musicals and romantic comedies and uniformly detests violence, for example, can not be of much service to the moviegoing public.

In order to encompass a wide variety of tastes, this book extols the virtues of the best examples of satire, farce, slapstick, parody, screwball comedy, romantic comedy, and black comedy, all of which I admire. Still, saying that I like all kinds of comedies is not the same as saying that I like all styles and genres—or their practitioners—equally.

For example, I am particularly fond of black comedy, which accounts for the preponderance of such dark delights as *Dr. Strangelove, M*A*S*H, Harold and Maude, The Ladykillers, After Hours,* and *Prizzi's Honor.* I had to restrain myself from adding several other notable examples of the genre, including one of my favorites, Chaplin's *Monsieur Verdoux,* which in the end I decided was just one black comedy too many. Other caustic comedies that didn't make the cut include Woody Allen's *Stardust Memories;* Robin Williams in *Good Morning, Vietnam;* Robert Altman's *The Player;* Alan Arkin's *Little Murders* and *Catch-22;* the Coen brothers' *Fargo;* Mike Nichols's *Postcards From the Edge;* Barry Sonnenfeld's *Get Shorty;* Tony Richardson's *The Loved One;*

Peter Sellers in *The Mouse That Roared;* Frank Capra's *Arsenic and Old Lace;* Alexander Mackendrick's *Tight Little Island* (a.k.a. *Whisky Galore*), and all the other Ealing Studios comedies.

As this list reveals, I favor acerbic wit and biting (even bitter) humor. Daring films that tackle serious subjects are dear to my heart, and I don't mind being made a little uncomfortable by comedy. That, I would argue, is one of humor's many invaluable functions. Humor is a mighty weapon that, in the right hands, can be used to attack our societal assumptions and lay bare the follies of human nature. Rebellion is a key element in comedy, which is frequently used to challenge authority and the prevailing wisdom. Clearly some of the world's most memorable comedies were perfectly attuned to the zeitgeist, reflecting a radical shift taking place in the culture.

Although I am a sucker for sharp-witted satires such as *This Is Spinal Tap* and *Monty Python and the Holy Grail* and finely played farces such as *The In-Laws, The Court Jester,* and *Soapdish,* I also have a soft spot for affectionate, effervescent, and embracing comedies. *Moonstruck, When Harry Met Sally. . . , Bull Durham, King of Hearts, The Gods Must Be Crazy, Local Hero, The Full Monty,* and *Annie Hall* are all heartwarming comedies that reveal the emotionally uplifting power of humor. Many of the cinema's most enduring comedies take potent advantage of humor's capacity to gladden our hearts.

While I also enjoy pure slapstick, I generally prefer comedies that blend physical humor with verbal wit. For that reason I am not as keen on Jerry Lewis as I am on the Marx Brothers or even the Pink Panther films. I also adore physical comedy that is tempered with pathos and poetry, which is why Charlie Chaplin and Buster Keaton rank higher in my regard than Laurel and Hardy or Abbott and Costello. All of the above-mentioned comedy legends are, of course, represented in this survey of film comedy.

Because this book serves as an homage to the world's great screen humorists, I struggled to find a Bob Hope movie that could be considered a great comedy. *Son of Paleface* and *The Road to Utopia* came close, but I couldn't summon sufficient enthusiasm for them. I also fully intended to include at least one comedy by Robin Williams, who is the Bob Hope of our generation—and in my opinion not only much funnier, but a much better actor. But for some reason Williams has done his best work in more serious films, such as *Dead Poets Society, The Fisher King, Awakenings,* and *Good Will Hunting,* rather than in his pure comedies, such as *Mrs. Doubtfire, The Birdcage,* and *Flubber.* Since I decided not to include comic dramas, I was also forced to eliminate my top Williams choice, *Good Morning, Vietnam.*

If I had expanded my definition of the world's funniest films to include comic dramas, I would surely have chosen classics such as *The Graduate,*

The Apartment, Sunset Boulevard, All About Eve, One Flew Over the Cuckoo's Nest, Mr. Smith Goes to Washington, Forrest Gump, Guess Who's Coming to Dinner?, and possibly even *Pulp Fiction*.

Because I find literate dialogue so appealing and treasure clever comedies with vivid characters and well-written stories, I had an especially difficult time narrowing down the list of classic comedies from the 1930s and 1940s, a glorious period when intelligent and sophisticated filmmakers ruled a glittering comedy kingdom. One of my greatest regrets—and arguably my most egregious omission—was not including *The Philadelphia Story*. I also might well have added *The Awful Truth*, one of the Thin Man comedies, *Topper*, and *The Front Page* to the films culled from the golden age of screen comedy.

In an effort to include a healthy balance of genres and periods and to include work by all the great comic directors and stars, I limited myself to one film by each of the great directors of classical comedies. I picked Preston Sturges's wackiest comedy, *The Lady Eve*, although *Sullivan's Travels, The Miracle of Morgan's Creek, Palm Beach Story,* and *Unfaithfully Yours* were all given consideration and not found wanting. I couldn't very well overlook Frank Capra's legendary romantic comedy *It Happened One Night*, although it meant forgoing his whimsical Oscar-winning celebration of eccentricity, *You Can't Take It With You*.

I opted for Howard Hawks's definitive screwball comedy *Bringing Up Baby* after considering his other strong contenders, *Twentieth Century* and *His Girl Friday*. Although Ernst Lubitsch's *Ninotchka* and *Heaven Can Wait* tempted me, I gave in to his more controversial and risky comedy, *To Be or Not to Be*, featuring Jack Benny in his best screen performance. I also couldn't resist Judy Holliday's brilliant performance as a not-so-dumb blonde in George Cukor's *Born Yesterday*, although it meant eliminating Cukor's *The Philadelphia Story*. Besides, I reasoned, I already had one Katharine Hepburn-Cary Grant comedy (*Bringing Up Baby*) and one Jimmy Stewart comedy (*Harvey*). If I had picked another Hepburn comedy, it would have been one of her Spencer Tracy pairings, probably *Adam's Rib* or *Pat and Mike*, both also directed by Cukor.

It was also pure agony restricting myself to one Charlie Chaplin comedy. *Modern Times* and *The Gold Rush* were close runners-up to *City Lights*. Similarly, the Marx Brothers' *Duck Soup* narrowly edged out *Animal Crackers, A Night at the Opera,* and *Horse Feathers*. It was only a little less difficult choosing between Buster Keaton's slightly funnier *Sherlock Jr.* and his more satisfying masterpiece, *The General*.

Picking the top film, however, was surprisingly easy. Billy Wilder is, in my opinion, the finest comedy writer and director of the modern era. Although *The Apartment* is an undeniably great comic drama and I hold *Irma La Douce, Stalag 17, Sabrina,* and *The Seven Year Itch* in the highest regard, I have never seen a more perfectly realized comedy—or a funnier one—than *Some Like It Hot.*

If I had a hard time narrowing the field of classic comedies, selecting the best of the contemporary crop of comedies was absolutely excruciating. Comedy, it has been said, is best appreciated in retrospect. Who can know which of today's favorites will stand the test of time? I was enormously relieved to find that *A Fish Called Wanda* was as funny as I remembered it. I happen to be a big fan of the Coen brothers, despite their erratic output, and was happy to discover how well *Raising Arizona* held up. I included 1997's *The Full Monty* because I almost fell off my chair laughing when I first saw it, which is more than can be said of most recent comedies, and I laughed almost as hard on a second viewing. I did consider and do recommend such recent youth-oriented crowd pleasers as *Clueless, Reality Bites, Flirting With Disaster,* and *There's Something About Mary* and the more mature comedies *As Good as It Gets* and *Wag the Dog.*

I made sure to include a film by Steve Martin (*All of Me*), John Belushi (*Animal House*), Billy Crystal (*When Harry Met Sally. . .*), and Eddie Murphy (*Beverly Hills Cop*). Whoopi Goldberg (*Sister Act*) has only a small role in *Soapdish,* and Bill Murray (*Groundhog Day*) is a supporting player in *Tootsie,* but at least these two very funny comedy stars are represented. I could not, however, squeeze in the talented Richard Pryor, whose best work is in his concert films. After watching *Stir Crazy* and *Silver Streak* again, I concluded they were not as funny as the action comedy *Beverly Hills Cop,* which I included, or even *Midnight Run,* which I did not.

I also regret not being able to find a place for Dan Aykroyd, who was very funny in Hollywood's first big-budget scare comedy, *Ghostbusters,* and in his teaming with Belushi in *The Blues Brothers.* I was also tempted to include Albert Brooks's *Defending Your Life,* but concluded that despite its hilarious moments it was too uneven.

Every time I reluctantly set aside a comedy I liked to make room for one I enjoyed even more, I contented myself by making reference to the near misses in the appropriate places. Each review in this book will guide you to other films by the artists who created them or to movies with similar styles or subjects. For example, *Some Like It Hot* will refer you to other films by Billy Wilder, Marilyn Monroe, Jack Lemmon, and Tony Curtis, as well as to other cross-dressing comedies such as *Tootsie, Victor/Victoria,* and *La Cage Aux Folles.*

Although the family comedy is not really a distinct genre, many of the funniest films of various comedy styles are suitable for all ages. I revisited several hundred comedies as I researched this book, and my eight-year-old daughter, Shayna, watched many of them with me. She proved a shrewd judge of film comedy. We spent many an evening laughing together as I shared classics from the past with her. I was surprised and delighted by what she found funny, as well as by what comedies held the attention of her little sister, Naomi. Parents looking for films to watch with their children might well consider digging into the comedy treasure trove. For the record, Shayna's favorite comedies in this book were *Some Like It Hot, What's Up, Doc?, Duck Soup, Tootsie, All of Me, Abbott and Costello Meet Frankenstein, Airplane!, The Pink Panther Strikes Again, My Little Chickadee,* and *Raising Arizona.*

It is my hope you will share the rib-tickling, side-splitting, thigh-slapping comedies in this book with your children, your parents, your friends, and your loved ones. And when you're all alone, there's no better company than a good comedy. May this book bring the gift of laughter into your life.

THE
50 Funniest Movies of All Time

1

Some Like It Hot

United Artists (1959)
CAST: Jack Lemmon, Tony Curtis, Marilyn Monroe,
Joe E. Brown, George Raft, Pat O'Brien
DIRECTED BY: Billy Wilder
119 minutes [Not rated]

Some Like It Hot has everything you could possibly want from a comedy and more. It has men wearing dresses and Marilyn Monroe wearing next to nothing. It has gangsters and show tunes, hilarious sight gags and even funnier dialogue, slapstick and romance, an ingenious, risqué premise, and the best closing line of any film comedy in history.

It is a subversive satire of Hollywood clichés and a sardonic spoof of sexual stereotypes, perfectly cast and expertly acted. A singular screen comedy triumph, Billy Wilder's cynical, scintillating comedy centers on a pair of musicians (Jack Lemmon and Tony Curtis) in 1929 Chicago who witness the St. Valentine's Day Massacre and take refuge in an all-girl jazz band bound for Miami to avoid being rubbed out by the Mob.

Some Like It Hot, one of the most continually popular and universally admired comedies in history, has been called "one of the most durable treasures of sound comedy," "sensational from start to finish," "one of the imperishable joys of film comedy," and "one of the better illustrations of dark, inverted film comedy." It is the first comedy listed in the American Film Institute's 1998 poll that ranks the top one hundred films of all time. With four films in the top one hundred, Wilder is also the most represented comedy director on the list.

The legendary, landmark comedy is also credited with opening new sexual ground in America as it tested the limits of audience tolerance for openly sexual films as the conservative, repressive 1950s were drawing to a close. Although the film caused discomfort in some viewers and critics, its astounding critical and popular success can, in part, be attributed to its overt rebellion against the tedium, conformity, and propriety of the era. Raucous and ribald, the film offered audiences a welcome escape from the constricting conventions of life on and off the screen.

By 1959 Wilder was the most successful director in Hollywood, having earned acclaim for *Double Indemnity,* a 1944 film noir that inspired *Body Heat;* his 1945 multi-Academy Award–winning *The Lost Weekend,* a landmark drama dealing with alcoholism; *A Foreign Affair,* a 1948 romantic comedy starring Marlene Dietrich and Jean Arthur; the bitterly humorous *Sunset Boulevard* (1950); the seminal antiwar dramatic comedy *Stalag 17* (1953); *Sabrina,* a 1954 romantic comedy starring Audrey Hepburn (which was remade in 1995); and the classic Marilyn Monroe comedy *The Seven Year Itch* (1955). Considered the last in the line of sophisticated auteurs that included Lubitsch, Capra, Hawks, and Sturges, Wilder was already well known for tackling taboo subjects and for ridiculing cultural and cinematic clichés of romance and success. He had pioneered military black comedy in *Stalag 17* (the basis for the TV sitcom *Hogan's Heroes*) and unleashed a scathingly funny yet poignant attack on Hollywood in *Sunset Boulevard,* for which he won an Oscar for best screenplay.

The director, an educated Jewish refugee and former journalist from Vienna, began his Hollywood career as a screenwriter, coauthoring (with Walter Brackett) Ernst Lubitsch's *Ninotchka* and Howard Hawks's *Ball of Fire.* Wilder, who continued to cowrite all his scripts when he began directing in 1942 with *The Major and the Minor,* took on some risky subjects in *Some Like It Hot.* The entire comedy is built on an elaborate and brilliantly sustained masquerade by its male stars, who spend most of the film in drag. It mixes the issues of transvestism, impotence, alcoholism, and gangland murder into its outrageous story of multiple deceptions and ever-escalating moral deceit.

Curtis, a pretty-boy actor who had won an Oscar for *The Defiant Ones* in 1958, may have been cast for his looks but proved remarkably proficient in his first pure comedy. Curtis plays a smooth-talking, saxophone-playing cad named Joe who easily metamorphoses into Josephine. Later, in order to woo the band's beautiful, boozy singer Sugar Kane (Monroe), Joe dons yet another disguise, masquerading as the kind of tame, dopey millionaire Sugar has described as her dream man. Adding another layer of deception, Joe, posing as the Shell Oil heir, pretends to be impotent so that softhearted Sugar will attempt to seduce him, which she does in one of the movie's most memorable and raciest scenes.

The final layer of pretense in Joe's charade is his impeccable Cary Grant impression. The idea of mimicking Hollywood's romantic male icon and undisputed master of screwball comedy, which originated with Curtis, deepens the astringent comedy's commentary on sexual stereotypes. Because Monroe was already an icon and a clichéd stereotype of female sexuality, pitting her against a phony Cary Grant—her male equivalent—was nothing short of pure genius.

RUNNING WILD   Tony Curtis, far left, Jack Lemmon, center, with cello, and Marilyn Monroe in Billy Wilder's *Some Like It Hot*. Curtis said his love scenes with Monroe were "like kissing Hitler." Monroe was not amused.

Other icons associated in the public's mind with certain genres and character types were similarly cast in this good-natured parody of Hollywood conventions. Tough-guy George Raft (*Scarface*) plays the feared gangster Spats Columbo, and frequent Irish cop Pat O'Brien costars as the federal agent on his tail. There are numerous Hollywood in-jokes peppered throughout the script, such as Raft deriding another mobster's coin tossing—which was Raft's own signature bit of business. When Jerry (Lemmon) first hears Joe doing his impeccable Cary Grant impersonation, he protests, "No one talks like that."

Jack Lemmon, who had won a best supporting actor Oscar for his role as the irrepressibly lecherous Ensign Pulver in *Mister Roberts* but was not yet a box office star, was Wilder's first choice as Jerry. Lemmon indeed gave what is generally considered the finest of several superlative performances in the film. Lemmon went on to work with Wilder the next year in *The Apartment*, for which Wilder became the second person in history to collect three Oscars in one night (for picture, director, and screenplay). The two men collaborated on five more film comedies, including *Irma La Douce* and *The Fortune Cookie*, which was the first film pairing of Lemmon and Walter Matthau.

Lemmon's Jerry is a study in sexual frustration. Disguised as Daphne, Jerry is like a kid in a candy shop—except that the sweets are strictly forbidden if he wants to maintain his deception and stay alive. In a capriciously comic turn of events, however, Jerry begins to warm to the role of Daphne, especially after "she" begins to be courted by a real millionaire, Osgood Fielding III. The lustily determined and blithely eccentric Osgood is wonderfully played by veteran comedian Joe E. Brown, who had frequently appeared in drag earlier in his screen career.

The film's comic highlight is the night on the town Daphne spends with Osgood, as they dance a wild, liberating tango. Returning from the pleasurable tryst, Daphne gaily announces, "I'm engaged!" Joe replies, "Who's the lucky girl?" "I am," Daphne responds, shaking her maracas euphorically. Jerry has clearly stepped over some invisible cross-dressing line, becoming his female alter ego, which gooses the sexual confusion that runs through the film. When Joe presses on, asking why a guy would marry another guy, Daphne speaks for women everywhere when, without missing a beat, she answers, "Security." Later, when Joe asks if the diamond bracelet Osgood has given Daphne is genuine, Daphne snaps, "Of course! Do you think my fiancé is a bum?"

Even today this unsettling gender bender carries a kick as it takes delicious delight in its sexual ambiguity. Osgood's startling final line, his unflappable response to Daphne's revelation that she's a man—"No one's perfect"—must have provided quite a jolt to audiences in 1959. The famous line, incidentally, was just a temporary idea cowriter and frequent Wilder collaborator I. A. L. Diamond suggested until he and Wilder could think of something better. Luckily, they never did.

Wilder, who began his career as a screenwriter, always cowrote his own screenplays. With the 1957 romantic comedy *Love in the Afternoon,* Wilder began a long and fruitful association with Diamond, a former math champion who had changed his first name, Izzy, to I. A. L., which stood for the Interscholastic Algebra League, of which he had been champion in 1936. Wilder once said of Diamond, "If I ever lost this guy, I'd feel like Abercrombie without Fitch."

Some Like It Hot, Wilder and Diamond's shocking assault on conventional morality, had one of the worst first previews in screen history. Only one person in the audience laughed. One of the century's most astute judges of comedy, Steve Allen, sitting in the front row, was the only one to find the future classic funny. Despite the disastrous screening, Wilder cut only one short scene. The film went on to earn rave reviews—*Time* magazine hailed it as the best comedy of the year—and became the third-highest-grossing film of 1959.

Come Oscar time, however, the comedy had the misfortune of competing against *Ben-Hur,* which still holds the record for the most Oscars (eleven) ever won by a film. The Hollywood foreign press bestowed a Golden Globe for best musical/comedy on the film and awarded its best actor award to Lemmon and best actress award to Monroe.

In the years since its release, *Some Like It Hot* has been often imitated but never bettered. *Tootsie* came the closest, picking up on the theme of a man becoming a better human being by spending time inside a woman's body and mind. The 1978 French hit comedy *La Cage Aux Folles* and Blake Edwards's *Victor/Victoria* (1982) continued to push the cross-dressing envelope with hilarious results. Tom Hanks also enjoyed some success starring in the TV sitcom *Bosom Buddies,* based on a similar premise. *Some Like It Hot* was also remade as a successful Broadway musical, *Sugar.*

Much of the credit for the daringly outrageous yet ultimately tasteful comedy lies with Wilder. One of Wilder's consistent accomplishments was his ability to engender audience sympathy for disreputable or unsavory characters, which gave his comedies emotional depth and a biting edge. His greatest triumph in this regard is *Irma La Douce,* the story—cowritten by Diamond—of an unrepentant Parisian prostitute (Shirley MacLaine), which was one of his biggest smash hits. In Wilder and Diamond's masterful, tough-minded, and sharp-witted comedy *The Apartment,* Lemmon plays an ambitious "schnook" who allows his apartment to be used for the assignations of executives who promise him promotion in return for his part in their extramarital affairs.

Joe and Jerry are by no means exemplary characters, yet we root for them every step of the way. Jerry is something of a sap who allows himself to be bullied by Joe, who in turn is exactly the kind of selfish scoundrel Sugar says she always has the misfortune of falling for. Only after getting to know Sugar as her "sister" does Joe realize that "no man is worth" the suffering Sugar has been through.

Sugar is also a sad character, really, a weak, vulnerable, abused woman lost in a haze of vermouth—which, in real life, Monroe reportedly brought to the set in a thermos as she engaged in her famously unprofessional behavior during the filming.

Nonetheless, as even the frustrated, furious Wilder had to admit, Monroe's performance was transcendent. Although an equally outraged Curtis compared his love scenes with Monroe to "kissing Hitler," Monroe gave one of the best performances of her career as the sultry singer in *Some Like It Hot.* Her rendition of "I'm Through with Love" offers a trenchant, poignant moment of Monroe at her finest.

One of the reasons *Some Like It Hot* is so consistently funny is that both Curtis and Lemmon, while not entirely convincing as women, are actually quite successful in creating realistic female characters with distinct personalities. Wilder decided to shoot the film in black and white to make the men in drag less garish and more believable. A drag queen was hired to tutor the stars, but much of the inspiration for Daphne and Josephine came from the actors, who both report they relished the challenge of playing men playing women.

Performed with joyful abandon, *Some Like It Hot* threw caution and convention to the wind. It remains a glorious demonstration of Wilder's consummate skill and a validation of his reputation as the most wickedly witty director in screen history. As its frequent revivals indicate, audiences continue to like it hot.

2

City Lights

United Artists (1931)
CAST: **Charles Chaplin, Virginia Cherrill, Harry Myers**
DIRECTED BY: **Charles Chaplin**
86 minutes [Not rated]

For proof of Charles Chaplin's inestimable contribution to the cinema, we need look no further than the term "Chaplinesque"—an adjective describing Chaplin's patented formula of one part pathos to two parts comedy—which has entered the English vocabulary as the highest form of compliment.

City Lights is Chaplin's most perfect blending of humor and poignancy, a fact that was not lost on the critics of the day. "Excruciatingly funny and terribly, terribly sad," wrote the reviewer for the *New York Daily News* in 1931. Subsequent critics have been no less enthusiastic. "The triumph of motion and emotion," wrote mime Dan Kamin. "The most ingeniously formed and immaculately interlocked of Chaplin's experiments combining comedy with pathos," gushed Walter Kerr. "Chaplin goes only so far with sentiment, then makes his getaway with a gag," Roger Ebert notes in his glowing review of *City Lights.*

City Lights, which Chaplin had begun to work on in 1928 after his mother's death, was his first film to be released after the advent of sound. It contained no spoken dialogue, relying instead on the artist's celebrated skill at pantomime, but it did have a score composed and conducted by Chaplin as well as numerous sound effects. Although by 1931 audiences were accustomed to talking pictures, they flocked to *City Lights,* which earned Chaplin the greatest adulation since his first feature-length film, *The Kid* (1921), and became the fourth-highest-grossing film of the year.

City Lights begins with an ingenious unveiling of the Little Tramp, the cherished child-poet character Chaplin had created in 1914 in the one-reeler *Making a Living* and continued to play for the next twenty-six years. In his 1964 autobiography Chaplin describes how he hastily assembled the tramp's famed costume, deliberately formed of contradictions: baggy pants and tight coat, small hat and big shoes. Chaplin claims the character evolved automatically and instantly once he put on the costume, which he wore in what is

BRIGHT LIGHTS, BIG CITY Charlie Chaplin as—what else?—the Little Tramp, and Virginia Cherrill as the blind flower girl in *City Lights*, the first Chaplin film released after the advent of sound.

considered his first masterpiece, *The Tramp* (1915). Chaplin recalls immediately recognizing the potential for the character, "a poet, a dreamer, a lonely fellow, always hopeful of romance and adventure." Part outcast and part rebel, part Bohemian and part hobo, the tramp was a symbol of both freedom and loneliness.

The inspired opening scene of *City Lights* finds a crowd gathered for the dedication of a huge new white marble sculpture. When the cloths draping the monument are lifted, the tramp is discovered sleeping peacefully, curled up in the lap of one figure. The wistful vagrant's efforts to extricate himself from his humiliation before the outraged crowd prove futile, as a giant sword becomes lodged in the seat of his pants. For the onlookers, the tramp's actions are a desecration. For the audience, they are an example of Chaplin thumbing his nose at the pretensions of polite society.

The scene also established the film's themes: the disparity of wealth and poverty; dignity and indignity; the vagaries of fortune; and the fickle nature of fate. One of the reasons Chaplin is regarded as the greatest film artist in motion picture history is that his marvelously funny comedies were beautifully constructed around serious themes that allowed for deep emotion.

While Buster Keaton was the stone-faced fatalist and Harold Lloyd the clean-cut nice guy who gamely rose to the challenges before him, Chaplin was an emotive actor who conveyed a wide range of feeling through facial expression and body language. He laughed, cried, sighed; showed fear, pain, anger, and pity. Playing impoverished and disenfranchised outsiders—a reflection no doubt of the physical and emotional hardships of his childhood—Chaplin earned huge audience sympathy. We never laugh *at* Chaplin, always *with* him.

Chaplin's ability to bring emotional depth to slapstick comedy is most perfectly displayed in *City Lights*, in which the tramp falls in love with a beautiful blind flower girl (Virginia Cherrill) and resolves to help her despite his own destitute state. His tenderness and tenacity are touching as he undertakes a series of improbable—and hilarious—schemes to make money, including prizefighting. The brilliant balletic staging of the boxing match is one of the film's rightly famous set pieces.

The tramp's luck seems about to change when he takes pity on a distraught, drunken millionaire (Harry Myers), whom he saves from suicide, almost drowning in the process. The grateful gentleman invites the tramp home to his mansion, where Charlie becomes humorously intoxicated. The next morning, however, the sober millionaire wants nothing more to do with his savior.

Meanwhile, the flower girl is under the mistaken impression that the tramp is a millionaire, adding another layer in the film's contrast between wealth and poverty. The cruelty of fate is underscored when the millionaire, once again inebriated, embraces his best friend, who again finds himself out in the cold after being ushered temporarily into the lap of luxury.

The final blow comes when the millionaire agrees to give the tramp $1,000 for an operation to restore the flower girl's sight. But because burglars break into the mansion, it is assumed Charlie stole the money, and he narrowly makes his escape. He succeeds in giving the money to his beloved but is apprehended and sent to jail. Upon his release, the shabby and despondent indigent comes upon a fancy flower shop and the woman he loves, who is no longer blind. When he stops and stares, she tries to give the beggar, a man she's never "seen," a few coins. Pressing them into his hands, she recognizes the hands that performed so many kind deeds for her. What will she think of her knight in tarnished armor? "You can see now?" he asks. "Yes, I can see now," she says, gazing at the hopeful yet forlorn face in front of her. The film ends ambiguously with the close-up of Chaplin's expression of pain and pleasure.

Much of the humor in *City Lights* derives from the tramp's many faux pas when he is admitted to high society and attempts to emulate the millionaire. In one especially funny act of misdirected valor, the tramp attempts to "rescue" a woman from her abusive partner during an apache dance at a nightclub.

The milestone movie is a comedy of mores and manners that hinges on the instability of life during the Depression. The theme of chance is beautifully illustrated in a bit of business in which the tramp stops to examine a store window. Every time he steps back to get a better angle on the statue he is admiring, a freight elevator rises just in time to prevent him from falling into the hole behind him. We expect the gag to end with a plummet. But fate smiles on our little hero this happy day, and he emerges unknowingly victorious over the impending disaster. Whether he will be so lucky when it comes to being rewarded for bestowing the gift of sight on his beloved is a question the film leaves open. Clearly, however, the tramp's decision to sacrifice his own desires for hers is presented as ineffably admirable.

Chaplin's next project, another semisilent film released after a five-year hiatus, was an even more direct social satire, coupled with an old-fashioned romance. *Modern Times,* which boasts the funniest fifteen-minute opening of any Chaplin film, satirizes the dehumanizing mechanization as well as the utter instability of modern life.

Chaplin finally broke his silence in the provocative and controversial black comedy *The Great Dictator* (1940), the first Hollywood film to directly challenge Hitler and his anti-Semitic policies. Chaplin got into even more hot water playing a wife murderer in the rich, darkly funny, unjustly overlooked comedy *Monsieur Verdoux* (1947), a film that caused consternation in its day but holds up extremely well. Chaplin left America in 1952, after *Limelight,* and spent the rest of his life in self-imposed exile. He returned to America only once, in 1972, to receive an Oscar for his "incalculable effect" on film art.

Chaplin, who wrote, directed, and starred in a remarkable series of film comedies during his forty-year heyday, began his unparalleled career at the age of twenty-five, already a seasoned veteran. Born to musical hall entertainers, Chaplin was a child stage star before signing on to work with Mack Sennett in 1914. After cutting his teeth at Keystone, Chaplin began to work independently and formed United Artists Studio with Mary Pickford, Douglas Fairbanks, and D. W. Griffith in 1919. He scored a huge critical and popular success in 1925 with *The Gold Rush,* the film Chaplin said he most wanted to be remembered for. The American Film Institute's ranking of the one hundred best films of all time places *The Gold Rush* in seventy-fourth place, with *City Lights* seventy-sixth and *Modern Times* eighty-first.

Chaplin won a special Oscar in 1927 for "versatility and genius in writing, directing, acting, and producing *The Circus.*" A peerless performer, Chaplin was also an accomplished and perfectionistic film technician. He shot hundreds of takes and spent months editing. His shooting ratio was an unheard-of one hundred to one. Chaplin always took his time, paying equal attention to the quality of form and content.

During his day he was championed by Alexander Woollcott, James Agee, and George Bernard Shaw, who called him "the only genius developed in motion pictures." Chaplin, who brought poetry to comedy, was also revered by his peers. Stan Laurel called him "the greatest film artist that was ever on the screen." Buster Keaton deemed him "the greatest artist that ever lived." W. C. Fields was the only one to openly acknowledge the jealousy that tempered his admiration: "He's the best ballet dancer that ever lived, and if I get a chance, I'll kill him with my bare hands."

3

Duck Soup

Paramount (1933)
CAST: Groucho, Harpo, Chico, and Zeppo Marx, Margaret Dumont
DIRECTED BY: Leo McCarey
70 minutes [Not rated]

Animal Crackers has Groucho's best monologues and his most cherished incarnation, Captain Spaulding. *A Night at the Opera* has the classic crowded stateroom scene and "the party of the first part" shtick. *The Cocoanuts* has the priceless "viaduct/why a duck" routine, Groucho's land auction bit, and Irving Berlin's music.

But *Duck Soup* has more of the Marx Brothers' frantic antics than any of the films made by the free-spirited iconoclasts during the twenty-one years they spent staging a full-front comic assault on all that American society holds sacred. *Duck Soup* is the Marx Brothers' purest comedy, undiluted by the silly romantic subplots and musical interludes that clog up their other films. It is the shortest, fastest, darkest, and most furiously focused of their thirteen movies, all of which remain eminently entertaining more than half a century after they first tickled the nation's fancy, appealing to intellectuals and low-brows alike.

The inimitably zany Marx Brothers were at their unbridled best in *Duck Soup,* the only Marx Brothers comedy listed in the American Film Institute's ranking of the one hundred best films of all time. This cheerfully demented comedy, written by Bert Kalmar and Harry Ruby, casts Groucho as the improbable ruler of the fictitious and fractious nation of Freedonia. It was the fifth and final film they made at Paramount, and its enduring appeal must be credited partly to strong direction by Leo McCarey, the man who launched the career of Laurel and Hardy and went on to win Oscars for *The Awful Truth* and *Going My Way.* Although the unruly Marx Brothers exerted less artistic control over their films than Keaton, Chaplin, or Lloyd, they enjoyed spontaneity, took a strong hand in shaping their material, and were considered "undirectable." McCarey also had forged a formidable reputation as a strong-willed and creative director. The result of this collaboration is a tight film that still feels spontaneous.

HAIL, FREEDONIA! Harpo Marx, left, Chico Marx, center, and Groucho Marx, right, in *Duck Soup.* Though it was a box office disappointment upon its release in 1934 (and nearly ended the Marx Brothers' film career), *Duck Soup* is revered today for its irreverent look at politics and government.

Another contribution McCarey made was his inventive showcasing of Harpo's unique talents. McCarey has said that because of his work in silent film and his tendency to think visually, he liked Harpo best. Harpo is given some wonderful pieces of business in *Duck Soup,* most famously in the mirror scene in which he shadows Groucho and does an excellent impression of his younger brother. McCarey also wisely cast Laurel and Hardy veteran Edgar Kennedy as the owner of a lemonade stand who engages in a hilarious running battle with Harpo and Chico.

Although today *Duck Soup* is revered for its relevant satire of government, its blistering pace, and its unrestrained and unrelieved humor, the movie did only middling business in 1933 and was not well received by the critics. *Variety* complained that the jokes came too fast and furious—an inane comment that calls to mind the accusation that Mozart's music had too many notes in *Amadeus.* The *New York Times* predicted that the Marx Brothers were all washed up.

The next year the popular success of *A Night at the Opera* proved that the

Times's opinion was not infallible. *Duck Soup* and *A Night at the Opera* are the only two Marx Brothers movies owned by the Museum of Modern Art. *A Night at the Opera* is indeed their second funniest film—and gets funnier if you fast-forward through the singing. Somehow arias don't seem to mix well with the absurdist, anarchic sensibility of the Marx Brothers.

Duck Soup is blissfully devoid of the supporting structures that comedy teams were thought to need in the 1930s. Today audiences prefer their comedy straight up, but in the golden age of Hollywood it was assumed that nonstop monkey business was too much of a good thing, and comedians were primarily charged with providing comic relief rather than trusted to carry the full weight of a movie. Not so *Duck Soup*, which put the burden squarely on Groucho's famously stooped shoulders. Here the backdrop functions not as a distraction from the Marx Brothers' mad mayhem, but as a target for their lacerating wit and gives rise to the inspired lunacy that plays out in front of it.

Margaret Dumont, that pigeon-breasted, imperious matron who served as the perfect Marx Brothers foil in seven of their films, is cast as the heiress who will donate money to Freedonia only if Rufus T. Firefly is appointed leader of the beleaguered nation. Groucho's Firefly swarms in to the solemn stateroom, annoying the diplomats and dignitaries with his indecorous manner and clearly disreputable air. An impertinent impostor, the rumpled, fast-talking swindler quickly deflates the pomp and circumstance around him.

The Marx Brothers, who grew up in poverty in the Jewish ghetto of Manhattan's Yorkville section, were forever crashing the gates of polite society. Urged on by their mother, Minnie Marx, Leonard (Chico), Adolph (Harpo), Julius (Groucho), Milton (Gummo), and Herbert (Zeppo) began their show business careers while still in their teens.

After finding early success in vaudeville, the brothers found even greater favor as a team on the Broadway stage. Gummo quit the act early, but the remaining four were still starring in *Animal Crackers* on Broadway when they began filming their earlier stage success, *The Cocoanuts*, in 1929. Three more films followed in quick succession: *Animal Crackers* (1930), *Monkey Business* (1931), and *Horse Feathers* (1932).

Duck Soup, originally titled *Cracked Ice* but changed to conform to the animal imagery of their previous successes, was the last film to be made by Zeppo, who had been relegated to small, noncomic roles and decided to quit rather than continue to be embarrassed.

By the time they began filming *Duck Soup* in 1933, Groucho, Harpo, and Chico had become anti-Establishment icons. Upstarts, misfits, and eternal outsiders, they wore their immigrant roots proudly. Chico even adopted an improbable Italian accent. The oddly dressed strangers thumbed their noses at authority, were forever on the make, and always got the last laugh as they lampooned cherished institutions.

Duck Soup was made as Hitler was storming onto the political horizon and America was in the grips of the Great Depression. As a result, it was even more finely attuned to the ironic absurdity of the modern world than their earlier movies. Although there is some debate as to the intended social significance of *Duck Soup* (which takes a dim view of international affairs, war, and the economy), there's no doubt that the film's suspicious view of government reflected the Marx Brothers' sentiments.

There's also no doubt that the influential movie had a dark, sardonic edge that would later resurface in black comedies such as *M*A*S*H* and *Dr. Strangelove*. The Marx Brothers also exerted a strong influence on Woody Allen's early films, and Allen tributes the team directly in *Hannah and Her Sisters,* in which the character he plays wanders into a screening of *Duck Soup.*

Long after the act broke up following 1949's *Love Happy* (their weakest film, which featured Harpo and Chico and relegated Groucho to a cameo part), the Marx Brothers' reputation for comic brilliance continued to grow with each passing year. Groucho, of course, went on with his solo career as the author of several humorous books and the acerbic host of *You Bet Your Life.* Hosting a quiz show seemed to some fans to be quite a comedown for a comic genius and the former president of Freedonia. Groucho was typically philosophical: "You know me," he quipped. "I have no shame."

Yes, we did know Groucho, and his shameless scheming, leering, lechery, and fortune hunting were exactly what we loved about him and his equally incorrigible brothers.

4

Dr. Strangelove or: How I Learned to Stop Worrying and Love the Bomb

Columbia (1964)
CAST: Peter Sellers, George C. Scott, Sterling Hayden,
Slim Pickens, Keenan Wynn
DIRECTED BY: Stanley Kubrick
93 minutes [Not rated]

Dr. Strangelove is one of the most deliberately provocative films in cinematic history—and one of the most savagely funny. Director Stanley Kubrick's one and only comedy exploded with astounding force on its release in 1964, and the fallout from the socially significant comedy can still be felt today. Its extreme irreverence and furious satiric irony set off a chain reaction, producing a series of paranoid black comedies that continue to shake the cultural landscape.

Everything in the scathing, apocalyptic assault on the military and political establishment is overstated—bigger, bolder, and brasher than any comedy had previously dared to be. The acting is wildly exaggerated, and the visual style is similarly arresting. Filled with overt sexual imagery, outrageous caricatures, and outlandish dialogue, *Dr. Strangelove* treats the subject of accidental nuclear annihilation as the world's biggest, sickest joke.

Audiences definitely got the grim joke, which was told with verve and nerve. In the year that *My Fair Lady* swept the Oscars, *Dr. Strangelove* was nominated for best picture, director, script, and actor (Peter Sellers), ushering in an era of black comedy that reflected the nihilism of the atomic age. Released in the post-Holocaust, post-Kennedy assassination age of Vietnam War protests, the civil rights movement, and the cold war, *Dr. Strangelove's* cynicism was astutely attuned to the times. This singular story of technology run amok cost the studio $1.5 million to produce—and grossed more than $5 million.

Dr. Strangelove was based on a dramatic novel by RAF officer Peter George, published in England under the pen name Peter Bryant as *Two Hours to Doom* and released in America as *Red Alert*. During the process of adapting the novel for the screen, Kubrick began to realize that it was the underlying absurdity of the situation that gave the story its kick. Deciding that the mind-numbing horror of the subject demanded a comic treatment, Kubrick enlisted renowned satirist Terry Southern (*The Loved One*) to sharpen and refine the screenplay's ferociously grotesque humor.

Kubrick had long been interested in the public acceptance of the possibility, and even probability, of nuclear war. Hoping to jolt the audience out of its complacency, Kubrick focused on the danger of accepting madness as normality, expanding on an idea that had been explored in Joseph Heller's 1961 darkly funny, absurdist antiwar novel, *Catch-22*.

Dr. Strangelove was not the first or last film to deal with the threat of nuclear annihilation. Director Stanley Kramer had broached the topic in 1959's *On the Beach,* and while American expatriate Kubrick was shooting *Dr. Strangelove* in England, director Sidney Lumet was filming *Fail-Safe* in America. But the iconoclastic Kubrick was the first to mine the somber subject for its absurd humor, starting a trend that continued with *How I Won the War, Oh! What a Lovely War, Slaughterhouse Five, Catch-22,* and *M*A*S*H.* Kubrick was correct in predicting that a brutally funny comedy would have a more shocking and disturbing effect than a predictably serious treatment could have produced.

Kubrick (*2001, A Clockwork Orange, The Shining*) elicited a string of bravura performances, one more dynamic than the next, from his superb cast. Sterling Hayden plays the cigar-chomping General Jack D. Ripper, who sets the story's wheels spinning when he goes around the bend and orders his thirty-four-plane bomb wing to drop 1,400 megatons of atomic bombs on Russia. The attack cannot be called off without a code that only Ripper knows and is not about to reveal. Indeed, he takes the secret code with him when he commits suicide.

Peter Sellers, who had worked with Kubrick on the screen adaptation of *Lolita* (1962), a disturbing comedy of obsession laced with black humor, was offered "the lead and the lead and the lead" in *Dr. Strangelove.* Sellers, who ended up playing only three of the five roles offered to him by Kubrick, was initially leery of playing several roles, which he had already done in *The Mouse That Roared* (1959). Kubrick convinced him that the multicasting was being done not as a gimmick, but because Sellers was simply the best actor for all the parts. The multiple casting of Sellers, whose *Pink Panther* was released in the same month and year as *Dr. Strangelove,* indeed proved instrumental to the film's success.

Sellers signed on to play the title character, the sinister scientist modeled on Wernher Von Braun (although sometimes mistakenly thought to be based on Henry Kissinger). With a mechanical arm that has a will of its own, a strangled Germanic falsetto voice, and a demonic gleam in his eye, Strangelove—a character who does not appear in the novel—is one of the

GENTLEMEN PREFER BOMBS Peter Bull, left, as the Russian ambassador, and Peter Sellers, right, as President Merkin Muffley, in Stanley Kubrick's nuclear war classic, *Dr. Strangelove*. Muffley was one of three roles played by Sellers.

screen's most outrageous comic inventions. Although Strangelove appears late in the film and only briefly, he is the title character because he represents the heart of evil insanity. The creator of the bomb is a deranged ex-Nazi who has been given a position of supreme power by the U.S. government. What could be more obscenely absurd—although utterly realistic—than that?

Sellers first appears on screen as Captain Lionel Mandrake, an RAF officer with a stiff upper lip but a streak of common sense and decency utterly lacking in his commanding officer, Ripper, who believes that fluoridation is a Communist plot to "sap all of our precious bodily fluids." The voice of reason, Mandrake is held hostage by Ripper but finally manages to figure out the code and almost saves the day.

Sellers turned down the role of General Buck Turgidson (originally called Buck Schmuck), a rabid "better dead than Red" hawk who relishes the opportunity to the wage war on the Commies. George C. Scott stepped in, giving the role its needed macho muscle and sexual energy. Not known as a comic actor, Scott goes wonderfully over the top playing the lewd, lecherous, warmongering cretin.

Sellers was also set to play Major King Kong, the pilot of the one plane that actually makes it to its target and sets off the Soviet's dreaded, irreversible doomsday device, designed to wipe all human life off the face of the earth in the event of a nuclear attack. But when Sellers broke his ankle, he was replaced by Slim Pickens, who drawls up a comic storm as the redneck pilot. When Kong gets the "go" code, he is initially leery. "I've been to two world fairs, a rodeo, and a picnic," he says, "but that's the stupidest thing I ever heard come out of a set of earphones." He is soon gung ho, however, gamely donning his cowboy hat to engage in "nuclear combat toe to toe with the Ruskies." In the end he gleefully rides the bomb like a bucking bronco, whooping and hollering into oblivion.

Sellers also agreed to play President Merkin Muffley, a sensible, intellectual, but ineffectual liberal egghead modeled on Adlai Stevenson. Muffley attempts to remain rational and calm amid the madness, but his efforts to resolve the crisis prove futile. Muffley's polite phone conversation with the drunken Russian Premier Dimitri Kissoff is one of the film's highlights. Muffley's restraint and decorum, while admirable, are glaringly at odds with the insanity, and inanity, of the situation. When Turgidson scuffles with the Russian ambassador de Sadesky (Peter Bull), Muffley indignantly admonishes them, "Gentlemen, you can't fight in here. This is the War Room."

There are only three major locations in *Dr. Strangelove*. One is the dark, round, isolated War Room. The other is Ripper's locked office. The third is the B-52 bomber, based exactly on a real plane. All three are claustrophobic, sealed spaces in which the characters are trapped. The relentless pace of the ninety-three-minute film, which unfolds more or less in real time, adds to the nightmarish quality of the comedy, in which events spin ever more erratically out of control.

Kubrick gave cogent, chilling expression to the nation's worst fears in this revered cautionary tale, which was embraced not only by the counterculture, but by the general public. One of the most original and continually inventive films ever made, it is the second comedy on the list of the one hundred best films of all time compiled by the American Film Institute in 1998. *Dr. Strangelove,* which spawned a sizable body of satirical comedy in the sixties and seventies, is the cinema's ultimate oddity, a mainstream cult classic.

5

Bringing Up Baby

RKO (1938)
CAST: Katharine Hepburn, Cary Grant, Charlie Ruggles
DIRECTED BY: Howard Hawks
102 minutes [Not rated]

Katharine Hepburn had never made a comedy when Howard Hawks cast her as the madcap heiress in *Bringing Up Baby,* the fastest, funniest, wildest, most demented screwball farce in movie history. This rousing romantic battle royal pits a scatterbrained socialite who inherits a tame leopard named Baby against a bumbling, bespectacled milquetoast whose idea of excitement is finding a rare dinosaur bone.

Cary Grant, who had established himself as a gifted light comedian the previous year with *Topper* and *The Awful Truth,* at first turned down the part of the absentminded professor who is driven to distraction by the ditzy debutante. Ray Milland, Fredric March, and Ronald Colman also turned down the unglamorous part. Convinced by Hawks that he could believably play a nerdy egghead by imitating Harold Lloyd, Grant undertook the part of stuffy paleontologist David Huxley. It was his first and last total departure from type. "I play myself to perfection," Grant later said of his customary role as a suave, debonair sophisticate.

Hawks recalls that while Grant was a natural in the role, Hepburn at first had trouble hitting her comic stride in her comedy debut and was coached by veteran comic actor Walter Catlett, who plays the constable in the film. An eager student, Hepburn caught on quickly and went on to distinguish herself in some of the greatest comedies of the 1940s, including another outing with Grant in the beloved romantic comedy *The Philadelphia Story* (1940) and her celebrated collaboration with Spencer Tracy in verbal sparring classics such as *Adam's Rib* (1948). *Bringing Up Baby* was her sole foray into slapstick comedy.

Bringing Up Baby, although something of an anomaly for its stars, was also an unusually high-spirited comedy that went gleefully over the top. All the staples of screwball comedy (the fantastic and improbable plot, the frenzied pace, the charmingly irresponsible heroine) are taken to the nth degree in what has aptly been called "the screwiest of screwball comedies." The barely controlled anarchy of *Bringing Up Baby,* a comedy of perpetual motion, was apparently more than audiences could take in 1938. It was a box office disappointment, deemed too silly and crazy by the critics. Still, the comedy had its admirers. Harold Lloyd called it "the best constructed comedy" he had ever seen.

It was not until the 1960s that it attained its status as one of Hollywood's most perfect and brilliant comedies. Its reputation was further enhanced by Peter Bogdanovich's 1972 homage, *What's Up, Doc?,* which created new interest in the revered classic. Fifty years after its release, *Bringing Up Baby* was listed in the American Film Institute's ranking of the one hundred best films of all time.

Recent years have also seen a reappraisal of director Howard Hawks. Although Hawks was not predominantly a director of comedy, no one made better comedies, as historian Gerald Mast points out. Along with Frank Capra's *It Happened One Night,* Hawks is credited with inventing screwball comedy in 1934 with *Twentieth Century,* starring Carole Lombard and John Barrymore. In *Ball of Fire* (1941), Hawks again explored the girl-gets-boy theme, casting Barbara Stanwyck as burlesque dancer Sugarpuss O'Shea, who wins and liberates prissy Professor Potts (Cary Cooper).

Hawks is appreciated today for his refusal to sentimentalize, moralize, or apologize for his characters. He never explains their consistent silliness, no matter how eccentric they might seem. In *Bringing Up Baby* Hawks did more than simply push the limits of lunacy in a story that consists of a series of mounting disasters that dismay and mortify David and delight the audience. Working from a screenplay by Dudley Nichols and Hagar Wilde, based on Wilde's short story published in 1937 in *Collier's,* Hawks also shrewdly created characters who seem to have nothing in common but are clearly destined for each other, a quality that resurfaced in Preston Sturges's definitive screwball comedy, *The Lady Eve* (1941).

David first meets Susan Vance (Hepburn) on the golf course, where she unwittingly steals his ball, causing him the first of many social embarrassments. She then wreaks havoc with his car, setting off a chain of events that will systematically destroy David's dignity. The irony is that in the process of ruining his life and sabotaging his career, Susan will liberate uptight David from his emotional constraints. Susan both entraps David and sets him free.

David resists Susan's slaphappy pursuit of him until the last possible moment, of course, greeting each catastrophe with growing chagrin and each new indignity with unalloyed aggravation. *Bringing Up Baby* is a brilliant example of comic exasperation, once again exaggerated to glorious excess. The comedy of liberation's theme is neatly expressed by the oddball psychiatrist Dr. Lehmann (Fritz Feld), who says, "All people who behave strangely are not insane." This celebration of eccentricity and human resilience has been described by critic Robin Wood as the triumph of the id over the super-ego in which the forces of disorder prevail over the forces of order.

Susan may make a mess of everything, but her comically destructive actions are not malicious. She is merely maddeningly oblivious. Opinionated, assured, and headstrong—classic Hepburn traits—she is also heedless, rash, and wrongheaded. She sets her sights on David, undeterred by the fact that he would sooner strangle her than kiss her—if she stopped moving long enough to permit him to do either. David himself comments on the impossibility of romance amid the relentless chaos when he says, "In moments of quiet I'm strangely drawn to you, but there haven't been any quiet moments."

Much of the humor in *Bringing Up Baby* rests on the characters' utter reasonableness in the midst of the ever-escalating insanity. The comedy stems from Susan's seemingly sensible but truly outlandish actions, which cause the normal David to appear dangerously unstable. She keeps making him act against his nature until he's permanently knocked off-kilter. "I love to put my characters into embarrassing situations," Hawks confessed in an interview, and in David he found the perfect stuffy character begging to be deflated by humiliations.

David completely lets go of his rational resolve only once in the famous cross-dressing scene. Susan has taken David's clothes in order to keep him captive, and David is wearing a frilly negligee when he answers the door of Susan's Connecticut home. Susan's rich aunt Elizabeth, whom David has hoped will make a million-dollar donation to his museum, is standing there, and she demands to know what he's doing in Susan's dressing gown. Leaping into the air, he proclaims giddily, "I suddenly went gay!" (No sexual reference intended.) In explaining David's presence, Susan says he's a friend of her brother's from Brazil who's had a breakdown. "I'm a nut from Brazil," David mutters in chagrined agreement.

The daringly risqué film, rife with sexual anxiety, features another hilarious episode that was filmed at Grant's suggestion. After Susan accidentally rips his coat ("Oh dear, you've ripped your coat," she says with typical refusal to take responsibility), David steps on the train of her dress, pulling it off and revealing her undergarments. At first he tries to rescue Susan from embarrassment with his top hat, but she deflects his actions and refuses to understand the situation. When she does grasp her predicament, David gallantly comes to her rescue by falling in lockstep behind her and awkwardly marching her out of the crowded country club.

Visual comedy doesn't get much better than this, but *Bringing Up Baby* is much more than an assemblage of inspired sight gags. Like many masterpieces, it is more than the sum of it parts. The delirious pace, the audacity of the plot, the wacky supporting performances, and the many clever mixups and mishaps do not fully account for its success. There's something else going on that gives this film its charge.

Two great performers, poised at early pivotal moments in their careers, took enormous risks in *Bringing Up Baby*. Hepburn found her comic voice in this full-throttle farce. It is her abandon that fuels the high-octane film. Grant, who starred in four Hawks comedies and became the undisputed king of screwball comedy, also cast caution to the wind as he allowed himself to be bested by the funniest femme fatale in screen history. In this heated and hilarious battle of the sexes, there were only winners.

BABY, IT'S YOU   Cary Grant and Katharine Hepburn take Baby out for a walk in Howard Hawks's 1938 *Bringing Up Baby,* which has been deemed by critics "the screwiest of all screwball comedies."

6

*M*A*S*H*

Twentieth Century-Fox (1970)
CAST: Donald Sutherland, Elliott Gould, Tom Skerritt, Sally Kellerman,
Robert Duvall, Roger Bowen, Gary Burghoff
DIRECTED BY: Robert Altman
116 minutes [Rated PG]

The American cinema's reigning skeptic, director Robert Altman, proved perfectly matched to screenwriter Ring Lardner Jr.'s social satire, which mocked the military mentality. Set during the Korean War, Altman's seminal antiwar comedy about a Mobile Army Surgical Hospital operating three miles from the front was hailed as "one of the most irreducibly funny films ever made" by *Sight and Sound* magazine and earned $30 million in its first year of release.

M*A*S*H, Altman's most commercially successful film, bore all of the director's now familiar trademarks: a large ensemble cast; colorful, nonconformist characters; overlapping dialogue; an episodic structure; natural, multilayered sound; an unpretentious visual style; and a loose, improvisational feel.

Altman was not the first choice to direct *M*A*S*H*. In fact, he was at the bottom of a very long list. At least seventeen well-established directors were offered the project before producers Ingo Preminger and Richard Zanuck decided to give the relative newcomer a crack at it. Altman had worked in television for seven years, primarily directing episodes of *Bonanza, Combat!,* and *Alfred Hitchcock Presents,* and had just directed his first, inauspicious feature, *That Cold Day in the Park.* Altman, who served as a bomber pilot during World War II, had tried unsuccessfully for five years to make a World War II farce and relished the opportunity to film the story of a group of surgeons attempting to maintain their sanity—and their humanity—amid the madness of military service.

The unproven director proceeded to cast his film with unknown actors who were just beginning their promising careers. Altman set up tents on the Twentieth Century-Fox back lot, where the entire cast camped out during the filming, thus creating a community akin to the one depicted on the screen. Altman established an authenticity and spontaneity that were essential to the success of an audacious, acerbic comedy that, as Rex Reed wrote in 1970, "topples the American system of cornball idealism so perfectly."

Reed, who added that he hadn't laughed so hard since the release of *Some Like it Hot* eleven years earlier, was one of many critics who recognized that the story benefited from Altman's offhand, natural treatment. The gruesome, blood-spurting surgery scenes were more shocking because of the doctors' casual banter. The characters' attitude is what makes the ridiculous situations mordantly comical.

Altman's coolness was indeed well suited to the irreverent, anti-Establishment comedy about the lunacy and obscenity of war, based on a 1968 picaresque novel by Richard Hooker. Altman's first major film remains his funniest, although humor percolates through the film many consider his best, 1975's *Nashville*. He also injected dark humor into his deviously hilarious satire of Hollywood, *The Player* (1995).

Black comedy had entered the modern age in 1964 with *Dr. Strangelove* and continued to thrive in films such as Mel Brooks's *The Producers* (1967), *Where's Poppa?*, and *Little Big Man,* the latter two released in 1970 at the height of the Vietnam War. The other 1970 film *M*A*S*H* most closely resembled, however, was *Catch-22,* based on Joseph Heller's 1961 bestselling novel emphasizing the absurdity of war. But *M*A*S*H* was distinguished from the other black comedies of the era by its amiable, affable scruffiness, understated sophistication, and easygoing sarcasm. The jolting yet jolly effect of Altman's almost plotless film is inextricably linked to his impromptu style as well as to the nonchalant tone of the performances.

Donald Sutherland had played only minor supporting film roles when he was cast as the film's central iconoclast, Captain Hawkeye Pierce. Tall, unconventionally handsome, and uninhibited, Sutherland embodied the rebellious spirit of the freewheeling movie. Hawkeye is intelligent, free-spirited, anti-authoritarian, and charming. He can be compassionate or cruel, reasonable or rascally, as the situation demands.

When we first meet Hawkeye he is awaiting transport to his *M*A*S*H* unit. His disheveled, unassuming appearance leads Duke Forrest (Tom Skerritt), another surgeon en route to the same unit, to assume he's his driver. Hawkeye, who likes to go with the flow, obliges, stealing the jeep. Duke and Hawkeye share a bottle on the way to their outfit, and a friendship is born. The two men take an instant dislike to their tentmate, a Bible-thumping, teetotaling hypocrite and incompetent surgeon, Major Frank Burns (Robert Duvall). They are supported by the camp commander, the befuddled, non-military-minded Colonel Henry Blake (Roger Bowen), whose company clerk, Radar O'Reilly (Gary Burghoff), is always one step ahead of him.

When Captain "Trapper" John MacIntyre (Elliott Gould), a chest cutter

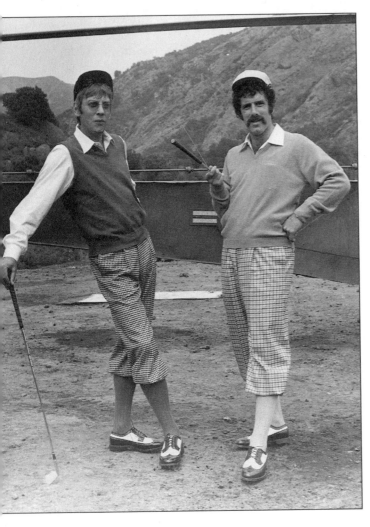

M*A*S*H*HUGGENAH Donald Sutherland, left, and Elliott Gould, right, in Robert Altman's brilliant 1970 antiwar satire, *M*A*S*H.* The film's success catapulted Altman to A-list director and spawned a megasuccessful television sitcom that ran for thirteen years—eleven years more than the Korean War it was based on.

from Boston, arrives, he joins the Hawkeye-Duke-Henry alliance by sharing martinis with his new bunkmates (he carries his own olives) and by socking Frank Burns in the jaw for blaming a patient's death on a sensitive orderly (Bud Cort, who would make a big splash in another black comedy, *Harold and Maude,* two years later).

Burns, the literal "odd" man out, gets his own ally when Major Margaret Houlihan (Sally Kellerman) arrives as chief nurse. Hawkeye, who initially finds her attractive, is the first to recognize that the uptight, by-the-book, straight arrow is "what we call a regular army clown." Attempting to retaliate for the insult, she asks aloud how "a degenerate like that could rise to a position of authority in the Army Medical Corps." The unit's mild-mannered chaplain replies, "He was drafted."

When Frank and Margaret join forces and begin an affair, the boys can't resist playing a prank on the overly officious officers and broadcast their tryst over the unit's loudspeakers. Frank, a religious zealot, is exposed as a hypocrite, leading the *New York Times* to conclude that *M*A*S*H* was the first major American film to openly ridicule the belief in God. Frank is pushed over the brink and leaves in a straitjacket (although the script makes it clear that the pranksters have actually done him a favor by sending him home), and Margaret is forevermore known as Hot Lips. Hot Lips suffers further indignities and finds no support from Blake.

But the film ultimately softens somewhat toward her, too, late in the film, when she gleefully leads idiotic cheers at a football game against a rival unit. Although she's still incredibly out of it—"My God, they shot him!" she exclaims when the third-quarter gun goes off—she has apparently found her niche and is no longer an outcast.

The football scene, a hilarious slapstick finale that borrows from Harold Lloyd's *The Freshman,* is the ultimate expression of anarchy in the film, in which all rules of America's sacred sport are broken and "the symbol of the American way of life" is roundly ridiculed. Much of the film's humor comes from the characters' attempts to maintain a semblance of normal life in this artificial community far from home and family. Colonel Blake wears a fly-fishing hat and vest and spends his off hours tying flies or bedding his favorite nurse. The men play poker, drink, and party with the nurses. Hawk-eye and Trapper play golf on the helicopter landing pad.

That's where they are when they are summoned to Tokyo to operate on a congressman's kid. In this very funny comic sequence, Hawkeye and Trap-per engage in some inspired antics as they outwit yet another "army clown" and save the life of a Korean infant. Another famously funny section of the film is the assisted suicide of the company's well-endowed dentist Painless, who is convinced he is impotent and hence homosexual. The elaborate "last supper" and phony funeral staged by the men are brilliant moments of macabre humor.

M*A*S*H, listed fifty-sixth in the American Film Institute's 1998 ranking of the one hundred best films of all time, won the grand prize at the Cannes Film Festival, the New York Film Critics Award for best film, and the Golden Globe for best musical/comedy. It was nominated for Oscars for best picture, director, and supporting actress (Kellerman) but won only for Ring Lardner Jr.'s screenplay.

The wildly popular movie took on a life of its own in 1971 with the TV spin-off series of the same name that enjoyed enormous success for twelve seasons. The excellent show became such an accepted part of the cultural landscape, it's hard to imagine the profoundly unsettling effect of the original film. Lewd and graphic, the film was so disturbing that it was originally rated X but was eventually modified to an R. It has since been released on video with a PG rating.

M*A*S*H turned the war movie genre inside out, and it's never been the same since.

7

Annie Hall

United Artists (1977)
CAST: Woody Allen, Diane Keaton, Tony Roberts, Paul Simon
DIRECTED BY: Woody Allen
94 minutes [Rated PG]

Woody Allen was already known as the director of the funniest American films of the 1970s when he scored his greatest commercial and critical success with the heartfelt and hilarious *Annie Hall,* which remains one of Allen's most beloved films and the best odd-couple, interethnic romantic comedy of all time. *Annie Hall* was the first comedy since *Tom Jones* to win an Oscar and also garnered the most top nominations since *Citizen Kane.* Smart, sweet, and uncommonly insightful, *Annie Hall* earned Oscars for best picture, best director, best screenplay, and best actress and established the popular screen comedian as a serious film artist who has become the most prolific and consistently successful director of screen comedies working today.

Annie Hall also marked a change of direction for the writer, director, and actor, whose previous work consisted of inspired, slapstick larks such as *Bananas* and *Sleeper,* which many fans still consider his funniest films. Working in the physical comedy tradition of the Marx Brothers and Charlie Chaplin, Allen had created wildly anarchic comedies that established Allen's comic persona as the lovable loser. But Allen's patented comic personality blossomed in *Annie Hall,* the first film in which he left freewheeling fantasy and farce for the richer rewards of reality-based humor. In fact, Allen seemed to be playing himself—and presumably based the film's lead character on his own life—in this relationship-oriented, character-driven, confessional comedy about the doomed love affair between cranky comic Alvy Singer (Allen) and a ditzy aspiring singer (Diane Keaton).

A chronically dissatisfied romantic antihero, Alvy finds himself in a relationship doomed by the characters' culturally ingrained differences. The humor of *Annie Hall,* coauthored by Allen's frequent collaborator Marshall Brickman, is based on contrasts, including the dichotomies within Allen's own personality. The hopeful pessimist, Allen sums up his conflicted philosophy when he observes, "Life is filled with loneliness and misery and suffering and unhappiness—and it's all over much too quickly."

Alvy may be self-absorbed, analytical, and overly sensitive to suffering, but he contrasts his morbid worldview with those he considers unthinking and unfeeling. On the street he stops a handsome, happy couple to ask the secret of their relationship. "I'm shallow, empty, with no ideas and nothing interesting to say," the woman blithely replies. "And I'm the same way," her strapping mate adds cheerfully. It's easy to be happy, Allen seems to be saying, if you're oblivious.

As this bit reveals, Allen's absolute sense of superiority is coupled with a profound sense of alienation from mainstream American culture. This distinctly Jewish combination—the arrogant misfit—is a large part of Allen's appeal. He makes fun of himself, but he is also proud to be different. An intellectual who parodies pseudointellectuals, he makes fun of others but also makes fun of himself making fun of others.

The relationship between neurotic New Yorker Alvy and all-American Annie provides Allen with the perfect opportunity to mine his favorite themes, chief among them the difference between Jews and gentiles. Annie is, in her own way, just as neurotic and eccentric as Alvy, but she's pure midwestern WASP. Alvy is caustic, cerebral, and cynical, given to exaggeration, often hostile, and usually contemptuous. Annie is open, naive, intuitive, unsophisticated, unassertive, unsure of her own intellect, and eager for approval. Annie's anxieties, however, don't inhibit her enjoyment of life and other people. As Alvy fondly looks back on their failed relationship, he remembers how much fun it was just to be with her. Although during the relationship Alvy egotistically takes the role of mentor, molding and cultivating and encouraging Annie, in the end she has ironically blossomed and outgrown him. It could also be said that she has a more profound effect on him than he does on her, which is quite a gracious admission from Allen.

Because of his unprepossessing appearance, Allen's casting of himself in a romantic role is, in itself, funny. But it is also touching, defying the movie myth that only perfect-looking people can be sexual beings. Despite his looks, Alvy/Allen is actually quite attractive to the opposite sex. Allen's alter ego is a man who is not afraid to express his feelings; in fact, he is unable to be anything less than ruthlessly honest. This rare degree of self-knowledge and vulnerability allows us to laugh at Alvy and genuinely care about him at the same time.

Although Allen is an intensely private person, he has revealed more about himself to the audience than almost any other contemporary film artist. Allen is especially unsparing in his depiction of Alvy's hypercritical nature, which, of course, allows the character to unleash a series of seriously funny zingers.

ANNIE SEZ Diane Keaton, left, Woody Allen, center, and Colleen Dewhurst, bottom right, enjoy some laughs during the filming of *Annie Hall* (1977), which won four Oscars and established the Woodman as a serious filmmaker.

Although Allen is often self-demeaning, we like him precisely because he is so hard on himself. On the whole, Allen engenders a huge amount of sympathy for his screen persona.

Alvy is wise enough to know when it's time to let go of Annie. "Relationships are like sharks. They have to move forward or die," he tells Annie. "What we have on our hands is a dead shark."

While *Annie Hall* is still considered by many to be his best comedy, it is clearly a precursor to such subsequent complex classics as *Hannah and Her Sisters* and *Crimes and Misdemeanors*. Although he has frequently moved in a more serious direction, Allen has let his funny side hang out in recent years in a number of extremely amusing comedies. Although 1980's *Stardust Memories* was not well received by the critics, who accused him of indulging in sour grapes and self-pity, it is actually one of his best comedies, albeit one of his darkest. *Broadway Danny Rose* (1984) is a personal favorite and features one of Allen's best comic performances—again brilliantly contrasted with Mia Farrow's Mob-connected Italian bimbo. *The Purple Rose of Cairo* (1995), also starring Farrow, was sweet and inventive. One of Allen's most endearing, vivid, and imaginative comedies was his segment of the trilogy *New York Stories* (1989), the short film "Oedipus Wrecks," in which Allen's disapproving mother (Mae Questal) magically appears in the sky.

Although *Manhattan Murder Mystery* (1993) failed to find an audience, it features funny work by Allen, reunited again with his perfect foil and ex-flame, Diane Keaton. *Bullets over Broadway* (1994), in which John Cusack plays a pretentious playwright who could easily have been played by Allen, is one of his most hilarious and original films. *Mighty Aphrodite* (1995), an uncharacteristically bawdy comedy starring Mira Sorvino as a happy hooker, was also laugh-out-loud funny.

Allen, who has been churning out comedies for thirty years, will no doubt go down in cinema history as the Chaplin of his times. His comic vision has matured marvelously, with *Annie Hall* marking the beginning of his increasing artistic sophistication. Yet a film like 1973's *Sleeper* hold up remarkably well. In his first collaboration with Marshall Brickman, Allen placed himself two hundred years into the future to parody popular culture. In this zany Keystone Kops comedy, Allen's Miles Monroe, an involuntary subject of cryogenic immersion, awakens to find the worst attributes of today's chic, hedonistic, materialistic lifestyle grossly magnified. Realizing he's missed two hundred years of appointments with his analyst, he moans that he'd almost be cured by now.

Allen has continued to parade his neuroses before the public in comedies steeped in anxiety, sexual frustration, vulnerability, obsessiveness, and morbidity. Allen uses humor to vent his hostility and as a defense mechanism to hide his feelings of inadequacy. No other comic filmmaker mines his complex psyche with such honesty or humorous results. We can only hope he's never cured.

8

The Ladykillers

Ealing Studios (1955)
CAST: Alec Guinness, Cecil Parker, Katie Johnson, Peter Sellers
DIRECTED BY: Alexander Mackendrick
87 minutes [Not rated]

A master of disguises, Alec Guinness was the quintessential character actor and the ultimate chameleon, rivaling Lon Chaney in his ability to disappear into his roles. He titled his autobiography *Blessings in Disguise,* an apt reference to his talent for transformation. Early in his screen career he set a record for the number of roles played by a single actor in a film. In the classic *Kind Hearts and Coronets* (1949), which some critics consider his best comedy, he created eight vivid characters (including a lady suffragette)—one more than Paul Muni had played in *Seven Faces.*

In the gleefully macabre *The Ladykillers,* Guinness plays the demented leader of a gang of bumbling crooks who are inadvertently outwitted by a sweet little old lady. True to form, Guinness adopted a look, manner, voice, and physical demeanor that was intrinsically amusing, creating one of the most memorable portraits in his rogue's gallery of off-kilter characters. As Leonard Maltin observes of Guinness's odd appearance and peerless performance in *The Ladykillers,* ". . . even his *teeth* are funny."

An accomplished London stage actor who shone in plays by Shakespeare, Shaw, and Chekhov, Guinness burst onto the English film scene in 1946 in David Lean's masterpiece *Great Expectations.* It was in Lean's next Dickens adaptation, however, that Guinness established his ability to render himself unrecognizable. In *Oliver Twist* (1948), Guinness created such a vividly vile interpretation of Fagin that his portrayal of the notorious character, which was slavishly faithful to the book, was greeted with charges of anti-Semitism.

Working for the Ealing Studios during the next decade, Guinness played lovable rascals and oddballs in a series of sophisticated black comedies that established his reputation as one of the most versatile actors of his generation, as well as one of the funniest. The dark and daring Ealing comedies dealt with grim subjects—murder, crime, insanity—in an irreverent and satirical manner, earning international acclaim.

Guinness, who was nominated for an Oscar for his role as the mild-mannered, late-blooming criminal mastermind in *The Lavender Hill Mob* (1952), was the perfect actor for these devious, delightfully wicked and dry comedies that foreshadowed the black humor that emerged in the 1960s in American films such as *Dr. Strangelove, M*A*S*H,* and *Harold and Maude.*

Guinness was a serious actor who played comedy straight. He underplayed emotion, turning in subtle and realistic performances. It was the events around him and his reaction to them that were comical. In *The Ladykillers* Guinness does a slow burn as his brilliant plan is undone by the seemingly harmless, presumably gullible Mrs. Wilberforce, whom he has chosen to play a role as an unwitting accomplice in his robbery because she is trusting and innocent. The humor rests on the reversal of expectations. Instead of being manipulated and exploited as the perfect front for the crime, the prim, proper, but feisty Mrs. Wilberforce proves an obstacle that cannot be overcome.

In the end, the gang is left with no choice but to knock her off. However, like Martha Raye in Charlie Chaplin's excellent black comedy *Monsieur Verdoux,* she is not so easily disposed of. (*Monsieur Verdoux,* which introduced the idea of the lovable murderer, influenced *Kind Hearts and Coronets* as well as *The Ladykillers.*) As in *Monsieur Verdoux,* the intended victim in *The Ladykillers* remains oblivious of the murderous intentions she manages to elude and emerges unscathed.

Katie Johnson, a sprightly seventy-seven, won the British Academy Award for her performance as the indomitable and unfailingly sensible old biddy who thwarts the robbery and drives her would-be cohorts to distraction. Mrs. Wilberforce is one of the cinema's great comic inventions, a cheerful senior citizen who cannot be taken for a fool. She is high on the list of little old ladies who have been put to fine use in film comedy, a tradition that includes the sweet, murderous sisters in *Arsenic and Old Lace,* Margaret Rutherford as Miss Marple in four Agatha Christie mysteries of the 1960s, and Ruth Gordon in *Harold and Maude.*

The devious, bucktoothed Professor Marcus (Guinness) rents a room in Mrs. Wilberforce's house and tells her that the other gentlemen who will be gathering there are members of a string quartet. His distinctly nonmusical cohorts in crime include a seemingly brutish but softhearted thug (Danny Green), a genteel crook known as the Major (Cecil Parker), and a dim-witted young punk played by relative newcomer Peter Sellers, who was soon being called "the next Alec Guinness." Sellers played three roles, including a woman, in *The Mouse That Roared* (1959).

The motley mobsters plan the stick-up caper while a record plays classical music to fool the landlady downstairs. The disparity between the elegant

NO WAY TO TREAT A LADY   The cast of Alexander Mackendrick's 1955 black comedy *The Ladykillers*. Top row, from left: Herbert Lom, Peter Sellers, and Cecil Parker. Bottom row, from left: Alec Guinness, Katie Johnson, and Danny Green. Sellers and Lom would reteam twenty years later in *The Return of the Pink Panther*.

and refined music and the men who are supposed to be playing it is an ongoing source of humor in this polished screen gem.

In movies, "professor" is often a code word for "mad," and Professor Marcus is no exception. Guinness makes it clear that the character is indeed cracked by the wild look in his eye as well as by his reaction to the protest that his plan "sounds like something someone thought up in the booby hatch." It is this undercurrent of madness that makes *The Ladykillers* unnerving as well as funny. The British reputation for order, civility, respectability, and adherence to convention is set on its head in this impudent comedy.

American-born screenwriter William Rose, who won a British Academy Award for his witty screenplay, eventually returned to Hollywood, where he continued to tread on the dark and daffy side of comedy. He wrote *It's a Mad Mad Mad Mad World* and *The Russians are Coming! The Russians Are*

Coming! and won an Oscar for *Guess Who's Coming to Dinner*. Director Alexander Mackendrick also made his way to Hollywood, where he earned acclaim for the caustic satirical drama *The Sweet Smell of Success*.

Guinness finally earned his Oscar in 1957 for *Bridge on the River Kwai*, after which he began to take on challenging roles in more serious films. He did create one more truly outstanding comic character, playing the eccentric, irritating painter Gully Jimsin in *The Horse's Mouth* (1958). Guinness wrote the screenplay for this superb and disturbing comedy, based on the novel by Joyce Cary.

Knighted in 1959, Sir Alec Guinness is best known to the younger generation as Obi Wan-Kenobi in the venerable *Star Wars* saga. Guinness indeed proved sage in taking the part in return for 2.5 percent of the profits.

Over the years Guinness has played an Arab king (in Lean's *Lawrence of Arabia*), an Indian (in Lean's *A Passage to India*), a Japanese widower (in *A Majority of One*), Marcus Aurelius (in *The Fall of the Roman Empire*), and Disraeli (in *The Mudlark*). But during the heyday of British black comedy, he was as indispensable to the genre as Cary Grant was to American screwball comedy. In each comic incarnation he found the quiet, peculiar center of madness. The effect of his comedies, in which chaos battled the forces of order, was liberating. Guinness was at his unbridled best in *The Ladykillers*, in which the perfect crime indeed comes to a perfect, if completely unpredictable, conclusion.

9

Tootsie

Columbia (1982)
Cast: Dustin Hoffman, Jessica Lange, Teri Garr, Bill Murray,
Sydney Pollack, Charles Durning, Dabney Coleman
Directed by: Sydney Pollack
116 minutes [Rated PG]

In *Tootsie*, Dustin Hoffman landed the best female role of 1982 when he was cast as an out-of-work actor who learns to be a better man by spending time as a woman. A smash hit and a smashing comedy, *Tootsie* is a nimble, vigorous farce that manages to be funny from beginning to end and still deliver a cogent gender-bending message about sexism.

The feminist fun begins when Michael Dorsey disguises himself as Dorothy Michaels and lands a plum part on a daytime soap opera, which solves his financial problems but precipitates a transformative personal crisis. Michael begins to see things quite differently as Dorothy, who gradually takes on a life of her own. Dorothy is none too pleased by the condescending, patronizing, dismissive, and lecherous way men (Michael included) tend to treat women. By spending time on the receiving end of male chauvinism, Michael gets a wake-up call. In the end, the movie offers a perceptive social commentary on the maleness and femaleness that exist in every person and the importance of finding a healthy balance.

Tootsie originated when Hoffman wondered out loud what it would be like to play a woman. Writer Murray Schisgal took the idea of a comedy of mistaken sexual identities and ran with it. Hoffman also wanted to make a movie about the stress and strains of acting, and the two ideas were merged in a script revised by Larry Gelbart.

Before committing to the part, Hoffman wanted to make sure he could pass as a woman. He went around in drag, even attending his children's school functions and making an indecent proposal to Jose Ferrer in an elevator without being detected. Hoffman decided he could get away with the part, although he reports he was deeply affected by the realization that as a woman he was not attractive enough to interest him as a man.

Directors came and went, including Hal Ashby, who hired Charles Durn-

BOYS WILL BE GIRLS Sydney Pollack, left, and Dustin Hoffman, right, in the 1982 instant classic *Tootsie*. In addition to directing, Pollack scored nicely as Hoffman's flustered theatrical agent.

ing; and Elaine May, who hired Teri Garr. After three directors and twenty rewrites, the project was about to be shelved when Columbia put Hoffman together with power-house director Sydney Pollack, who was known not for comedy, but for intelligent entertainments such as *They Shoot Horses, Don't They?, Jeremiah Johnson, The Way We Were, The Yakuza, The Electric Horseman,* and *Absence of Malice.*

Pollack, while known for eliciting fine performances from his stars, was a director who insisted on complete artistic control of his films; and Hoffman was known as a perfectionist who also liked to exercise creative freedom. Despite the potential for conflict, the two men hit it off and agreed to work together. Pollack, however, was less interested in making a tribute to the actor's art than in creating a story about a man transformed by his masquer-ade as a woman, and Hoffman acquiesced. (Hoffman does say that he'd still like to make that homage to acting.)

Tootsie does begin as a portrait of the quintessential New York actor, offer-ing an inside look at the struggling theater community. The first shot is of a makeup table. Michael, not unlike Hoffman, is tenaciously dedicated to his craft. Almost obnoxiously obsessive and narcissistic, Michael is a demanding and difficult actor who insists on playing roles the way he thinks they should be played, which has alienated everyone who might hire him. Unemployed— and unemployable—Michael is desperate to work. Although his friends admire his integrity ("He makes you remember what acting is all about!"), the script makes it clear that Michael, while talented, is also arrogant and pretentious. "I did an evening of vegetables Off Broadway," he brags. He tells the students who take his drama class, "If you can't make the part yourself, then you can't play it," a point he is about to prove with his reckless ruse.

When his student and sometime girlfriend Sandy (Garr) auditions for a soap, Michael goes along for moral support. When Sandy isn't even allowed to read because she's not the right type for the middle-aged hospital admin-istrator, Michael dons a dress and gets the part himself. He even fools his agent, wonderfully played by Pollack at Hoffman's insistence. The agent is naturally appalled, but Michael is unfazed by the risk he's taking—he's totally jazzed by his ultimate acting coup.

Michael's playwright roommate (Bill Murray, who improvised his lines) is also skeptical, especially when Michael seems to have crossed the imaginary line between fantasy and reality. "I have something to say to women, to other women like me," Michael insists. "There *are* no other women like you," Murray reminds him.

Matters become complicated on the first day of shooting. Michael learns he's supposed to kiss the leading man, whom the other actresses have dubbed "the tongue." When the moment of truth arrives, Dorothy hits her costar on the head, claiming to the director (Dabney Coleman) that it felt right for her character. The scene stands as played. But more serious complications arise when Dorothy meets the actress playing "the hospital slut." Julie (Jessica Lange) takes an instant liking to tough, resourceful Dorothy, and the two become close confidantes. Michael's interest in Julie is romantic, however, and he can barely contain his amorous feelings, which leads Julie to think Dorothy is a lesbian. And when Sandy catches Michael trying on her clothes, she decides he must be gay.

Meanwhile, Julie's father (Charles Durning), a sweet, down-to-earth widower, develops a crush on Dorothy and proposes marriage. This turn of events calls to mind the classic cross-dressing comedy *Some Like It Hot*, in which Joe E. Brown falls hard for Jack Lemmon in drag. Backed into a corner by the hilarious ramifications of his deceptions, Michael has no choice but to reveal the truth, which he does on live television in an inspired piece of improv that is just ludicrous enough to fly on daytime TV.

A satire of the New York theater scene as well as the soaps, *Tootsie* is a farce with feeling, moving and incisive, played with total conviction by an excellent cast. Garr is delightfully ditsy as the insecure but feisty actress. Lange is luminous as the unhappy, confused woman struggling to make it on her own. Lange's rapport with Dorothy is so real, we too almost forget there's a man behind the glasses and under the wig. Murray, whose performance was unbilled and who was recruited by Hoffman, is side-splittingly funny in his bemused and sarcastic reactions to his roommate. Sizing Michael up in his latest ensemble, he offers a bit of advice: "Don't play hard to get."

Taking his cue from Lemmon and his *Some Like It Hot* costar Tony Curtis, Hoffman plays it absolutely straight, without a trace of self-consciousness or any attempt to ham it up. The sincerity of Hoffman's performance makes the wildly improbable story richly funny.

Cross-dressing comedies have long enjoyed popularity with the American public, and Hoffman joins a long list of actors who have gladly undergone a sexual transformation on the screen. Before Curtis and Lemmon hit it big in drag, Cary Grant gamely donned a dress in Howard Hawks's 1949 comedy, *I Was a Male War Bride*. Robin Williams was less fetching, but just as funny, disguised as a woman in *Mrs. Doubtfire* and appeared opposite cross-dressing Nathan Lane in *The Birdcage,* Mike Nichols's remake of the classic 1978 French comedy, *La Cage Aux Folles.* Julie Andrews played a woman posing as a female impersonator in Blake Edwards's popular comedy *Victor/Victoria* (1982), released the same year as *The World According to Garp,* which featured John Lithgow as a man who undergoes a sex change. Harvey Fierstein earned acclaim as a witty drag queen in 1988's *Torch Song Trilogy.* Patrick Swayze, Wesley Snipes, and John Leguizamo played drag queens in the comic road movie *To Wong Foo, Thanks for Everything, Julie Newmar,* which was preceded by a better drag queen road comedy, *The Adventures of Priscilla, Queen of the Desert,* an Australian comedy released in 1994. In that same year Johnny Depp played a director with a fondness for angora sweaters in Tim Burton's odd yet amusing *Ed Wood.*

Hailed as an instant classic on its release, *Tootsie* earned Oscar nominations for best picture, best screenplay, best actor (Hoffman), and best director. Lange won the best supporting actress Oscar. *Tootsie* won the Golden Globe for best musical comedy, and Hoffman won as best actor in a musical/ comedy. The Writers Guild bestowed its best original screenplay award on the script, which was also voted best screenplay by the New York Film Critics, who gave Hoffman the acting nod as well. The American Film Institute's 1998 ranking of the one hundred best films of all time places *Tootsie* in sixty-second place.

Wildly successful at the box office, *Tootsie* was greeted with cheers from most of the nation's critics. It was hailed as "funnier than farce and more forthright than camp." The *Los Angeles Times* proclaimed it a "generous, wonderfully funny entertainment with a backbone of intelligence." Not all the reviews were raves, however. It was called *Some Like It Warmed Over* and criticized for its "alleged feminist intent" by reviewers who complained that the real women in the film are weak, pathetic creatures.

Indeed, the film's irony demands that Dorothy be a role model to the actual women, who learn to be more assertive and to stand up for what they believe from someone who has been culturally conditioned to take control. But Michael discovers that "being a woman in the eighties is complicated" and learns a lesson in compassion and empathy from Dorothy, which is where the story's feminism really kicks in. "I was a better man with you as a woman than I ever was as a man," Michael tells Julie at the film's conclusion, adding the comic kicker, "I just have to learn to do it without the dress."

10

The Lady Eve

Paramount (1941)
CAST: Barbara Stanwyck, Henry Fonda, Charles Coburn,
Eugene Pallette, William Demarest
DIRECTED BY: Preston Sturges
93 minutes [Not rated]

Slapstick and sophistication were wrapped into one bright shiny package by Preston Sturges, the undisputed king of sharp-witted and surefooted screwball comedy in the 1940s. Of all the dazzling presents Sturges bestowed on a grateful American public during his brief reign, *The Lady Eve* is his most beguiling.

Sturges began his celebrated career as a screenwriter and turned to directing in order to protect his delicately constructed creations. He was no stranger to pratfalls and no slouch when it came to visual humor. But he is remembered for his skill with words, for the way perfectly articulated sentiments flew fast and furious from the lips of his quick-witted, sharp-tongued characters, especially from his saucy, red-lipped heroines.

Sturges himself described his dialogue as "the bright things you would like to have said except you didn't think of in time." Looking back on the 1940s, comedy scholar Gerald Mast decreed, "No one wrote better 'dialogue comedies,' because no one wrote better dialogue." Sturges's scripts crackled with snappy repartee, delivered at a breathless pace by strong women and antiheroic men. Sturges's style was idiosyncratic, but beneath the distinctive artifice of his work lurked a cynical, satiric view of society, particularly of what passes for success in the land of plenty.

Based on the story "The Faithful Heart" by Monckton Hoffe, *The Lady Eve* was originally written for Claudette Colbert but reshaped for Barbara Stanwyck. The story, which opens on an ocean liner, focuses on a smart, shrewd swindler and cardsharp who, for fun and profit, parts fools from their money, assisted by her debonair, crafty father (Charles Coburn). Jean Harrington is an elegant, exuberant femme fatale, a pretty predator who is an exaggerated extreme of the typical, independent, worldly screwball heroine who generally falls for a less worldly, simpler mate.

ACE IN THE HOLE   Charles Coburn, left, and Barbara Stanwyck, center, as a father-daughter team of cardsharps, prepare to fleece naive Henry Fonda, right, in Preston Sturges's 1941 *The Lady Eve.* Critics regard *Eve* as writer-director Sturges's finest film.

The man who stumbles into her lair is about as unworldly as they come, despite his convenient, unearned millions. "Hopsy" is a gullible rube who loves snakes and cares little for the family's ale empire. Played by Henry Fonda, Hopsy is also an exaggeration of the screwball male who is outclassed and outwitted by a clever (although usually less maliciously duplicitous) woman.

Sturges thus tightens the screws on screwball comedy, creating tension and placing the story in the hard, cold grip of irony. The effect is further intensified by the casting of Stanwyck and Fonda, neither of them known for light comedy and worlds apart in temperament. Stanwyck is hot, commanding, and aggressive. Fonda is cool, soft, and sincere. Fonda's Hopsy is no match for Jean's professional feminine wiles, and he succumbs at once. Jean begins to appreciate the gentle ophiologist (snake specialist) and decides that instead of fleecing him, she'll marry the devoted dolt. Rather than a triumph of treachery over gullibility, innocence proves more seductive and powerful in this comedy of twists and turns.

The movie takes a hard right when Hopsy's suspicious and protective bodyguard (Sturges regular William Demarest) proves to Hopsy that he's being taken by pros. Hopsy glumly gives the shady lady the heave-ho. Bent on revenge, Jean stages an elaborate scam, posing as her own virtuous, upstanding, and completely fictitious sister, Lady Eve Sedgwick. She once again seduces the too trusting romantic. On their wedding night aboard a train, she gleefully subjects Hopsy to cruel and unusual punishment by rattling off the long list of her old lovers.

Although reconciled in the final frames, the pair spend most of the film at odds. In this romantic comedy the emphasis is decidedly on the comedy. The romance, in fact, is a little cool, a complaint sometimes lodged against Sturges, who preferred satire to sentiment even in his love stories. Still, as renowned film critic Manny Farber observed, Sturges was "probably the most spectacular manipulator of sheer humor since Mark Twain."

A freewheeling comedy classic, *The Lady Eve* is the story of a deceitful dame who gets her man by hook or crook. Along the way, the story pokes gentle fun at class bias, as we notice how much better the poseurs are at playing rich folks than the true moneyed gentry. The impersonators play their parts with relish and skill; their exuberance is quite intoxicating.

The Lady Eve screenplay is also rife with biblical references. When Jean/Eve first spies her mate, she initiates her temptation by hitting him on the head with an apple. Later, one of Hopsy's snakes gets loose, rattling the cool operator, who runs screaming from his cabin. The knowledge Hopsy gleans after tasting her forbidden fruit results in his being expelled from the ship, a Garden of Eden, which he leaves sadder but wiser. Eve twice disabuses her mate of his illusions of her innocence. Sturges, an educated sophisticate, loved literary allusions and symbolism.

The Lady Eve is now regarded as one of the great screwball comedies of all time and Sturges's best movie. It was the first bona fide commercial triumph for the writer-director, who had based the Oscar-nominated screenplay on personal experience. In particular, Jean was said to be loosely based on his mother, a much married bohemian adventuress. *The Lady Eve* topped the *New York Times'* "10 Best" list for 1941 and established Sturges as Paramount's fair-haired boy.

Sturges followed his success with three back-to-back hits, *Sullivan's Travels, The Palm Beach Story,* and *The Miracle of Morgan's Creek.* His last great comedy was *Unfaithfully Yours* (1948), starring Rex Harrison as a conductor unhinged by jealousy and remade with Dudley Moore in 1984. His career then floundered, and he died in 1959.

The Lady Eve was also remade in 1956 as *The Birds and the Bees,* starring Mitzi Gaynor, who was unable to fill Stanwyck's deadly stilettos. *The Lady Eve* was a personal triumph for Stanwyck. The versatile actress proved she could be glamorous in Edith Head's sexy costumes and funny in her first true comedy. Both fit perfectly.

11

A Fish Called Wanda

MGM (1988)
CAST: Jamie Lee Curtis, Kevin Kline, John Cleese,
Michael Palin, Tom Georgeson
DIRECTED BY: Charles Crichton
108 minutes [Rated R]

The happy collision between two legendary, long-defunct British comedy traditions—Monty Python and the Ealing Studio comedies—*A Fish Called Wanda* was written by John Cleese and expertly directed and cowritten by Charles Crichton.

Cleese, who also stars in the fast and furious comedy, has woven a wicked and wacky tale of treachery that owes much in spirit to the naughty nuttiness of Monty Python. Crichton, best known for the ingenious black comedy *The Lavender Hill Mob* (1951), is from an entirely different and far more elegant and understated school of film comedy. Although the style and content of the Ealing comedies and the Monty Python films are radically dissimilar, the two do share a self-deprecating wit and an irreverent tone. Like the botched-crime comedies that were Ealing's specialty, *A Fish Called Wanda* is a blithely amoral romp about a group of ruthless people whose greed, lust, and betrayals are humorously rendered.

The improbable intergenerational collaboration works like a charm. Crichton's refinement, precision, and cultivation provide the perfect balance to Cleese's singularly bizarre vision. Crichton brings structure and order to Cleese's erratic comic chaos. The result is one of the flat-out funniest farces and most inventive comedies of the 1980s.

The viciously funny *A Fish Called Wanda* was a triumphant comeback for the seventy-eight-year-old Crichton, who hadn't made a film in twenty years. Nominated for an Academy Award for best director, Crichton proved that he hadn't lost his flair for eccentricity. Nominated for a best original screenplay Oscar, *A Fish Called Wanda* was also a triumph for Cleese, who scored his greatest commercial and critical success to date with the heralded hit comedy.

There are two Wandas in this celebrated comic crime caper, sophisticated

THE WANDA YEARS   Michael Palin, left, John Cleese, center, and Kevin Kline, right, in the 1988 *A Fish Called Wanda.* Jamie Lee Curtis is squeezing Palin's rear end. *Wanda* combined the legendary traditions of British comedy of the 1950s with the irreverent lunacy of Monty Python—with hilarious results.

sex farce, and culture-clash comedy. One is a fish, the other is a dish. Jamie Lee Curtis stars as the latter, a farcical femme fatale who uses her wiles to ensnare men unfortunate enough to cross her path. Her first victim is George (Tom Georgeson), a smug and smarmy little jewel thief who has orchestrated a thirteen-million-pound diamond heist. Wanda, George's ostensible moll, has recruited weapons man Otto (Kevin Kline), whom she introduces as her brother but who is another of her duped lovers. Ken (Michael Palin), a competent crook with an excruciatingly funny stutter, is also smitten by Wanda. A devoted animal lover, Ken has named his pet fish Wanda in her honor.

The robbery goes like clockwork, except that during the getaway the thieves almost run over a little old lady (Patricia Hayes) walking her three dogs. Wanda and Otto double-cross George, fingering him to the police, and Wanda is about to triple-cross Otto when she discovers that George has moved the loot. Unable to weasel the whereabouts of the stash out of George when she visits him in prison, Wanda sets her sights on George's barrister, Archie Leach (Cleese). (In a tribute to the style of screwball farce personified by Cary Grant and emulated by *A Fish Called Wanda,* Cleese borrowed Cary Grant's real name for the role. Indeed, Leach, a dull fellow whose well-ordered universe is about to spin gleefully out of control, calls to mind Grant's hapless paleontologist in *Bringing Up Baby*.)

Posing as a law student interested in his work, Wanda wins Archie's lustful admiration but still can't find out where George has hidden the diamonds. Wanda's seduction of Archie, who has an unhappy home life with a shrewish wife (Maria Aitken) and is bored stiff being stiff and proper, is complicated by Otto. Jealous beyond all reason, Otto stalks Wanda and her intended paramour, popping up in the most unlikely places and at the most inopportune moments.

Otto, who hates to be called stupid, is a first-class harebrain with a hair-trigger temper who dresses in terrorist chic and reads Nietzsche. One of the film's funniest running gags involves Otto's lack of discernible intelligence. "He thought the Gettysburg Address is where Lincoln lived," Wanda laughingly confides to Archie. Later, when she calls Otto an ape, he defends himself by retorting, "Apes don't read philosophy." "Yes, they do," she counters. "They just don't understand it." She then proceeds to point out some of his other blunders. "Aristotle was *not* Belgian. The central message of Buddhism is *not* every man for himself. The London underground is *not* a political movement."

Otto's idiocy is brilliantly played by Kline, a versatile actor especially adept at farce, at which he also excelled in *Soapdish* and *In and Out*. Kline deservedly won the best actor Oscar for his role as the hotheaded American hit man in *A Fish Called Wanda*.

One of the prime sources of humor in *A Fish Called Wanda* is the contrast between the wild and woolly Americans (Wanda and Otto) and the Brits: Ken, Archie, and George. Otto continually makes fun of English decorum and assumes most English men are gay. "I love robbing the English. They are so polite," he jokes. Later he observes that rigor mortis sets in before "limeys" hit middle age. Archie, too, complains that "we're all so dead." "Do you have any idea what it's like to be English?" he asks Wanda, noting that he lives in mortal dread of embarrassment. His fears come true when he's caught in the buff by old acquaintances at an apartment he has borrowed for a tryst with Wanda.

Wanda and Otto, on the other hand, may be without taste, class, or principles, but they are utterly uninhibited. Archie ultimately finds Wanda so liberating, he decides to chuck it all and run off to Rio with her and the stolen goods. Otto also loves to bully and berate the utterly British Ken, a sensitive and sweet man marvelously played by Palin. Ken's unfortunate stutter, while a source of great amusement, betrays a slight cruel streak in the comedy. The cruelty escalates when the animal-loving Ken tries to bump off the old lady who is the only witness to the crime—but keeps accidentally killing her dogs. Then there's the scene in which Otto, in order to discover where George has hidden the diamonds, tortures Ken by eating his beloved fish one by one. Clearly *A Fish Called Wanda* is not for the faint of heart.

Although a few critics noted that the comedy goes a bit too far at times, *A Fish Called Wanda* earned the kind of universal praise that is rare for a comedy, particularly one so bold and indelicate. *Sight and Sound* magazine attributed the film's success to Crichton. "To those who appreciate Ealing comedy (which is to say all right-thinking people), watching the film is like chancing on a Hogarth sketch in grandmother's attic, clearly and unmistakably signed by the Master." *Time* magazine noted that the buoyant comedy "defies gravity, in both senses of the word, and redefines a great comic tradition." The *Village Voice* described Wanda as "a saggy, overloaded cargo plane of comedy that lumbers down the runway and manages—through sheer, manic resourcefulness—not merely to fly but to soar." The *Los Angeles Times* dubbed it "low comedy at high speed," lauding Kline's "deliriously dotty" performance. *Newsday* proclaimed it a "zany, sexy, witty romp with a superb cast of British and American farceurs."

The comedy bolstered the career of Curtis, who had successfully played a tramp in the 1983 hit comedy *Trading Places.* Curtis took full charge of the flagrantly sexy role, playing Wanda with steely determination and a bright spirit. Cleese, who won the British Academy Award for best actor, works wonders with a straight role, mining subtle humor from his character's psychic distress and ultimate liberation. Palin, who won the British supporting actor Academy Award, also scored a major post-Python success with *A Fish Called Wanda,* which required him to play a fully fleshed-out role rather than sketch a quick caricature.

In 1995 Cleese reunited his costars for *Fierce Creatures,* a farce directed by Robert Young concerning the complications that ensue when a corporation takes over a British zoo. The film was shelved, then reworked under the direction of Fred Schepsi and released in 1997. Although sporadically funny, with fine work by Kline in a dual role, *Fierce Creatures* was a flop that tried but failed to create the riotous comic energy that fed *A Fish Called Wanda.*

12

The General

United Artists (1927)
CAST: **Buster Keaton, Marion Mack**
DIRECTED BY: **Buster Keaton and Clyde Bruckman**
74 minutes [Not rated]

Buster Keaton's acclaimed masterpiece is also ranked as "the most formally perfect and funniest of all silent film comedies" in the *Videohound's Golden Movie Retriever.* When the American Film Institute polled the nation's critics in 1977 to pick the fifty greatest films ever made, *The General* was the only silent film on the list. *The General* was Keaton's most personal film as well as his favorite. "I'm more proud of that picture than any I ever made," Keaton said.

The General deserves every accolade heaped upon it. It stands unrivaled for sustained humor, not to mention suspense. It is a seamless, flawless film that moves with the speed and power of a steaming locomotive. It is also graceful and poignant, visually stunning and exciting. And it has more hilarious and perfectly executed sight gags and inventive comic set pieces than any other silent comedy.

Watching the film today, I find it impossible to fathom how its greatness could have gone unappreciated in its day. *Variety* deemed it "a flop" on its release in 1927, an opinion shared by most of the nation's critics, who failed to see either its humor or its beauty.

Written and directed by Keaton, *The General* combined the star's two great loves, trains and history. The story was based on an actual event that took place during the Civil War, and Keaton paid painstaking attention to historical detail in his monumental epic, which achieves a level of authenticity and realism rare in silent film. The film's climactic scene, in which a train passing over a flaming bridge falls into the river canyon below, was the most expensive single shot in silent film history.

Known as the Great Stone Face for his trademark stoicism, Keaton was at the height of his fame when he undertook this labor of love. The actor, who mined humor from his impassive reaction to whatever fate hurled at him, had learned growing up in vaudeville that the best way to get a laugh was not to smile. Always unflappable, Keaton was funny not because of what he did, but because of how he reacted. His comedy hinged on his nonplused attitude and nonchalant deportment. He virtually invented deadpan comedy.

A master at underplaying a scene, Keaton also had a knack for making the difficult look effortless. He found the perfect part in Johnnie Gray, the engineer of a Confederate steam engine called the *General*. Johnnie is a simple man devoted to his engine and his girl, Annabelle Lee (Marion Mack), in that order. When war comes to Georgia, Johnnie tries to enlist but is rejected because he's more valuable as an engineer. Annabelle thinks he's a coward and spurns him. Johnnie is thus placed in the classic Keaton position, the object of scorn and contempt who must prove his worth to the world. Again and again Keaton played little guys battling a hostile world, fighting the forces of nature or the monsters of modern technology.

In *The General* Johnnie single-handedly wages battle against the entire Union army. To accomplish the impossible task he must also control a complex and mighty piece of machinery. When his beloved train is stolen by the North, with Annabelle Lee aboard, Johnnie rushes to the rescue. Despite every obstacle thrown in his tracks, he manages to save the day, his girl, and the South.

The General is one long, extended, and incredibly elaborated chase, intercut with moments of respite that move the story along. Johnnie remains in continual motion throughout the film as he doggedly surmounts one challenge after another. Through all the comic disasters, Johnnie never reveals his fear or his frustration as he finds pragmatic solutions to each new problem. Yet underneath his unruffled manner we feel urgency and determination building.

The General was almost Keaton's swan song—and was certainly his last great film. The movie lost money and sent Keaton into a slow tailspin. By the early 1930s he was washed up and remained forgotten until 1952, when Chaplin gave him a small part in *Limelight*. In 1957 he served as technical supervisor of *The Buster Keaton Story*, which starred Donald O'Connor. In 1959 he was awarded a special Academy Award. These events rescued him from anonymity and brought him new audiences and appreciation. Until his death in 1966, Keaton made guest appearances in several films.

Today Keaton is remembered not just for *The General*, but for a string of classic comedies. *The Navigator* (1924) was his most financially successful film, although modern audiences delight in *Sherlock Jr.*, made the same year. Keaton is credited with numerous cinematic advances. He was the first director to film comedy at standard speed so that it did not have the manic look popular at the time. Although his stories often had a surrealistic quality (which might account for their popularity with modern audiences), he insisted on

BEST FOOT FORWARD   The one and only poker face, Buster Keaton, in 1927's *The General.*
Though the film fared poorly at the box office when first released, critics now recognize *The
General* as Keaton's finest hour. "I'm more proud of *The General* than any [other film] I ever
made," Keaton has said.

creating a natural look. He favored long shots and tracking shots and
employed the camera in creative ways, yet he never resorted to camera tricks
to fake his stuntwork.

Although he left behind a canon of work for us to enjoy, *The General*
encapsulates all of Keaton's best qualities. Keaton's daring, imagination, physical grace, and deft comic touch are all on ample display in this dazzling
series of sight gags. His humorous heroics make us laugh, even as we hold
our breath.

13

Born Yesterday

Columbia (1950)
CAST: Judy Holliday, Broderick Crawford, William Holden
DIRECTED BY: George Cukor
103 minutes [Not rated]

It is impossible to imagine anyone other than brassy, sassy Judy Holliday playing the prototypical dumb blonde Billie Dawn in *Born Yesterday.* Holliday gave one of the flat-out funniest (as well as most appealing) female comedy performances in film history as the irrepressibly brash Billie—playing both her vulgarity and vulnerability—in the screen adaptation of Garson Kanin's play about an uncouth millionaire junk dealer who hires a genteel reporter to turn his coarse, ex–chorus girl mistress into a lady.

Although Holliday had created and played the role for four years on the Broadway stage, when Columbia head Harry Cohn optioned the hit play for a record $1 million, he refused even to grant a screen test to Holliday, whom he dismissed as "a fat Jewish broad." Rita Hayworth was Cohn's first choice. Luckily George Cukor, who had landed the plum assignment of directing the comedy, was above all else a fine judge of female acting talent. The highest-paid director in Hollywood at the time, Cukor was known as a literate, witty, sophisticated "women's director." In a career that spanned fifty years, he guided Greta Garbo in *Camille,* Jean Harlow in *Dinner at Eight,* Ingrid Bergman in *Gaslight,* Judy Garland in *A Star Is Born,* and Katharine Hepburn in ten films, including *The Philadelphia Story* (ranked fifty-one in the American Film Institute's 1998 list of the one hundred best films).

Cukor had given Holliday her first screen role, a small part in *Winged Victory* in 1947. He had to find a way to convince the despotic and crass Columbia boss (who ironically served as Kanin's model for junk dealer Harry Brock in *Born Yesterday*) to give Holliday a chance. Cukor delayed the project two years in order to convince Cohn to cast her. On the advice of playwright Kanin, who also wanted Holliday to star in the screen adaptation, Cukor cast Holliday in *Adam's Rib* (1949), written by Kanin and his wife, Ruth Gordon. Holliday played a dim-witted but plucky woman on trial for shooting her no-good husband (Tom Ewell). Katharine Hepburn played her defense attorney, Spencer Tracy the prosecuting attorney. Cukor and Kanin enlisted his stars in his campaign to show Holliday off to her best advantage to impress Cohn. The conspiracy worked.

When Cohn saw Holliday's shaded performance in *Adam's Rib,* he gave her the green light and was so pleased with her performance in *Born Yesterday,* he predicted she'd win an Oscar. Holliday did win the Academy Award, as well as a Golden Globe, for best actress in 1950, beating out Bette Davis in *All About Eve* and Gloria Swanson in *Sunset Boulevard. Born Yesterday* received five Oscar nominations, including best picture, director, and screenplay.

Launched into stardom, Holliday next appeared in Cukor's *The Marrying Kind,* written for her by Kanin and Gordon. Although she continued to be a leading screen comedian until she died of cancer at the age of forty-four in 1965, she entered screen immortality as Billie Dawn.

Kanin had originally written the part of Billie for Jean Arthur, who became nervous about playing the "stunningly beautiful, stunningly stupid" dynamo and dropped out during the out-of-town run. Holliday stepped in on three days' notice and opened on Broadway, playing the role of the unrefined and uninhibited Billie—half vixen, half waif—to enormous acclaim.

Billie Dawn is a marvelous invention, a comic character of unusual depth who undergoes a remarkable transition and exacts a delicious revenge on her abusive mate. She also has the funniest voice this side of Betty Boop. At first Billie seems hilariously stupid as well as gloriously, unabashedly vulgar. In time we see that she is merely ignorant and has an innate intelligence, a keen wit, and a good heart. She is, in fact, much smarter—as well as more honest and ethical—than her loutish mate, who bullies and belittles her at every turn. Paul Douglas had played the part of the brutish junk dealer on the stage, but tough guy Broderick Crawford was cast to make the character of Harry Brock even more unattractive, thus encouraging the movie audience to root for Billie to fall in love with her kind and principled tutor, played by William Holden.

Well matched in pitch and crudity, Holliday and Crawford have some of the funniest moments on screen, including the famous silent gin game that remains one of the brightest scenes in screen comedy history. Holliday, whose shrill voice punctures the air with every untutored pronouncement, is shushed into silence by her partner, who is annoyed by her winning streak. Lustily singing a wordless burlesque melody, she beats him anyway.

Billie, who doesn't know what the Supreme Court is and doesn't know the difference between a peninsula and penicillin, has been signing papers for Harry for years without question. Harry tells her she's his "silent partner—so shut up." In fact, she owns more of Harry than Harry, who is involved in dozens of crooked deals and has come to Washington to buy government influence.

HOLLIDAY FOR LOVERS   Broderick Crawford, left, William Holden, center, and Judy Holliday, right, in George Cukor's 1950 *Born Yesterday*. Holliday won both an Oscar and a Golden Globe for her portrayal of not-so-dumb blonde Billie Dawn.

Under the tutelage of Paul Varall (Holden), Billie begins to read voraciously, devouring books on American history that teach her valuable moral, political, and ethical lessons. When Harry asks her to sign more papers, she decides to read them first, setting in motion her plan to free herself from Harry and put him over a barrel. Billie learns that knowledge is power and that "there's a better kind of life" than the shallow, materialistic one she's been leading with Harry, a greedy, mean, selfish man whom she comes to call "a fascist" and, later, "antisocial" (after looking it up in the dictionary).

Born Yesterday is considered a dialogue comedy, and with good reason. Line after line is wickedly funny, and Holliday's ripe repartee is made even funnier by her delivery. It's Holliday's intonation and accent, as well as her timing, that make us laugh. When Harry's crooked lawyer patiently tries to explain what a merger is, Billie suddenly cries, "A cartel!" Her voice lets us know she's proud of herself for figuring it out as well as outraged by the concept. Later, her voice is similarly full of glee and scorn as she recognizes Harry's misuse of language. "Double negative! Right?" she squawks, turning to Paul for confirmation.

One of the triumphs of *Born Yesterday* is that while Billie does smarten up, she is not totally transformed into a lady, as in *My Fair Lady* (for which Cukor won his fifth Oscar nomination and his first win in 1964). Billie never becomes dull and refined. She retains her hilarious speech patterns and continues to employ vulgar vernacular: "As far as I'm *concoined*—visa *voysa*"; "Don't knock yourself out, you gotta lotta surprises comin'"; "Do me a favor: Drop dead."

In the tepid 1992 remake of *Born Yesterday,* Melanie Griffith failed to make Billie's ignorance as amusing. Where Holliday crafted a comic persona, Griffith merely played dumb. The remake lacked the elegance, precision, and zest of the original.

Cukor's tastefully outrageous classic delights in Billie's commonness, but the humor is not condescending. Billie is shown to have good common sense, a great joy for life, and an indomitable spirit. She even gives Paul a lesson in the merits of writing clearly and simply. Billie tells Paul that an article he wrote was the best thing she'd ever read but confesses she didn't understand a word, even after she looked each one up. He explains what he meant with the high-flown phrases and convoluted structure. "Well, why didn't you say that?" she asks. The look he gives her tells us he realizes she's right.

Billie, it turns out, was not born yesterday. She's one smart cookie. In a sense, however, she's born during the course of the movie. We've watched the caterpillar turn into a brilliant, if garish, butterfly—with glasses. Billie gets the last laugh and the last line of the film. Stopped by a police officer after marrying Paul, she tells the cop that the union was a case of predestination. "What's that?" the cop asks. "Look it up," she tells him with a loopy grin, victory lighting up her baby-doll face.

14

The Producers

Avco Embassy (1967)
CAST: Zero Mostel, Gene Wilder, Kenneth Mars, Dick Shawn
WRITTEN AND DIRECTED BY: Mel Brooks
88 minutes [Not rated]

In 1961 a struggling comedy writer and performer named Mel Brooks announced his intention to write a play called *Springtime for Hitler* and to marry the acclaimed actress Anne Bancroft, whom he had just met. His friends scoffed at both ideas. The play, about a pair of producers who stage a Nazi musical to scam investors, was deemed too offensive to ever see the light of day. Friends also dismissed the notion that the largely unknown Jewish funnyman could win the hand of the Italian American starlet turned serious stage actress. His friends underestimated the crazy comic's chutzpah on both counts.

Mad Mel persevered with both projects. Brooks, born Melvin Kaminsky, married Bancroft, born Anne Italiano, in 1964. Three years later principal photography began on *The Producers,* which had evolved from a premise of dubious taste to an outrageous screenplay. Brooks had shopped the script around Hollywood with no success until his friend Barry Levinson (*Avalon, Diner, Rain Man*) introduced him to an independent producer who not only loved the screenplay, but insisted Brooks make his directing debut with it. *The Producers* was hailed as a comic masterpiece, and although it did only moderate business, it earned Brooks an Oscar for best original screenplay.

The Producers launched the film career of the actor, director, and writer, who joined the swelling ranks of urban Jewish directors, taking his place alongside two other major film artists who rose to prominence in the late 1960s, Woody Allen and Paul Mazursky. Brooks, the ultimate extrovert, is the flip side of introverted, cynical, and cerebral Woody Allen. Crude and vulgar, Brooks represents the Borscht Belt tradition of wacky, irreverent, anything-goes burlesque. "Over the top" is a compliment when applied to a Mel Brooks movie.

Much of the enduring popularity of *The Producers* rests on the performances of its superb comic stars, who appear to be having the time of their life hamming it up. The script was written expressly for Zero Mostel, who was at the height of his fame, and Gene Wilder, here cast in only his second film and his first comedy. Wilder was nominated for a best supporting actor Oscar for his work in *The Producers* and went on to work with Brooks again in the hugely popular *Blazing Saddles* and the hilariously outrageous *Young Frankenstein,* considered by some to be Brooks's funniest film.

The Producers is a broad farce featuring two stock Jewish caricatures. Boisterous has-been producer Max Bialystock (Mostel) is an uncouth, scheming, money-loving lout who bilks little old ladies, seducing them into investing in terrible plays. Timid accountant Leo Bloom (Wilder) is a classic schnook. Phobic, hysterical, repressed, and socially inept, Bloom stumbles upon a get-rich-quick scheme, and Bialystock convinces him to become his partner in crime.

They plan to raise more money than they need for a show that they are sure will close after one night—and then abscond with the excess cash. Their success depends on finding a surefire flop. *Springtime for Hitler,* a musical romp extolling life in the Third Reich, written by rabid ex-Nazi Franz Liebkind (Kenneth Mars), is so offensive and awful, they are positive it will fail. (In one of those classic Hollywood coincidences, Brooks's neighbor Dustin Hoffman, then an unknown actor, wanted to play the part of the dumb and demented German playwright but instead was cast in the career-making title role in *The Graduate*—playing opposite Brooks's wife, Anne Bancroft.)

To further ensure failure, the producers hire the worst possible actor to play Hitler, a zonked-out singer and overgrown flower child named LSD, hilariously enacted by Dick Shawn. They find an incompetent gay director, played by Christopher Hewett, who is pretentious and difficult. To seal their doom, on opening night they insult the drama critic by offering him a bribe.

The brilliantly devious plan backfires when the show, perceived by the public as a parody, becomes a sensation. This turn of events provides a bit of social commentary, suggesting that audiences are so undiscriminating, they can't tell trash from travesty. Perhaps not coincidentally, however, Brooks went on to build a career on the idea that audiences will mistake the truly tasteless for campy satire; if something is bad enough, it becomes good.

Similarly, although many viewers find his work distasteful, others feel Brooks has elevated poor taste to a fine art. In spoof after spoof Brooks parodies genres such as horror films, the western, Hitchcock thrillers—and whatever film is popular at the moment—by mimicking them amateurishly. Because his later work is deliberately derivative, *The Producers* is widely considered his most original comedy. Certainly the staging of *Springtime for Hitler* is an incomparably outlandish scene that ranks among the all-time funniest moments in movie history.

Gloriously uninhibited and crass, *The Producers* is actually more polished and inspired than much of Brooks's later work, which has become increas-

BIALYSTOCK AND BLOOM   Gene Wilder, left, and Zero Mostel, right, in Mel Brooks's 1967 laugh fest, *The Producers.* "Didja ever think you'd love a show called *Springtime for Hitler?*" is what the folks behind Wilder and Mostel are asking. With *The Producers* and, six years later, *Blazing Saddles,* Mad Mel elevated bad taste into a fine art.

ingly juvenile, repetitive, and scattered. In 1967 the comic excess of *The Producers* was hailed as liberating and novel, although some critics found his caricatures to be offensive. Indeed, Brooks is an equal opportunity offender and routinely makes use of negative stereotypes. But while he has some fun at the expense of the swishy gay director, for example, he is really condemning him for his artistic pretensions.

Although they are both playing stock figures, Wilder and Mostel bring infectious exuberance to their parts. And while the Jewish character types are unflattering, Bialystock and Bloom are by far the most sympathetic, sane characters in the film, which is peopled with raving lunatics. Bialystock may be unethical, but he exudes life force. Although he leads Bloom astray, he also teaches him to enjoy life, to take risks, to break out of his shell.

Some critics have argued that *The Producers* makes an important point, expressing outrage against the Holocaust by ridiculing the obscene absurdity of the Nazis. Comparisons have been made between *The Producers* and Chaplin's *The Great Dictator* and Ernst Lubitsch's *To Be or Not to Be,* both of which deflate the menace of the Master Race by satirizing it. Brooks went on to remake *To Be or Not to Be,* a 1942 anti-Fascist comedy that once again allowed him to thumb his nose at the Nazis.

Still, it would be a mistake to credit Brooks with too grand a political agenda. Brooks is a compulsive clown whose one great, desperate desire is to induce belly laughs. In *The Producers* he gets his wish.

15

All of Me

Universal (1984)
CAST: **Steve Martin, Lily Tomlin, Victoria Tennant,
Selma Diamond, Richard Libertini**
DIRECTED BY: **Carl Reiner**
93 minutes [Rated PG]

Steve Martin and Lily Tomlin give new meaning to the term "costar" in *All of Me,* Carl Reiner's quirky role reversal comedy. Martin and Tomlin, two of the most inventive, intelligent, and original comics to emerge in the 1970s, share screen time, and a body, in this fabulously funny fantasy about love, money, happiness, and spirit transmigration.

Martin plays Roger Cobb, a lawyer and frustrated jazz musician facing a midlife crisis that renders him incapable of reconciling his desire for respect, success, and stability with the nagging suspicion that there must be more to life. Roger, who is dating the boss's daughter in his halfhearted attempt to get ahead, is assigned the thankless task of overseeing the affairs of the firm's richest, crankiest, and most eccentric client. Edwina Cutwater (Tomlin), who has spent her life as an invalid unable to enjoy her vast wealth, is about to die, alone and unfulfilled. Determined to buy a second chance at health and happiness, she has hired an Eastern mystic to transfer her departing soul into the comely young body of her stableman's daughter, Terry (Victoria Tennant). Terry is Edwina's sole—and "soul"—beneficiary. Terry, however, has agreed to vacate her own body because she doesn't believe for a second that the hare-brained heiress's crackpot plan will work.

The first meeting does not go well. Edwina dismisses Roger as the firm's "tedious one" and "a presumptuous ambulance chaser." Outraged by her imperious manner and appalled by her daft plan, Roger can't resist informing Edwina that she's obviously nuts.

Beatific, befuddled mystic Prahka Lasa (hilariously played by Richard Libertini) may wear a funny hat and speak not a word of intelligible English, but he is the genuine article and is indeed able to extract Edwina's ephemeral being from her dying body. An accident at the moment of transmigration sends Edwina's soul into Roger's body, however, creating the ultimate split

57

personality. Much to the chagrin of both parties, who detest each other, Roger and Edwina control separate sides of Roger's body, leading to bang-up physical humor.

But *All of Me,* the fourth collaboration between Martin and director Reiner, is much more than a deftly directed slapstick comedy expertly performed by one of contemporary cinema's finest physical comedians. Based on the novel *Me Two* by Ed Davis, *All of Me* was written by Phil Alden Robinson (*Field of Dreams*), who creates an unexpectedly affecting screwball romance and a liberating, freewheeling fantasy that lightly touches on serious themes.

Just as actor Michael Dorsey (Dustin Hoffman) learned to be a better male by inhabiting the female character he created in *Tootsie,* Roger becomes a better human being when his body is inhabited by a woman. Hilariously struggling to coordinate his female side with his male side, Roger also finds himself suddenly speaking in Edwina's refreshingly frank voice and begins to see things through her eyes. Edwina liberates the free spirit trapped in Roger, who begins to feel Edwina's sadness at a life spent cruelly denied the pleasures most people take for granted.

Again echoing the theme of *Tootsie,* the film contains a message about integrating the male and female aspects of human experience into a balanced whole. It also comments on the possibility of male and female coexisting in close quarters by cooperating. In one of the funniest scenes, Roger falls asleep in court while defending his boss in a messy divorce, and Edwina, now in total command, saves the day as only a woman could. Martin is brilliant as a man playing a woman who is playing a man—a reversal of the gender bending in *Victor/Victoria,* in which Julie Andrews plays a woman masquerading as a man who plays a woman on stage.

Martin, a gifted physical comedian who specializes in portraying a mixture of arrogant, cynical superiority and vulnerable self-doubt, is perfectly suited to the physical and emotional challenge of the split persona. Tomlin is also well cast as the lonely, bossy oddball, whose voice we hear inside Roger's head and whose reflection we see each time Roger looks in the mirror, a device that keeps Tomlin from disappearing completely. Still, the movie belongs to Martin.

Martin, honored with the best actor award from the New York Film Critics for his tour-de-force performance as Roger/Edwina, began his comedy career as a stand-up comic. Known for his "wild and crazy guy" caricatures on TV's *Saturday Night Live,* his Grammy Award–winning comedy albums, concerts, and his novelty single, "King Tut," Martin was already a megastar when he made the leap onto the big screen with an Academy Award–nominated short film he wrote and directed in 1977, *The Absent-Minded Waiter.*

In 1979 Martin and Reiner scored a huge hit with *The Jerk,* a goofy, juvenile comedy that grossed over $100 million and made Martin a certified movie

SHALL WE DANCE Lily Tomlin and Steve Martin trip the light fantastic in Carl Reiner's 1984 *All of Me*. Fifteen years after its initial release, this underrated comedy about role reversal is finally being appreciated for the true comedy classic it is, due in no small part to Martin's amazing performance.

star. He went on to make the underrated, unconventional *Pennies from Heaven*, directed by Herbert Ross, then reteamed with Reiner for the lighter comedies *Dead Men Don't Wear Plaid* and *The Man with Two Brains* and starred in *The Lonely Guy*. Although not without merit, none of these amusing but slight comedies were big hits.

Martin returned to public favor with a vengeance with *All of Me,* which earned mixed reviews from the critics. Dismissed by Rex Reed as "an absurd trifle," and by the *Los Angeles Times* as "fitfully funny," *All of Me* was called "an uproarious slapstick farce" by *Newsday* and recommended, with reservations, by the majority of critics.

Martin went on to make one of the most appealing romantic comedies of the 1980s, *Roxanne,* an updating of *Cyrano de Bergerac* that earned him a best actor award from the Los Angeles Film Critics and an award for best screenplay by the Writers Guild of America. Martin has also graced notable comedies such as *Dirty Rotten Scoundrels, Parenthood, My Blue Heaven, Planes, Trains and Automobiles,* and *Father of the Bride.* As both an actor for hire and the creative force behind risky, sophisticated comedies such as 1991's *L.A. Story,* Martin has successfully made the transition from stand-up comic to major comedy star and respected actor. With the possible exception of Robin Williams, he has made more outstanding comedies than any of his fellow stand-up and TV comedy graduates, including Bill Murray, Dan Aykroyd, Chevy Chase, Eddie Murphy, Whoopi Goldberg, Bette Midler—or Lily Tomlin.

Tomlin, who also rose through the ranks of TV and concert comedy, made an auspicious screen debut in 1975 as the distraught gospel singer in Robert Altman's ruefully amusing *Nashville,* followed by another brilliantly wacky performance in *The Late Show.* She had a popular hit with *Nine to Five* in 1980 and again earned accolades for *All of Me,* even though she was overshadowed by Martin's virtuoso performance. She was similarly upstaged by Bette Midler in *Big Business* (1988) and in recent years has enjoyed more success with smaller roles in Altman's *Short Cuts* and *The Player.*

Reiner also began his film comedy career in TV, writing for *Your Show of Shows* and *The Dick Van Dyke Show.* He began acting in TV and film before making his directing debut with *Enter Laughing* in 1967, based on his autobiographical novel, followed by the bleakly funny cult comedy classic *Where's Poppa?* in 1970. Reiner enjoyed wide popular success with 1977's *Oh God!,* followed by *The Jerk,* one of the screen's biggest comedy hits. His collaboration with Martin continued revitalizing his career for a period, although his recent film comedies—*Summer Rental, Summer School, Sibling Rivalry, Fatal Instinct,* and *That Old Feeling*—have been disappointing and he is, sadly, better known today as Rob Reiner's father. *All of Me* remains his most artistically accomplished comedy.

The pairing of Martin and Tomlin, well matched in comic maturity, intensity, and idiosyncrasy, was an inspiration. Combining them into a single schizophrenic character was a stroke of genius.

16

After Hours

Warner Bros. (1985)
CAST: Griffin Dunne, Rosanna Arquette, Teri Garr, John Heard,
Catherine O'Hara, Linda Fiorentino, Verna Bloom
DIRECTED BY: Martin Scorsese
97 minutes [Rated R]

Martin Scorsese is not a name that springs to mind in association with comedy: he is better known for serious, brutal, provocative, and generally humorless examinations of the human condition, the director of such hard-hitting dramas as *Raging Bull, Taxi Driver, The Last Temptation of Christ, Goodfellas, Cape Fear,* and *Casino.* Scorsese first turned his attention to the comic genre with *The King of Comedy* in 1983, testing the limits of humor with his gripping portrait of the comedian as obsessive psychopath. *The King of Comedy* plays like the flip side of *Taxi Driver,* with frustrated would-be comedian Rupert Pupkin (Robert De Niro) as Travis Bickle's comic soulmate.

More disturbing than funny, the edgy comedy of psychic alienation led to Scorsese's next foray into the world of dark humor. Naturally interested in the hallucinatory side of humor, specifically the comic manifestation of paranoia and panic, Scorsese created one of the best nightmare comedies ever made, *After Hours,* for which he earned the best director prize at the Cannes Film Festival.

The Kafkaesque story of Paul Hackett (Griffin Dunne), a bored word processor who craves a little romance, adventure, and excitement and gets more than he bargains for, *After Hours* depicts a hellishly funny evening in which everything that can possibly go wrong does. The film operates on the slippery slope of dream logic, dominated by absurdity and anxiety, frustration and fear; it is anything but a happy or comforting comedy. Still, we laugh—at times heartily and at others hesitantly—at the bizarre twists and creepy turns of Paul's escalating misadventures, sensing it is all a bad dream from which he will soon wake . . . or so we hope.

Scorsese had just been through his own nightmare, trying—as yet unsuccessfully—to get *The Last Temptation of Christ* onto the screen. When the project fell through at the last minute, he had to find another film quickly but

61

A NIGHT IN SoHo   Griffin Dunne, center, flanked by Cheech Marin, left, and Tommy Chong, right, in Martin Scorsese's 1985 *After Hours.* After such hard-hitting movies as *Taxi Driver* and *Raging Bull,* Scorsese decided to turn his talents to comedy; *After Hours* was the result.

turned down *Beverly Hills Cop* and *Witness.* Then he read *Lies* (later titled *A Night in SoHo*), a script written as a class project by Columbia student Joseph Minion. Minion's teacher, Dusan Makavejev (the director of the very funny comedy *Montenegro*), had given him an A and taken the script to Robert Redford's Sundance Institute. Coincidentally, the script was optioned by Amy Robinson, who had acted in Scorsese's *Mean Streets.* Robinson enlisted Griffin Dunne, with whom she had produced *Chilly Scenes of Winter* and *Baby, It's You,* who was immediately attracted to the role of an average guy caught in a vortex of escalating madness.

Minion's dark comedy drew on an odd variety of sources, including Orson Welles's films noir (*Touch of Evil, The Lady From Shanghai*), Hitchcock's romantic mysteries (*Marnie, Rear Window, The Birds*), the Keystone Kops, Charlie Chaplin, and the plays of Ionesco, Beckett, and Pinter. Wanting to do a surrealistic movie realistically, Scorsese hired the brilliant, now famous European cinematographer Michael Ballhaus to help him achieve the subjective perspective and the effect of a heightened reality. Scorsese was particularly attracted to the low-key project, which he made for $4.5 million, by the possibility of parodying Hitchcock's subject and style. Indeed, Paul closely resembles the "wrong man" heroes who fall victim to calamity in Hitchcock's films.

When Paul walks out of his office at the end of the film's opening scene, he dreams of escaping his sterile, lonely life and his dull workaday world. Before long he's plunged into a parallel universe, proving the maxim "Be careful what you wish for because you just might get it." Reading *The Tropic of Cancer* at a coffee shop that night, Paul meets a lovely yet slightly strange young woman named Marcie (Rosanna Arquette), who shares his passion for Henry Miller. Paul eventually follows Marcie home to SoHo, losing his twenty-dollar bill during the wild cab ride. Arriving well after midnight, Paul finds Marcie's roommate, Kiki (Linda Fiorentino), a sexy sculptress, working on an anguished papier-mâché human figure. Marcie appears to be in some kind of crisis, which may involve mysterious second-degree burns. Appealing but flaky, Marcie tells Paul odd stories about her life that both repel and fascinate the essentially ordinary, normal guy. When things get too weird, Paul makes his escape into the rainy night but finds he lacks subway fare home owing to a rate hike that went into effect at midnight—the witching hour, when different rules apply.

Taking refuge from the rain in a bar, he hooks up with the kooky waitress Julie (Teri Garr) and her kindly boss, Tom (John Heard), who offers Paul subway fare in return for a favor. There have been a rash of burglaries in the neighborhood, and Paul is sent to Tom's apartment to make sure his alarm is on. Accosted by Tom's suspicious neighbors, Paul is presumed to be the burglar, and he ends up being chased by an angry vigilante mob.

Returning to Marcie's loft, he sees two men (Cheech and Chong) putting Kiki's sculpture into a van and assumes they are the thieves. In fact they have bought the sculpture, but in a story where nothing is as it seems, they really are the robbers. Things go from bad to worse when Paul finds Marcie dead from an overdose of sleeping pills. In one of the many bizarre coincidences in this tale of tangled lives, Marcie turns out to have been Tom's girlfriend.

As Paul recounts, with mounting hysteria, the fantastic events of the evening—each one possible yet improbable—to an incredulous gay man who has taken him home, the hilarity of the ludicrous situation reaches full expression. "All I wanted to do was go out with a girl and have a nice time. Do I have to die for it?" Paul asks in desperation.

Paul is plunged not only into a nightmare of mistakes and confusions, but also into a bohemian subculture that operates outside the rules that govern normal human society. In this fearful fascination with society's rebels, *After Hours* resembles a number of other comedies of the period, most notably Susan Seidelman's *Desperately Seeking Susan*. Released the same year as *After Hours* and also starring Rosanna Arquette, the box office hit featured a strikingly similar story. Arquette plays a bored housewife who, through a case of amnesia, is mistaken for a free-living, amoral hustler played by Madonna. In Seidelman's highly original and captivating comedy, however, the walk on the wild side has a liberating effect. Although *Desperately Seeking Susan* holds a more romantic view of alternative lifestyles, both films imagine life on the fringe as dangerous, sexy, exciting—starkly contrasted with the empty, materialistic, middle-class life. These films reflect a cultural malaise, a general discontentment with convention, and a latent desire to let go of our inhibitions.

This liberating joyride premise was also explored in 1986 in *Something Wild,* Jonathan Demme's comedy about a mild-mannered businessman who hooks up with a wacky vamp (Melanie Griffith) and finds himself on a terrifying but enthralling adventure. Demme had earlier explored eccentricity in his acclaimed 1980 bittersweet comedy, *Melvin and Howard.* Also in 1986, David Lynch released *Blue Velvet,* about an innocent young man who is thrust into a world of danger and depravity. Lynch explored the theme again in *Wild at Heart,* his much lighter and brighter, funny and frightening, 1990 excursion into the heart of erotic passion.

These rigorous films, *After Hours* chief among them, were all made by thoughtful, accomplished directors. Andrew Sarris proclaimed that *After Hours* established Scorsese as "the most talented of his generation's non-mainstream filmmakers." *Variety* called the comedy "a must for serious-minded filmgoers." *After Hours* was part of a comedy trend that emerged in the 1980s, when hip, eccentric comedies aimed at a young but intelligent and educated audience became popular. Offering the antithesis of the dumb, adolescent humor of *Animal House,* but sharing its anarchic sensibility, comedies such as *After Hours* appealed to sophisticated audiences hungry for fresh humor that reflected the tensions and anxiety of modern life.

Scorsese shrewdly cast his comedy, beginning with Dunne as the straight but not uncool Manhattan yuppie whose encounters with the denizens of darkness leave him feeling awkward and alienated. At first Dunne's Paul struggles to maintain his composure in the face of his increasingly outlandish situation. As time wears on, his patience grows thin and he begins to become unhinged by the events that seem continually to be conspiring against him. Dunne is the perfect Everyman, and our own reactions closely mirror his. Scorsese has said that *After Hours* is the only film of his he can comfortably watch, because "Griffith acts out all my reactions . . . to watch him squirm in and out of all these situations is therapeutic."

Each of the women Paul encounters is stranger than the next. Arquette's Marcie is more than a little loony. Garr's waitress, who wears a beehive, listens to the Monkees, and has mousetraps around her bed, is a mass of neuroses. Catherine O'Hara, as the woman who takes Paul in and then leads the war party with her ice-cream truck, is a paranoid vigilante. Paul ends up being rescued from the mob by a lonely woman (Verna Bloom) who saves him by turning him into a papier-mâché sculpture—and then refuses to set him free from his prison. Luckily he's stolen by the burglars as the convoluted story comes full circle.

After Hours, like many of Scorsese's movies, is about an altered state of mind and is perfectly attuned to the psychically distressed and alternative-oriented age. This emotionally troubled comedy addresses a generation's pressures, apprehensions, disappointments, and longing for fulfillment in a hostile world. *After Hours* is the story of Job reimagined as a ultracontemporary comedy.

17

It Happened One Night

Columbia (1934)
CAST: Clark Gable, Claudette Colbert, Walter Connolly
DIRECTED BY: Frank Capra
105 minutes [Not rated]

A recalcitrant Clark Gable was cast against his will in *It Happened One Night* by angry MGM boss Louis Mayer as punishment for the actor's rebelliousness. Claudette Colbert was also reluctant to appear in Frank Capra's unpromising comedy about a headstrong heiress and a worldly newspaperman whose lives are changed on a bus ride from Florida to New York. Shot on a tight budget and a short schedule, the film proved a turning point in both actors' careers.

Gable and Colbert both won Oscars for their performances in the first of the 1930's screwball comedies, which also earned Academy Awards for best picture, director, and screenplay (by Capra's frequent collaborator, Robert Riskin). A huge hit with Depression-era audiences, the movie set the tone for romantic comedies for years to come. Poor little rich girls found love in dozens of subsequent comedies, and the antagonistic courtship became a staple of the genre.

With its bright banter and freewheeling spirit, the story of a spoiled, snobbish heiress who finds love and adventure with a commoner also redefined the on-screen relationship between the genders and the classes. Equality became the watchword of the day in screwball comedies, which cut through social barriers and frequently ridiculed the pretensions of high society.

Having almost single-handedly invented screwball comedy—some credit is generally also afforded to two other films of 1934, *Twentieth Century* and *The Thin Man*—Capra all but abandoned it as he proceeded to more seriously develop his democratic screen populism in the stirring, sentimental films for which he is best remembered. Capra found his true métier in his masterpiece, *It's a Wonderful Life,* and other seriocomic dramas that extolled his strong social values, such as *Mr. Deeds Goes to Town* and *Mr. Smith Goes to Washington.*

The acclaimed director of idealistic fables returned to the screwball genre only twice, both times in adaptations of popular stage plays. *Arsenic and Old Lace,* Capra's only black comedy (although a singularly brilliant one), is uncharacteristic of the director's humanism and sentimentality but is unrivaled in the Capra canon for sheer hilarity. *You Can't Take It with You,* a winning comic celebration of eccentricity and individuality, earned Oscars for best picture and best director in 1938.

The term "Capracorn" has been coined to convey the idealization and moralizing of Capra's optimistic vision. But Capra's affection for American life, which was warmly welcomed by audiences during the nation's hard times, remains infectious today. Its egalitarian spirit is still striking, and audiences continue to derive satisfaction from the humbling of a spoiled brat by a genial workingman.

It Happened One Night was listed thirty-fifth in the American Film Institute's 1998 ranking of the one hundred best films of all time. It has a deeper human dimension than many of the comedies that were patterned after it, including such classics as *My Man Godfrey* (1936) and *Nothing Sacred, Topper,* and *The Awful Truth,* all released in 1937. Although consistently amusing and engaging, *It Happened One Night* never sacrifices believability for a laugh. Less frantic, daffy, and exaggerated than latter screwball comedies, *It Happened One Night* is stamped with Capra's distinctive visual style and features the sympathetic characters for which he is known.

When we first meet Ellen (Colbert) she is aboard a yacht, being held captive by her protective father (Walter Connolly), who does not approve of her recent, secret marriage to playboy King Westley. Determined to live her own life, the pampered and isolated heiress jumps overboard and swims to freedom. After pawning her watch, she buys a bus ticket to New York, where she plans to join her new husband. As fate would have it, the last seat on the bus is already taken but is just wide enough for two. Squeezed in beside her is Peter Warne (Gable), a newspaper reporter who has just been fired. When he recognizes his famous traveling companion, Peter offers to accompany Ellen to New York in exchange for her exclusive story, which will salvage his career. Although wary, Ellen is also tired and broke, and she agrees to the arrangement.

The journey, however, is filled with unexpected detours and complications that prove Peter's character and serve to open Ellen's eyes to the real world. The difficulties turn the trip into an adventure, and pretty soon the pair is having fun despite their animosity and mutual suspicions. A final misunderstanding almost dead-ends the budding romance, but it is set back in motion by Ellen's father, who realizes his daughter must follow her heart to find happiness.

The term "screwball" entered the English vocabulary in the mid-thirties as a reference to an eccentric person, probably related to the already established expression "to have a screw loose." Although the circumstances in which they find themselves are unusual and unexpected, Ellen and Peter are not themselves screwballs. That requirement of screwball comedy came later. Peter, in particu-

THUMBS UP   Clark Gable and Claudette Colbert attempting to hitch a ride in Frank Capra's 1934 smash hit, *It Happened One Night*. The movie won Oscars for Capra, Gable, Colbert, and frequent Capra screenwriter Robert Riskin. It also launched Gable's career as a Hollywood superstar, a ranking that lasted until his death in 1959.

lar, is a practical career man and a solid, competent member of the middle class. He is upstanding and principled, as are all of Capra's common-man heroes. Time and time again Capra expressed his faith in the essential decency of the average citizen, who invariably triumphs over the evils of materialism, greed, cynicism, and injustice.

Ellen has lived a sheltered life and is innocent of the ways of the world, but she is only mildly snooty. She becomes "alive and real" (Peter's stated requirements for a mate) through her experiences. Although she faces hardship, she also finds the pleasures in everyday life. Eventually she acquires humility, another quality Capra always insisted upon.

Although the bickering and bantering of their courtship is typical of screwball comedy, Ellen and Peter are unlike later couples in that they fall in love without deceptions or manipulations. Unlike Katharine Hepburn in *Bringing Up Baby* or Barbara Stanwyck in *The Lady Eve,* Ellen does not set out to win her man. The humor in *It Happened One Night* does not rest on one party pursuing the other. Rather, it hinges on both parties' complete resistance to the idea of romance even as they are obviously falling in love. Although opposites in many regards, Ellen and Peter are well matched in stubbornness.

The sparks fly as they spat and spar, each trying to gain the upper hand and maintain their dignity and independence. This is what made them admirable as well as amusing to audiences in a troubled time when resourcefulness was an increasingly valued commodity. This struggle for self-reliance is also what makes *It Happened One Night* seem surprisingly fresh and modern more than half a century later.

18

To Be or Not to Be

United Artists (1942)
Cast: Jack Benny, Carole Lombard, Robert Stack
Directed by: Ernst Lubitsch
99 minutes [Not rated]

Jack Benny was always better than the films he was cast in—until he landed the plum part in Ernst Lubitsch's *To Be or Not to Be*. In this audacious, darkly funny tale of chicanery in the name of liberty, Benny was cast as "that great, great actor" Joseph Tura. The facetious description fit Benny's vain, self-absorbed comic persona like a glove. And well it should: the starring role in *To Be or Not to Be* was written expressly for Benny, who in 1942 was already well on his way to becoming one of the most beloved and influential comedians of his time.

Benny gave the performance of his career as Tura, an egotistical ham actor who gives the greatest performance of *his* career impersonating a Nazi spy in an elaborate ruse to dupe the Gestapo. The high-spirited film's boldly imagined plot is a convoluted series of impersonations, tricks, mistaken identity, sexual snares, and close calls. Tension builds as the quick-witted actors scramble to foil a plot to destroy the Polish Resistance. Benny's droll, unflappable demeanor relieves the tension and keeps the film from flying off into screwball comedy.

Known for his sarcasm and impeccable timing, Jack Benny, born Benjamin (or Benny) Kubelsky, continued to define his trademark character on his popular TV series, which aired from 1950 to 1965. Throughout his career Benny capitalized on this jealous, cheap, selfish, self-deprecating persona—qualities utterly lacking in the kind and humble man behind the comic mask.

Carole Lombard was perfectly cast opposite Benny as Tura's glamorous, faithless, yet politically principled wife, Maria. Her acclaimed performance was also her last. The consummate screwball comedienne, who made a name for herself in classics such as *Twentieth Century,* was tragically killed in a plane crash before the film was released.

A seriously funny comedy that took steady aim at the Nazi menace, *To Be or Not to Be* depicts the heroic yet amusing exploits of a Polish theatrical troupe in wartime Warsaw that engages in a desperate charade to save the Underground. The story, which drew on Lubitsch's early experiences with the Deutsches Theater, was the director's most personal film as well as his most thoroughly political work. Perhaps not surprisingly, it was also his most controversial.

Although today *To Be or Not to Be* is regarded as Lubitsch's greatest film and is hailed as the first black comedy in Hollywood history, it was not well received by the critics when it was released in 1942. His only critical and commercial flop, Lubitsch's anti-Fascist movie was criticized as insensitive and tasteless for taking a satirical approach to such a deadly serious and "too real" subject. *New York Times* critic Bosley Crowther called it "callous and macabre."

Although the film was a box office disappointment, not all critics were uncomfortable with the idea of a comedy taking on world events. Hitler's ravaging of Europe and his attack on the Jews had been a taboo film subject, and many welcomed a film that dared to raise a voice against the Third Reich and enjoyed seeing Hitler ridiculed. Nor were all reviewers troubled by the movie's mixture of comic and dramatic modes and moods. In fact, outside of New York the positive reviews outnumbered the negative ones.

Lubitsch defended the film until his death. "One might call it a tragical farce or a farcical tragedy—I do not care and neither do the audiences," he wrote. He was also very aware that he was creating a new genre, continuing to explore ground broken by Charlie Chaplin's 1940 anti-Nazi comedy, *The Great Dictator.* Although the edgy dark humor of *To Be or Not to Be,* which flirts openly with sex and death, was new to Hollywood film, it owed much to a style of humor popular in Lubitsch's native Berlin in the years prior to his departure for America. (Think *Cabaret.*)

The son of a prosperous Jewish tailor, Lubitsch had become Germany's favorite film comic as well as an accomplished director of historical costume dramas before emigrating to America in 1922. After he was imported to Hollywood by Douglas Fairbanks and Mary Pickford, Lubitsch began to direct an astonishing string of critical and commercial hits—including such quality comedies as *Ninotchka, The Shop Around the Corner,* and *Heaven Can Wait*—that continued until his death in 1947. Lubitsch enjoyed astounding success in his adopted homeland, bringing cosmopolitan flair to his sophisticated and witty films. Like Chaplin, who chose to launch a comic assault on Nazi ideology in his popular but similarly controversial *The Great Dictator,* Lubitsch was in the unique position of having the clout to produce a film that reflected his conscience rather than the climate of caution that gripped the wartime movie world.

Much of the film's humor comes from Joseph Tura's halting heroism in the face of danger. Tura is a normally timid man who puts aside self-interest and

HAMMY HAMLET   Carole Lombard, seated, and Jack Benny in Ernst Lubitsch's 1942 *To Be or Not To Be*. The gifted Lombard (who was Mrs. Clark Gable offscreen) died tragically shortly after filming.

jealousy when his wife stumbles on a plot by the Polish traitor Siletsky (Stanley Ridges). The discovery is made by Maria's paramour, an aviator played by Robert Stack, who became best known playing Eliot Ness on TV's *The Untouchables*. Every night, while Tura is mangling Hamlet on stage, Maria's lover slips out of the audience for a tryst during the "To be or not to be" soliloquy—hence the film's title. (The title is also a barb aimed at those artists who were paralyzed by indecision and stood silent in the face of Hitler's totalitarian onslaught.)

Along with Maria and her valiant would-be lover, Tura summons his skill and his courage to outwit the German invading forces. "I'm going to meet Herr Siletsky at Gestapo headquarters. And after I've killed him, I hope you will be kind enough to tell me what it was all about," Tura says, comically revealing his blind faith in his wife and his willingness to fight for the cause without bothering with the details. One of the film's funniest lines—an indirectly obscene one that also aroused the wrath of prudish critics—is a direct reference from a Nazi officer to the vain actor's lack of talent. "What he does to Hamlet, we are now doing to Poland," a Nazi says.

Although *To Be or Not to Be* relies on Benny's well-established and beloved comic persona, the movie is not without real suspense or a clearly defined sense of moral outrage. With a screenplay by Edwin Justus Mayer from a story by Lubitsch and Melchior Lengyel, this early and rare screen indictment of Hitler offers a stinging condemnation of discrimination in its climactic scene, in which the Jewish bit player Greenberg (German refugee and Lubitsch regular Felix Bressart) gets to deliver the "Hath not a Jew eyes?" speech from *The Merchant of Venice.* Reality and illusion frequently collide in this manner in *To Be or Not to Be,* which cleverly juxtaposes the reality of politics with the illusion of the theater.

The vitality of the sharply written screenplay is evidenced by Mel Brooks's 1983 remake, which repeats most of the scenes verbatim and follows the plot exactly. No doubt attracted by the classic's daring subject and boldly comic style, Brooks also clearly relished the role of the ham actor played by Benny. Brooks assigned his stage-trained wife, Anne Bancroft, to Lombard's sexy saboteur role. Brooks may not have improved upon the original in his broader, more slapstick comedy, but he proved the maxim that imitation is the sincerest form of flattery.

19

This Is Spinal Tap

Embassy (1984)
CAST: Christopher Guest, Michael McKean, Harry Shearer, Rob Reiner,
Tony Hendra, Fran Drescher, with cameos by Billy Crystal and Paul Schaffer
DIRECTED BY: Rob Reiner
82 minutes [Rated R]

Marty DiBergi is a hack director and faithful fan of the English heavy metal band Spinal Tap. Oblivious of the aging rockers' stunning lack of talent and precipitous decline in popularity, DiBergi sets out to document the band's first American tour in six years, which proves an unmitigated disaster. The results of the devoted director's earnestly inept effort to "capture the sights, sounds, and smells of a hardworking rock band on the road" is the classic rockumentary, *This Is Spinal Tap.*

But wait. As much as it may look like the real thing, it's all a gag—the world's first smash hit "mockumentary." The surefooted spoof is so convincing, it could almost fool viewers into thinking Spinal Tap—which proudly proclaims itself "England's loudest band"—is a real rock group instead of the creation of its writers and stars. If you didn't know better, you might also think DiBergi—clad in baseball cap and safari jacket with a light meter around his neck—is an actual director instead of a character played by actor Rob Reiner, who really did direct *This Is Spinal Tap.*

An utterly original comedy that came out of left field to capture wide public acclaim, *This Is Spinal Tap* is both a savage satire of the noisy stupidity of heavy metal and a letter-perfect parody of the musical documentary. The success of the straight-faced send-up of both the pretensions of cinema verité filmmaking and the rude, crude, and lewd inanity of heavy metal lies with the very hip sensibilities of its makers. Because the mindless, tasteless excess of the heavy metal music scene is so rife for satire, anyone could make fun of it. But only someone who understands its appeal and comes from the music's own generation could produce such a knowing satire. And only young, comically inclined film industry insiders could come up with such a hilariously dead-on spoof of the popular new musical genre typified by Martin Scorsese's tribute to the Band, *The Last Waltz* (1978).

ENGLAND'S LOUDEST BAND   Christopher Guest, Michael McKean, and the rest of the band in Rob Reiner's 1984 "mockumentary," *This Is Spinal Tap*. This spoof of heavy metal rock bands was a surprise hit and launched Rob "Meathead" Reiner's directorial career.

Reiner, then known largely as Meathead on TV's *All in the Family,* made his directing debut with *This Is Spinal Tap,* which he cowrote with the actors who play the dim-wit Brits and proficiently perform their amusingly atrocious music. Christopher Guest stars as Nigel Tufnel, one of two lead guitarists in the band. His fellow front man is David St. Hubbins, who is played by Michael McKean. Harry Shearer, the film's fourth cocreator, is the bass player Derek Smalls, the only other surviving member of the band, which has gone through thirty-seven musicians in its rocky seventeen-year history. Drummers in particular have come and gone, quite literally, with alarming regularity. One died after choking on vomit, not his own. Another fell victim to spontaneous combustion midconcert.

Using archival footage and interviews with the performers, DiBergi reverentially traces the evolution of the "band that, for me, redefined rock and roll" when he heard them first in 1967 and again in 1976 at the Electric Banana. The intrepid musicians began life as the Originals, but because there was already another band named the Originals, they changed their name to the New Originals and later became the Thamesmen. We see the group in its early Beatles-clone phase in a clip from the *Pop, Look and Listen* show and later in its psychedelic incarnation on *Jamboreebop.*

By the time the band arrives in America to plug its new and controversial album *Smell the Glove*—so named for the cover photo of a naked, kneeling woman sniffing a man's black leather gloved hand—the motley crew is attired in full heavy metal regalia: oversize chains, industrial studs, shiny, tight vinyl pants, and leopard-skin vests over bare, hairy chests.

They are also singing incredibly vulgar songs like "Big Bottom," with offensive lyrics that include "The sweeter the cushion, the better the pushin'" and "Big bottom, talk about bun cakes, my girl's got 'em" and, best of all, "How could I leave this behind?"

The critics have not responded favorably to albums such as *IntraVenus DeMilo,* which found Spinal Tap drowning in "a sea of retarded sexuality." Nigel dismisses the criticism as nit-picking. And when Polymer Records balks at the sexist cover for *Smell the Glove,* St. Hubbins wonders what's wrong with being sexy. Indeed, sexism is a foreign concept to these groupie-loving guys who pad their crotches. In one of the movie's many brilliant bits targeting the bad boys' sexual immaturity, an alarm at airport security is set off by a cucumber wrapped in aluminum foil that Smalls has stuffed into his pants.

Polymer's objections, voiced by the company's high society PR director (played with aplomb by Fran Drescher), are only the beginning of the boys' problems on the disaster-plagued tour. Their incompetent manager, Ian Faith (Tony Hendra, one of the authors of the parody *Not the New York Times*), assures them that losing the Boston gig isn't a big deal because "Boston isn't a big college town." When the Memphis show is canceled, the boys morosely gather by the grave of Elvis Presley and hilariously try to harmonize on "Heartbreak Hotel." In Cleveland they can't find their way out of the cavernous basement and onto the stage. At the Holiday Inn they are given second billing to *The Wiz* road show. Their eighteen-inch-tall Stonehenge set is delivered as per the specifications doodled on a bar napkin. They play an air force base where the straight crowd plugs their ears and shake their heads in disgust at the song "Sex Farm Woman."

How do the lads feel about the humiliations? "I'd feel much worse if I weren't under heavy medication," St. Hubbins reports. There are problems within the band as well. St. Hubbins's astrologist girlfriend has joined the tour and alienated Nigel as well as Ian with her meddling. Jealousy mounts and tempers flare until Nigel walks out in a huff. It looks as though Spinal Tap is finished for good. St. Hubbins and Smalls contemplate making a musical based on the life of Jack the Ripper or recording a collection of acoustic numbers with the London Philharmonic. But then Nigel comes back with a message from Ian. They are on the charts in Japan, and Spinal Tap is back in the business of "making eardrums bleed."

Well versed in both comedy and rock and roll, Reiner, Guest, Shearer, and McKean improvise their way through the film, adding to the offhand feel of cinema verité with their moronic rambling. Although the songs were written before filming began, the script was a bare-bones affair that allowed the actors plenty of room for invention. Reiner filmed take after take of improvisation and shot the film with a handheld 16-millimeter camera to add to the pseudorealistic effect.

Reiner, the son of famed comedy writer and director Carl Reiner, got his start appearing with improvisational comedy troupes and writing for *The Smothers Brothers Comedy Hour* and other TV shows before playing the long-haired liberal who went head-to-head with Archie Bunker on *All in the Family.* Reiner first got the idea for a mock rockumentary while playing Wolfman Jack in a TV special. Guest and McKean were songwriting partners who cut their comedy teeth with *National Lampoon's Lemmings,* the Off Broadway comedy show where John Belushi first performed his Joe Cocker impression. Guest and McKean had worked with *Saturday Night Live* veteran Shearer in the Credibility Gap, a Los Angeles comedy troupe that often satirized rock stars.

Reiner also recruited Billy Crystal to play a small role as the owner of Shut Up and Eat, a catering company that uses mimes to serve the food. Much of Crystal's inspired improv ended up on the cutting room floor but is restored in "the outtakes, alternate takes, and abandoned subplots" featured on the laser disc and 1995 video release. Paul Schaeffer also makes a vivid impression as an obsequious ad man who sets up a dismal record promo.

All of the actors create caricatures of glorious mediocrity that are oddly endearing despite their delusions of grandeur and general stupidity. Part oafs, part naïfs, the boys in the band are classic bumbling boobs who stumbled onto success—as many a band no doubt has—and can't quite fathom why they're now plummeting into ignominious obscurity in the " 'Where are they now?' file." There's just a touch of affection in the mockery, which may account for the popularity of the pop culture parody. Critics applauded the novelty, invention, and skill of the deadpan comedy, which generated genuine Spinal Tapmania and attracted legions of fans in numbers usually restricted to rock. To meet the overwhelming public demand, Spinal Tap went on tour, appeared in a TV special, and reunited for *The Return of Spinal Tap* in the 1990s.

Reiner has gone on to prove himself adept at romantic comedy with *When Harry Met Sally . . .* (1989). His *Princess Bride* is also a wonderfully funny fairy tale for all ages. Reiner also occasionally plays small comic roles and was especially funny in *Sleepless in Seattle.* Christopher Guest returned to the mock documentary form as the writer, director, and star of 1997's *Waiting for Guffman,* a frequently funny behind-the-scenes look at an amateur theater company.

This Is Spinal Tap did not start a trend of phony documentaries, but it did set a standard for parody that few films have been able to reach and none have surpassed.

20

The Pink Panther Strikes Again

MGM/United Artists (1976)
CAST: Peter Sellers, Herbert Lom, Burt Kwouk, Omar Sharif
DIRECTED BY: Blake Edwards
103 minutes [Rated PG]

Inspector Clouseau is the most famously funny film character of the sixties and seventies and as brilliantly foolish a figure as has ever graced the screen. With his ridiculous, vowel-mangling French accent and his misplaced arrogant assurance, the accident-prone klutz raised comic incompetence to new heights. The inadvertently indestructible comic hero also single-handedly returned slapstick comedy to public favor.

Jacques Clouseau, an idiotic oaf who considers himself one of the world's greatest detectives, was a role master impersonator Peter Sellers was born to play. However, Peter Ustinov, another fine English comic actor, was writer-director-producer Blake Edwards's first choice to star in his 1964 comedy about a bumbling French detective. When Ustinov backed out at the last minute, Sellers jumped at the opportunity to make his first full-force foray into slapstick comedy.

Sellers was not the star of *The Pink Panther,* which gave top billing to David Niven, cast as the cat burglar who steals the priceless pink diamond with a panther-shaped flaw. Sellers stole the show, however, and his role as the maladroit nincompoop was expanded in the subsequent sequels. Although the first film ends with Clouseau framed for the crime and headed for jail, all the films that followed rest on the premise that Clouseau unintentionally succeeds in solving the crime despite his incredible ineptitude.

The Pink Panther was released at the same time as Seller's next assignment, the much more serious and original comedy *Dr. Strangelove,* for which Sellers received an Oscar nomination. *The Pink Panther* was not as critically successful as *Dr. Strangelove,* but it was a much bigger commercial success. The reviews were mixed, with many less than glowing reactions and a few raves, most notably from Pauline Kael.

Audiences, however, couldn't get enough of Clouseau's clowning, and the first Pink Panther sequel, *A Shot in the Dark,* was shrewdly tailored to showcase Clouseau's clumsy stupidity. The excellent comedy eliminated Sellers's previous costars, Niven, Claudia Cardinale, Capucine, and Robert Wagner, and introduced two new characters that became staples of the subsequent sequels. Herbert Lom (who had co-starred with Sellers in *The Ladykillers* and *Mr. Topaze*) was cast as Chief Inspector Dreyfus, who is Clouseau's boss and eventual nemesis. Burt Kwouk appeared as Cato, Clouseau's servant and karate master, whose job description includes launching surprise attacks on his employer, which he always stages at the most inopportune moments. *A Shot in the Dark,* the racy highlight of which features Clouseau at a nudist colony, was rightfully described by *Newsweek* as being "twice as funny" as *The Pink Panther.*

In 1968, citing artistic differences with Edwards, Sellers decided against reprising his most famous role in *Inspector Clouseau,* written by Edwards and directed by Bud Yorkin. Despite good work by Alan Arkin as Clouseau, the film was a dismal failure. By 1975 Edwards and Sellers were both desperate for a hit and reunited for *The Return of the Pink Panther.* Excessively violent and juvenile, the comedy was a critical disappointment but a box office smash.

The pair bounced back the next year with the very best in the series, *The Pink Panther Strikes Again.* Sellers was in top form in this tightly scripted comedy that manages to sustain its energy with one inspired sight gag and plot twist after another. The plot picks up where *Return* left off—with Dreyfus, who has developed a pathological hatred for Clouseau, in a prison for the criminally insane. The twitching Dreyfus, who has been driven mad by Clouseau's continued accidental success, escapes the loony bin and turns terrorist. He kidnaps a scientist and his daughter, forcing Professor Fassbender (Richard Vernon) to use his doomsday machine (a nod to *Dr. Strangelove*) to blackmail the world's governments into eliminating Clouseau, who is now chief inspector of the Sûreté. Threatened with annihilation, the world powers send their top assassins to kill Clouseau, who is in Munich for Oktoberfest. In a comic plot device borrowed from the central conceit in Chaplin's *Monsieur Verdoux,* the attempts are unwittingly thwarted by the intended victim, who remains oblivious of each failed assault.

Only the Egyptian and Russian assassins are still alive as the film hurtles toward its conclusion. The Egyptian (Omar Sharif) mistakenly kills one of Dreyfus's henchmen, who has disguised himself as Clouseau, and then, in another case of mistaken identity, beds the Russian agent (Lesley-Anne Down) sent to kill Clouseau. She is so smitten by the accomplished lovemaking, she decides not to carry out the contract, unaware that the real Clouseau is not the lover who has undone her resolve.

Clouseau tracks Dreyfus down at the German castle, where he is staging

DWARF TOSSING   Peter Sellers as the bumbling Inspector Jacques Clouseau in Blake Edwards's 1976 *The Pink Panther Strikes Again.* Sellers earned an Oscar nomination three years later for his portrayal of a simple-minded gardener in *Being There.*

his mad plan to rid the world of Clouseau. Clouseau, who takes a "rhum" at the local inn, dresses as an Austrian alpinist and attempts to gain entry to the castle, which is surrounded by a moat; but each inventive attempt lands him in the drink. He then dons the disguise of a doddering German dentist, who looks a little like Einstein, and arrives at the castle to treat Dreyfus, whose terrible toothache is inhibiting his enjoyment of his deranged villainy. Clouseau administers too much laughing gas, to himself as well as to Dreyfus, and the archenemies are reduced to hysterics before Clouseau's disguise melts and Dreyfus recognizes him. Wearing a suit of armor, Clouseau again saves the day by chance, turning the doomsday machine on Dreyfus, who disappears— only to reappear in Sellers's final outing as the bungling buffoon, *The Revenge of the Pink Panther* (1978).

　　Sellers gave up the ghost in 1980, but Edwards refused to give up Clouseau. He strung together outtakes from earlier Sellers films for *The Trail of the Pink Panther,* then cast Ted Wass as Clouseau's replacement in *The*

Curse of the Pink Panther, and finally cast Roberto Benigni as Clouseau Jr. in *Son of the Pink Panther.*

Edwards and Sellers, whose careers were similarly uneven, both rose to prominence in 1959—Edwards as the director of the submarine comedy *Operation Petticoat,* Sellers—à la Alec Guinness—playing three roles (including a grand duchess) in *The Mouse That Roared.* Edwards, who went on to make the hit comedies *Breakfast at Tiffany's, 10, S.O.B.,* and *Victor/Victoria,* was known for his strong sense of style and his affinity for farce. He was just the kind of strong, disciplined director Sellers needed to hone his erratic talents.

Sellers, a brilliant comic who made some singularly unfunny films, got his start with the surrealistic BBC radio program *The Goon Show,* which inspired the creation of *Monty Python's Flying Circus.* He made more than fifty films despite suffering a series of heart attacks that contributed to his personal unhappiness, which manifested itself in strange, unprofessional behavior. According to Edwards, Sellers was at his most difficult on the set of *The Pink Panther Strikes Again,* after which his career went into a rapid decline.

Sellers did make one more great film before dying of a massive heart attack at the age of fifty-five. In fact, some consider his performance in 1979's *Being There* to be his finest. It is surely his most subtle, subdued comic role and one of the most interesting comedies of the decade, directed by Hal Ashby (*Harold and Maude*). Sellers had wanted to play the simple-minded gardener whose reticence is interpreted as wisdom ever since he'd read Jerzy Kosinski's novel in 1971, and he personally tapped Ashby to direct. The role earned him an Oscar nomination and the critical praise that had so often eluded him.

But to the vast majority of moviegoers Sellers will forever be equated with Clouseau. The gallantry and dignity with which he endowed the character, who attracted disaster like a magnet, endeared Clouseau to audiences, who loved seeing the loser win. He was a cartoon character come to life, impervious to indignity and pain. A "bimp" on the head never really hurt. He rose from each pratfall unscathed and unfazed. He performed the oldest and most predictable gags in the book—walking into closets and vaulting off the parallel bars down a staircase—with such blithe assurance that they seemed fresh again. Audiences couldn't help but root for the hapless stooge who, at the end of *The Pink Panther Strikes Again,* finally gets the girl—but can't get his clothes off.

21

The Sunshine Boys

MGM (1975)
CAST: Walter Matthau, George Burns, Richard Benjamin
DIRECTED BY: Herbert Ross
111 minutes [Rated PG]

A comedy about comedy, *The Sunshine Boys* is both a valentine to the glory days of vaudeville and a showcase for two veteran practitioners of the lost art of shtick. Simon's screen adaptation of his bitterly funny play is as funny today as it was in 1975, thanks in large part to the masterful performances by Walter Matthau and George Burns as feuding former vaudeville stars who reunite for an appearance on a TV variety show honoring the history of comedy.

One surefire way to create funny characters is to make them talented comics and then cast gifted comedians in the roles. Neil Simon shrewdly did just that in *The Sunshine Boys,* the playwright's most continually amusing and enduringly popular comedy. If directing is 90 percent casting, then director Herbert Ross is to be credited for finding the two perfect actors to play the cranky old vaudevillians once known as Lewis and Clark, who still turn every event in their lives into a comedy routine. Providence, however, played a large part in the felicitous pairing of Matthau and Burns.

When Jack Benny died at age eighty shortly before filming was set to begin on *The Sunshine Boys,* the part of Al Lewis fell to his old friend and fellow comic George Burns. Burns, who had not made a movie since 1939's *Honolulu,* had been in a long and presumably fatal slump since the death of his wife and partner, Gracie, in 1964. Casting Burns opposite the well-established Walter Matthau, who was set to play cantankerous comic Willy Clark, was a calculated risk for director Ross (who went on to direct Simon's *The Goodbye Girl*). It paid off handsomely, however, precipitating one of the most remarkable comebacks in show business history. A veteran of vaudeville, radio, TV, and film, Burns (born Nathan Birnbaum) won an Oscar for his impeccably timed and nuanced performance and became a bona fide movie star at the age of seventy-nine.

Matthau, then only fifty-five, was too young to have experienced vaudeville firsthand. However, Matthau—a veteran of Broadway and TV—special-

GRUMPY OLD MEN   George Burns, left, gives Walter Matthau, right, the finger in Herbert Ross's 1975 *The Sunshine Boys*. The film marked a major comeback for Burns, who stepped in after his pal Jack Benny passed on. Neil Simon hailed the film version of *The Sunshine Boys* as the best screen adaptation of any of his plays.

ized in grouchy comic characters, making him the obvious choice for the curmudgeonly Willy. Simon had written the stage role of sloppy, testy Oscar Madison in *The Odd Couple* expressly for Matthau, and the popular 1968 screen version catapulted Matthau to fame. He earned his second Oscar nomination and won a Golden Globe for his role as the quintessential grumpy old man in *The Sunshine Boys*.

Lewis and Clark, a comedy team also known as the Sunshine Boys, spent forty-three years together working in perfect harmony—on the stage, at least. Off stage, however, they couldn't stand each other. When Al quit the act without warning, Willy stopped speaking to his former partner. The action of *The Sunshine Boys* begins some twelve years later, as Willy is still trying to earn a living as a solo performer. His nephew, Ben (Richard Benjamin), is also his agent. But Willy is an exasperatingly difficult client—as well as an abrasive, unappreciative uncle. Willy can't remember his lines anymore and is argumentative and arrogant. When the long-suffering Ben lands Willy a guest appearance on an upcoming TV variety show, he knows it's the perfect opportunity to boost his uncle's moribund career. There's only one hitch: He has to talk Willy into working with Al, who is now happily retired and living in New Jersey with his daughter.

Al is amenable, and Willy reluctantly agrees. "I'm against it, but I'll do it," he says. But when they get together, the old animosities quickly resurface. Their sparring, wonderfully worded by Simon and perfectly played by Burns and Matthau, forms the hilarious heart of the comedy. Simon understands the cadences, rhythms, and speech patterns peculiar to this brand of comedy, and the performers know just how to deliver the expertly crafted lines.

Buried beneath the barrage of barbs and bon mots is another classic odd couple comedy about friendship. Willy is the classic kvetch, Al a world-class kibbitzer. Al is a know-it-all like Willy, but more reasonable. Both men are clowns who love to perform. There is a good reason their teamwork is perfect: they are one of a kind. The doctor sketch they revive for the show is the film's comic centerpiece, a reminder that corny can still be very funny.

Despite their all-American-sounding names, a reference to famous explorers, Lewis and Clark are thoroughly Jewish comics who come from a Jewish-dominated comic industry. (Willy and Al are loosely modeled on Jewish comics Joe Smith and Charlie Dale.) There is a running gag in the film in which Al and Willy argue over the identity of someone whose obituary ran in *Variety*. Was it Saul Burton, Saul Bernstein, or Sid Weinstein who wrote those sappy song lyrics? In a marvelous reference to the way Jews often appeared in disguised form, Willy remembers that in the dance team of Ramona and Rodriguez, Bernie Eisenstein was Rodriguez—or was it Sam Hesselman or Jackie Aronstein?

All the names mentioned in the film are Jewish, from Mrs. Kugelman to Mr. Melnick. Most of the supporting characters are Jewish as well. When bewildered and befuddled Willy wanders into a garage at the film's opening, looking for an audition, the mechanic is played by F. Murray Abraham. The floor manager for the TV show is played by Ron Rifkin, emphasizing how Jews still play a prominent role in all aspects of entertainment. The show itself is hosted by Steve Allen, who in reality introduced a great many Jewish comics to the American public, thus adding to the authenticity of the homage.

Ben is another standard Jewish character, the devoted son, in this case the dutiful nephew. Benjamin, who won a Golden Globe for best supporting actor, plays Ben as sensible, decent, and patient, motivated by genuine affection for his vexatious uncle. A competent professional and sane family man, he's driven to distraction by Willy's stubborn, hostile behavior and his habit of not listening. Benjamin gives one of his best performances as the man torn between adoration and exasperation, an attitude the audience is invited to share.

Simon, who began his career writing for Catskills comics, got the idea for *The Sunshine Boys* from some of the fading, old-time stars he met as a struggling comedy writer. "I spent my life growing up with these men," Simon has said. "If they spoke in one-liners and punch lines instead of conversation, it's because it was the only language they knew." The play, directed by Alan Arkin, debuted in 1972 with Jack Albertson as Willie and Sam Levene as Al. It was another in Simon's unbroken string of hits.

Simon is without doubt the most prolific as well as popular and financially successful playwright in the history of the American theater, and his flourishing career has been dedicated almost exclusively to comedy. Simon rose to prominence with his first comedy, *Come Blow Your Horn,* based on his own family, which in 1963 was made into a movie with Frank Sinatra playing the writer as a young man. Simon continued to write comic plays and adapt them for the screen, launching a tandem career as one of the industry's most successful screenwriters. Simon earned Oscar nominations for *The Odd Couple, The Goodbye Girl, The Sunshine Boys,* and *California Suite.* The screen versions of *Plaza Suite, The Prisoner of Second Avenue, Barefoot in the Park, Chapter Two,* and *I Ought to Be in Pictures* were all commercially successful, as were his original screenplays *Seems Like Old Times, Murder by Death,* and *The Marrying Man.* His seriocomic autobiographical trilogy—*Brighton Beach Memoirs, Biloxi Blues,* and *Broadway Bound*—followed by the Pulitzer Prize–winning *Lost in Yonkers,* finally earned Simon acclaim as a playwright of substance rather than merely a facile stylist.

The Sunshine Boys, which pokes fun at old age while registering sympathy for the indignities that come with it, was surprisingly successful in the youth-oriented film market. Simon's script earned an Oscar nomination, and the film won a Golden Globe for best musical/comedy.

Coincidentally, *The Sunshine Boys* did for Burns what the film's TV show was supposed to do for Willy—renew appreciation for a performer who had fallen from favor. With his understated, natural performance, Burns proved himself a more than able actor as well as a superb comic. The late George Burns put it best when he said, "Acting is all about honesty. If you can fake that, you've got it made."

22

Tom Jones

United Artists (1963)
CAST: Albert Finney, Susannah York, Hugh Griffith,
Edith Evans, David Warner, Joyce Redman
DIRECTED BY: Tony Richardson
129 minutes [Not rated]

A movie that perfectly reflected the shifting social mores of the 1960s—
although set more than two hundred years earlier—*Tom Jones* captivated the
moviegoing public with its cheeky charm, ribald humor, and animated acting.
Director Tony Richardson brought Henry Fielding's famed eighteenth-century
novel to vigorous life in this bawdy, high-spirited English comedy, which is
both a faithful (although condensed) adaptation and a thoroughly modern
morality tale. Delightful and daring, wicked and winsome, the sexually liberated comedy captured the giddy, free-spirited mood of the times—and captured wide acclaim.

Winner of the Oscar for best picture, best director, best adapted screenplay, and best score, *Tom Jones* brazenly winked at the audience, and viewers instantly succumbed to the cinematic seduction. English actor Albert
Finney, then a rising stage and screen star, soared to international celebrity
with his exuberant embodiment of the life force in a story with a rogue as its
hero. The title character of Fielding's comic odyssey emerges as a virile rascal
blessed with an irrepressible love of life and a strong sentimental streak.
Although not one to resist temptation, Tom is steadfast in his love for the
lovely and lively Sophie (Susannah York), making him the ultimate romantic
hero for an increasingly permissive age. *Tom Jones* ridicules the hypocrisy
and prudery of the times, contrasting the uptight, class-conscious society with
the libertine sex symbol who crashes the gates of false modesty and decorum.

Although frank in its depiction of the character's sexual exploits, *Tom Jones*
is anything but graphic. Extremely discreet and tasteful, the film shows us nothing more explicit than two people tearing into their food with wanton abandon
and palpable pleasure. The unbridled lust and hedonism of this famous food-
as-sex scene remains as erotic as any sensual moment ever put on film, however. Its comic charge also proves that humor and passion are not mutually

exclusive. The movie, which was embraced as an expression of the cultural revolution sweeping the Western world, argued that sex can be fun—and funny.

Richardson sets the frisky tone of the comedy in the opening precredit scenes, which are played as though in a silent film and set to sprightly harpsichord music composed by John Addison. A narrator (Michael MacLiammoir) informs us with mock solemnity that we are in the west of England at the home of Squire Allworthy, who is just returning from a trip. The squire is astonished to find a baby in his bed, the apparent product of an illicit union between his maid, Jenny Jones, and his manservant, Mr. Partridge. A decent sort, Squire Allworthy charitably decides to raise the boy as his own.

"The opinion was that he was born to be hanged," the narrator informs us of Tom, whom we next see as a strapping young man with a twinkle in his eye who looks quite smashing in his buckskin boots, velvet vest, and voluminous white shirt. Tom, we are informed, has a weakness for women and a fondness for country life and the woods. "It's a good night to be abroad and looking for game," we hear just before Tom encounters the gamekeeper's licentious daughter Molly. As the two fall to the forest floor, the camera cuts away and the narrator explains, "It shall be our custom to relieve such scenes as taste, decorum, and the censors dictate."

Tom, who has "no sense of religion or virtue," next encounters a woman of quite another character when he visits the home of the neighboring land baron, Squire Western (Hugh Griffith). Although the squire is an uncouth, whoremongering, drunken lout, his daughter, Sophie, is every inch a lady, although no snobbish prude. Tom is smitten, and Sophie returns his affections, but she is dismayed to learn of Tom's sexual indiscretions. At the local hunt, a scene that scorns the wanton excesses and cavalier cruelty of the ruling class, Sophie's horse bolts and Tom rescues her, breaking his arm in the process. The courtship is in full swing when events conspire against Tom. Undone by his rival, Squire Allworthy's pompous nephew Blifil (David Warner, in his screen debut), Tom is turned out of the house and makes his way to London, where his sexual misadventures continue apace. When Sophie arrives in town, Tom tries to win her back but is again hampered by the forces that jealously conspire against him. The story concludes with Tom saved from hanging, proved to be the rightful heir to Squire Allworthy's fortune, and reunited with his love.

The briskly paced comedy romps through the events of Fielding's *The History of Tom Jones, a Foundling,* deftly touching on its "I have lived today" theme and vividly evoking the era. Impressive in its authenticity, the film finds cinematic devices to approximate the picaresque effect of the 1749 novel, which takes a comically disparaging view of human nature. "We are all as God made us," the narrator comments, "and many of us much worse."

A STAR IS BORN   Albert Finney in the title role of *Tom Jones*. Tony Richardson's 1963 adaptation of the Henry Fielding novel launched Finney's film career and also managed to win four Academy Awards, including best picture.

An accomplished cast gamely assails the book's colorful characters, creating believable yet comic figures of fun. Allworthy (George Devine) is the dullest of the lot, but his prim and proper sister, Miss Western, is enacted with great comic verve by the distinguished Dame Edith Evans. York is soft and appealing as Sophie, a woman who is allowed to be playful and smart and who follows her heart. Joyce Redman does a sexy turn as the woman who gives birth to Tom and later unknowingly beds him. She is not his mother, after all, which lets everyone off the incest hook.

Griffith, who reportedly played the lecherous drunk off screen as well as on and drank himself into an early grave, is gleefully boisterous as the crude but dynamic reprobate. His behavior almost led to tragedy on the set, however, when he drunkenly turned his horse so quickly that it fell on him. Although far from funny at the moment, the scene looked like deliberate slapstick and stayed in the movie.

Surrounded by veteran actors, Finney shines as the ill-born, would-be gentleman who is unfairly treated by his supposed "betters." Playing the rakish young stud, Finney exudes animal magnetism yet creates a character of some sensitivity. It is an honest performance that makes us like Tom as he bounces from one amusing adventure to the next. Finney was not eager to play Tom, who he felt was too passive a character and too insubstantial a role. Finney, who was cajoled into taking the role by a share in the profits, made his reluctance felt on the set, Richardson recalls in his autobiography. Richardson had one temperamental star and another out-of-control actor to deal with on his first comedy, which was intended to be a "holiday" picture.

The distinguished director, then married to Vanessa Redgrave, had earned acclaim for his downbeat dramas—first on stage and then on film—*Look Back in Anger* and *The Entertainer*. After the success of the similarly serious films *A Taste of Honey* and *The Loneliness of the Long Distance Runner*, Richardson wanted a change of pace. When he realized that *Tom Jones* had never been filmed, he decided to attempt to translate Fielding's "unstoppable narrative" onto the screen. He hired playwright and frequent collaborator John Osborne to write the screenplay but did much of the rewriting himself.

When the problem-plagued location filming was completed, Richardson was disappointed with the results of the technically proficient comedy and feared the worst. United Artists' British distributor predicted *Tom Jones* would never turn a profit. Indeed, the first reviews were terrible. The *London Times* sniffed that "there was nothing in the film that could give any member of the audience one moment of enjoyment." Audiences refused to comply with the *Times*' assessment, however, and enjoyed the rollicking two-hour-plus comedy from beginning to end. Lines formed around the block of the London Pavillion, turning the comedy, which was unlike anything audiences had seen before, into a box office sensation. American critics generally appreciated the novelty and spirit of the film, which opened just as the Beatles were taking America by storm. "Prepare yourself for what is surely one of the wildest, bawdiest and funniest comedies that a refreshingly agile filmmaker has ever brought to the screen," the *New York Times* proclaimed, lauding the director's obvious "enjoyment of the absurd."

In addition to its Oscar wins, *Tom Jones* earned the Golden Globe for best musical/comedy and best foreign film. Richardson was named best director by the Directors Guild. *Tom Jones* won best film and best director at the British Academy Awards and earned numerous awards from critics groups.

The success of *Tom Jones* allowed Richardson the financial freedom to pursue his next project, the very dark and wickedly irreverent comedy *The Loved One,* based on the novel by Evelyn Waugh. Billed by MGM as the comedy "with something to offend everyone," the strange satire of Los Angeles, religion, and the funeral business was a critical failure but has developed a strong and well-deserved cult following. Unaccountably, Richardson's promising career went into a tailspin. The closest it ever came to recovering, before the high-living director died of AIDS in 1991, was with his adaptation of John Irving's seriocomic *The Hotel New Hampshire* (1986). Although Finney has also made only infrequent forays into comedy (*The Playboys* stands among the best), he has fared much better than Richardson, starring in powerful dramas such as *The Dresser, Shoot the Moon,* and *Under the Volcano.*

Richardson never shared the public and critical enthusiasm for *Tom Jones,* which he regarded as "incomplete and botched in much of its execution." Nevertheless, *Tom Jones* is widely considered a comic masterpiece. Devilishly diverting and irresistibly entertaining, *Tom Jones* offered a keen look at contemporary social values refracted through the long lens of the past.

23

Moonstruck

MGM (1987)
CAST: Cher, Nicolas Cage, Danny Aiello, Olympia Dukakis, Vincent Gardenia,
Julie Bovasso, Louis Guss, John Mahoney
DIRECTED BY: Norman Jewison
103 minutes [Rated PG]

Director Norman Jewison has a flair for ethnicity. The son of a Canadian father and English mother, the director of *Fiddler on the Roof* has proved equally at home in the shtetls of Eastern Europe as he is combing an Italian neighborhood in Brooklyn in *Moonstruck*. What he did for Eastern European Jews with *Fiddler on the Roof,* Jewison does for Italian Americans in *Moonstruck*, which is another glowing tribute to close-knit family life.

Directed with an irresistible combination of warmth and wit, *Moonstruck* is a good-natured, affectionate, and authentic celebration of Italian American culture rather than a satire that makes fun of its characters (like *Married to the Mob*). The Oscar-winning script by John Patrick Shanley (*Four Corners, January Man, Joe Versus the Volcano*) is steeped in ethnic detail that helps define the characters without stereotyping them. With an unpredictable plot full of surprises and colorful characters who speak their minds with astonishing candor, *Moonstruck* is a rare romantic comedy that is as sincere as it is cheering.

To create a comedy that is deeply felt and howlingly funny requires exceptional acting, and Jewison elicits perfectly pitched performances from his unlikely cast. Cher won an Oscar for her portrayal of Loretta Castorinni, a thirty-seven-year-old widow who falls in love with her fiancé's brother. Despite the fact that she's playing someone quite unlike her own persona, and although she is neither a great actress nor a skilled comedienne, Cher creates a completely believable woman whose frankness is profoundly funny.

Cage, an intense actor who tends to go over the top, plays the object of her affections with a passion that proves not so much excessive as endearing and goofy and smolderingly sexy. Olympia Dukakis, who won the best supporting actress Oscar for her role as Loretta's plain-speaking mother, Rose, manages to project unconditional love even as she tells her father-in-law

89

(Feodor Chaliapin), "Old man, you give those dogs another piece of my food and I'm gonna kick you till you're dead." As her husband, Cosmo, Oscar nominee Vincent Gardenia also gives an understated comic performance that has weight as well as wit.

Nominated for best picture and best director, *Moonstruck* cast a spell over audiences and critics alike with its captivating blend of loopy romance and cleverly played character comedy. Jewison sets the stage for his enchanting tale of romantic and family love in the opening credits, with Dean Martin singing "That's Amore" as the moon indeed hits our eye like a big pizza pie. The resplendent full moon—"*la bella luna*"—continues to make everyone act a little loony for the next forty-eight hours, changing Loretta's destiny and bringing her true happiness just as she is about to settle for contentment and security.

Loretta Castorinni, a no-nonsense bookkeeper who works for a mortician, a florist, and her uncle's Italian deli, has been dating the safe and dull mama's boy Johnny Cammareri (Danny Aiello), with an eye toward marriage. When he finally pops the question at the neighborhood restaurant, she makes him get down on his knees to do it right so she won't have bad luck, as with her last marriage. She believes her first husband was hit by a bus before they had children because they were married in city hall without the blessing of church and family. Johnny, who is about to visit his dying mother in Sicily, reluctantly agrees to set a date to plan a proper wedding. Before leaving, he asks that she invite his brother, Ronny, whom he hasn't seen in five years, to the wedding.

When Loretta comes home to tell her parents, she finds her father in the living room, listening to music. "I have news," she says. "Let's go in the kitchen," he replies, and they repair to the room where all important family discussions take place. When she tells her father she's getting married, his first response is, "What, again?" Cosmo doesn't like Johnny—"He's a big baby," he rightly complains—and refuses to pay for the wedding. Loretta's mother's reaction is similarly unexpected. She wants to know if Loretta loves Johnny. When Loretta tells her she doesn't love him but she likes him, her mother says, "Good, because when you love them they drive you crazy because they know they can." Indeed, Cosmo is driving Rose crazy with his philandering, which Rose handles matter-of-factly with her customary candor.

Loretta goes to see Johnny's brother at the bakery he owns and finds that the source of the bad blood is an accident that happened five years ago that caused Ronny to lose his hand as well as his fiancée. Still tormented by his personal tragedy, Ronny blames Johnny for his misfortune. Loretta doesn't buy it, but she is attracted to Ronny's intensity of feeling. He's a "luna-tic" who has fallen hopelessly under the moon's romantic spell. When he knocks

BIG HAIR DAY Cher and Nicholas Cage in Norman Jewison's *Moonstruck* (1987). This delightful romantic comedy was praised for its warm portrayal of a close-knit Italian family, none of whom are involved with organized crime.

over the table and kisses her passionately, she pulls away, crying, "Wait a minute, wait a minute!" then surprises him, and herself, by kissing him back with equally fierce passion. It is these little moments we don't expect that make *Moonstruck* such an unanticipated delight. Again and again the characters act on their impulses, suddenly moving the story in a new direction.

After a night of passion Loretta agrees to go to the opera with Ronny but insists that she's still going to marry his brother. "But I'm in love with you," Ronny protests. She slaps him hard and says, "Well, snap out of it!" When he tells her she should have waited for the right man to come along, she says she got tired of waiting. "But I'm here," he says. "You're late," she snaps.

After a charmed evening at *La Bohème,* Ronny delivers a crazily romantic speech that finally makes Loretta stop being sensible and give in to her feelings for him. "Love doesn't make things nice," Ronny tells her. "It ruins everything. It breaks your heart and makes things a mess. We are here to ruin ourselves and love the wrong people and die. Now I want you upstairs and in my bed."

The tangled love stories are finally resolved around the Castorinni family's kitchen table, where there's no such thing as a private conversation but there are such things as intimacy, support, and love. There's also exasperation, but that's accepted as a natural part of family life, well worth the price of knowing where you belong. Few films have expressed the connection that a family can offer with such conviction. Although the lushly photographed film sentimentalizes the joys of a family bonds, it offsets the sweetness with tart humor. For example, as the family sorts out the complicated love affairs and secrets come to light, Grandpa starts crying, presumably from joy. But when Cosmo asks him what's wrong, the old man sobs, "I'm confused." Without the plentiful laughs it so generously offers, this fairy tale would run the risk of becoming sappy instead of satisfying.

Sheila Benson of the *Los Angeles Times* accurately described the fulfilling effect of the comedy. "*Moonstruck* is such a nourishing comedy," she wrote. "It satisfies every hunger, especially the irrational ones that seem to hit hardest at holidays: hunger for impetuous romance and for the reassuring warmth of family, for reckless abandon and for knowing who we are and what we want."

Equal parts rapture and raucous humor, *Moonstruck* ends with a champagne toast: "To the family!" It's a fitting conclusion to an effervescent, intoxicating comedy that makes us giddy as it tickles our nose and warms our heart.

24

Safety Last

Pathé (1923)
CAST: Harold Lloyd, Mildred David
DIRECTED BY: Fred Newmeyer, Sam Taylor
83 minutes [Not rated]

Safety Last is not remembered for its title, even though it's a dandy evocation of the recklessness that categorized stuntwork in the silent film era. The 1923 film is known and loved for one single image: Harold Lloyd hanging from the hands of a clock at the top of a Los Angeles skyscraper he has scaled. This celebrated movie moment is indelibly etched into the minds of movie lovers everywhere. The memorable image is a symbol of daring in the days before doubles, computer-generated imagery, and high-tech special effects. The famous scene is also synonymous with the man dangling in midair high above a busy city street.

Forever remembered as the man on the clock, Harold Lloyd was one of the great silent film pioneers, as much revered in his day as Chaplin and Keaton. During the 1920s he was the highest-paid actor in Hollywood, and his films regularly made more money than those of his two great rivals. Some critics hailed him as the funniest silent screen actor of his day. Today, however, Lloyd is not as well known as the two other comic gods in the silent screen comedy pantheon. Although highly regarded by film scholars and critics, his films have been unjustly overlooked by the public.

Numerous explanations for Lloyd's lack of longevity have been offered, including his own tight control over the presentation of his films, which have not been widely seen in the last half century. Another theory is that his uneventful personal life, which lacked the drama of his rivals, created the impression that his comedies lacked the underpinning of tragedy. Additionally, the fact that his screen persona was conventional rather than eccentric may be one reason he has not stood the test of time as well as Chaplin and Keaton.

Lloyd's personality may not have been exciting, but his films certainly were. "Thrill pictures" is the term Lloyd coined for the action-packed comedies he wrote to showcase his unusual athletic abilities. *Safety Last* is the best example of this blend of stuntwork and humor, a genre that has become

TIME ON MY HANDS   Harold Lloyd executes a "high and dizzy," as these cliffhanging stunts were called, in the 1923 *Safety Last.* Hanging from skyscrapers, flagpoles, and even giant clocks thrilled and delighted movie audiences during the 1920s. It was not uncommon for some moviegoers to faint at the cinematic sight of Lloyd dangling seventy stories over a crowded avenue.

increasingly popular in recent years in films such as the *Lethal Weapon* series and the Jackie Chan movies. Known as the king of daredevil comedy, Lloyd made eighteen feature films, including his brilliant satire of college humor, *The Freshman* (1925), before retiring in 1938. Although he lived until 1971, he came out of retirement only once, in 1947, for the dismal *The Sin of Harold Diddlebrook,* recut as *Mad Wednesday.*

But thrill pictures such as *Safety Last* were only one part of his work. In fact, Lloyd preferred what he called his character pictures, which focused on his endearingly optimistic persona. While other screen comedians of the day played the clown, Lloyd went in another direction. When he first donned a pair of horn-rimmed glasses in 1917 for *Over the Fence,* he created a sympathetically bookish, mild-mannered Everyman. Usually called Harold (with different last names), or simply "the boy," the character was a game but gentle and timid soul who was the last person one might expect to climb a twelvestory building and swing from a giant clock. When pressed into daring and outlandish action, Harold always seemed over his head, which heightened the sense of danger as well as the humor. This incongruity was the key to Lloyd's remarkable success.

Handsome and ambitious, Lloyd came to Hollywood from Nebraska in

1913, found work as an extra, and befriended a fellow novice named Hal Roach, with whom he worked both before and after a stint with the legendary slapstick producer Mack Sennett at his famed Keystone studio. In 1924 Lloyd formed his own company and continued to enjoy great success. Although he wasn't quite able to make the transition to talking pictures, because he owned the rights to his own films he amassed a great fortune and lived to a ripe old age in his fabled Hollywood mansion. He was awarded a special Oscar in 1952 and released compilation films in 1962 and 1964, which helped reintroduce his work to a new generation of filmgoers.

The idea for *Safety Last* was born when Lloyd witnessed real-life daredevil Bill Strothers, a steel worker, scale a building in downtown Los Angeles. Impressed not only with the feat but with the enthusiastic, spellbound reaction of the crowd, Lloyd determined to record the human fly act on film. He hired Strothers to play his roommate in the movie but decided to do the climbing himself.

The beguilingly simple premise of the film is that Harold is a small-town boy who moves to the big city in search of fame and fortune. The best he can do is find work as a harried fabric sales clerk, but he writes letters home to his girl (Lloyd's wife and frequent leading lady, Mildred Davis), telling her he is the store manager. When she arrives, he is desperate to make good. Hoping to earn a bonus by having his roommate, Limpy Bill (Strothers), climb the building as a store promotion, Harold sets up the event. But Limpy Bill is in a little trouble with the law. Limpy Bill convinces Harold to climb the first story so that he can shake the cop on his tail and switch places with Harold. The cop, however, is not so easily shaken, and at every floor Harold has to keep climbing one more story. At each floor he is beset by problems, from pesky pigeons to protruding paint platforms.

In all of the shots, the street below is clearly visible, making this one of the most hair-raising, realistic action scenes ever put on film. Lloyd indeed risked life and limb to create the heart-stopping effect. Although small safety platforms were set up several stories below him, Lloyd worked without a double, rigging, or trick photography.

Lloyd broke box office records with *Safety Last,* which remains a milestone in silent comedy history. This finely crafted, skillfully executed, and deceptively simple story displays all the qualities for which Lloyd should be remembered. Above all, Lloyd understood how to get laughs not simply through a funny character, but by placing a seemingly average American, a nice lad audiences could identify with, in a riotously funny situation.

"If plain laughter is any criterion," critic James Agee wrote of Lloyd in 1949, "few people have ever equaled him and no one has ever beaten him."

25

Harvey

Universal (1950)
CAST: Jimmy Stewart, Josephine Hull, Victoria Horne
DIRECTED BY: Henry Koster
104 minutes [Not rated]

James Stewart had established an image of stalwart patriotism, unimpeach-able integrity, and incorruptible virtue when he eagerly undertook the role of amiable alcoholic Elwood P. Dowd, first in the Broadway production of Mary Chase's Pulitzer Prize–winning play and then in the 1950 screen adaptation. Only an actor as beloved and trusted as Stewart could bring an air of absolute innocence and honor to the character, a lovable eccentric whose best friend is a giant rabbit visible only to Elwood.

Stewart went out on a limb in *Harvey,* a gentle but subversive comedy that suggested reality and sanity were overrated commodities. The idea that insanity, eccentricity, and the escape offered by alcohol were acceptable alter-natives to a humdrum, hidebound existence was quite novel at the time, although the theme was later echoed in films such as *One Flew Over the Cuckoo's Nest, The King of Hearts,* and *Arthur.*

Audiences tend to forget that Stewart, that bastion of American normalcy, had a quirky, darker, and more daring side to his nature. This side of Stew-art, later revealed more fully in his Hitchcock films, first showed itself in *Harvey,* a fondly remembered comedy made both funny and human by Stew-art's dead-on, understated rendition of the role.

Elwood P. Dowd remained one of Stewart's favorite characters and is often cited as his best purely comedic performance. In this charming, goofy comedy, Stewart returned to the shy, hesitant, simple, absentminded, and awkward persona he had developed earlier in his career, particularly in Frank Capra's sentimental social comedies, *It's a Wonderful Life, Mr. Smith Goes to Washington,* and *You Can't Take It with You.* Stewart, who had won an Oscar in 1940 for the fabled drawing room comedy *The Philadelphia Story,* a Katharine Hepburn vehicle costarring Cary Grant, had been nominated again for *It's a Wonderful Life* in 1946, his first film following his military service.

WABBIT STEW James Stewart, as dipsomaniac Elwood P. Dowd, in 1950's *Harvey*. Here he introduces his invisible friend, a giant rabbit named Harvey, to some skeptical sanitarium workers. Dowd remained one of Stewart's favorite characters.

The renowned classic did little to boost his career, however, and by the late 1940s Stewart's popularity was waning.

Mary Chase's acclaimed play had been running on Broadway for three years when Stewart decided to return to the stage to revitalize his career. Although his performance in *Harvey* was not well reviewed, Stewart became firmly associated with the part in the public's mind after the film version was released, and he returned to the stage twenty-three years later in the Broadway revival of *Harvey* and appeared in a London production in 1975. He also made a TV version of *Harvey* in 1972.

Although *Harvey* was not the box office hit Stewart had hoped it might be, he was nominated for a best actor Oscar for his performance as a man who thinks every day is a beautiful day. His costar, Josephine Hull, did win a best supporting actress Oscar (as well as a Golden Globe Award) for her performance as Dowd's long-suffering sister. Hull, who had played the part on the stage, is marvelous as the exasperated, determined, sweet woman who almost comes to share her brother's hallucination. A stage actress who made only a handful of films, Hull was equally outstanding in Capra's fabulously funny black comedy, *Arsenic and Old Lace* (1944), another fine screen adaptation of a popular play.

Although Capra had expressed interest in adapting *Harvey,* the job fell to Henry Koster, a German Jewish refugee known for the charm and flair of his comedies. Koster, who had been nominated for an Oscar for *The Bishop's Wife* (1947), starring Cary Grant, went on to make *The Inspector General* with Danny Kaye. He worked with Stewart again in *No Highway in the Sky* (1951) and *Mr. Hobbs Takes a Vacation* (1963). Koster's faithful, straightforward adaptation places Dowd in the peaceful eye of a hurricane howling around him. Dowd is blissfully unaware that he is an embarrassment to his family or that others can't see his furry white friend and constant companion. Thus a sly irony is set up: Dowd sparks craziness around him but remains unaffected by it. He is so reasonable and genuine that he doesn't seem crazy at all. Absurdity permeates this daffy comedy, which gives off a strong whiff of whimsy that intoxicated audiences.

Unfailingly polite, sincere, and compassionate, a lover of beauty and poetry, Dowd is the ultimate harmless crackpot. "I wrestled with reality for thirty-five years, and I'm happy to state I finally won out over it," Dowd says, settling down to a drink. Due to Hollywood Production Code rules, Dowd never actually takes a sip of alcohol. He is seen spending his afternoons at taverns and bars, associates with "riffraff," orders drinks for himself and others, talks about drinking, and keeps flask behind a book in the library, however, and is clearly lost in an alcoholic haze that makes everything seem rosy. This haze, however, also keeps him from seeing the reality of the pain around him and the effect his drinking has on his loved ones.

This touch of rueful regret is minor, however, and the film accepts his condition as benign and even admirable. Dowd is perhaps the screen's most memorable happy drunk, a romantic representation of nonconformity that pops up less frequently these days but continues to exist.

Known as "a nice fella," Dowd in all his eccentricity is tolerated by his neighbors in this story, which champions individuality above respectability. Certainly the "cure" is depicted as being worse than the disease, as we see when Dowd is sent to a mental hospital and, owing to a misunderstanding, his flustered, dithering sister is committed instead.

Harvey does not seem terribly radical today, and it was warmly embraced by audiences of the period as an escapist fantasy. But it touched on serious issues and flouted unconventional attitudes toward work, family, and responsibility. At heart it expressed delight in one man's quiet rebellion.

Oddly, the title character, who is never seen or heard, struck a chord with viewers, who responded affectionately to Dowd's chosen companion, a six-foot one-and-a-half-inch rabbit. Stewart recounts that throughout his lifetime people would ask him—quite seriously, it seemed—how old Harvey was doing or where he was. "I'd tell them he's in bed with a cold," Stewart recalled, "or say he's right here with me now." In a way, *Harvey* did stick by Stewart's side, an enduring and endearing image of whimsical eccentricity that proved good company on the actor's long and varied screen journey.

26

Raising Arizona

Circle Films (1987)
CAST: Holly Hunter, Nicholas Cage, John Goodman, Trey Wilson,
William Forsythe, Randall "Tex" Cobb, Frances McDormand
DIRECTED BY: Joel Coen
92 minutes [Rated PG-13]

There's laugh-out-loud funny, there's comedy that makes you grin from ear to ear, and there's even comedy that brings a lump to your throat and lifts your spirits. And then there's humor so astonishingly inventive and odd and stylish, you just sit there shaking your head in disbelief and occasionally remembering to pick your chin up off your chest. *Raising Arizona,* which belongs in the latter category, is in a film comedy class by itself. An archly funny combination of irony, surrealism, and slapstick, it is like no other comedy, except, perhaps, for its slight resemblance to the Coen brothers' other strange and sometimes wonderful films.

The sons of college professors from Minneapolis, Joel and Ethan Coen operate in a realm one step removed from reality. Joel, an NYU film school grad, takes directing and screenwriting credit, while Ethan, who majored in philosophy at Princeton, is listed as cowriter and producer. But the collaboration between the brothers actually extends to all aspects of the filmmaking process. It is their shared vision that finds fantastic, flamboyant expression in the movies they have been making together since 1984, when their independent first feature, a maliciously witty film noir tale of intrigue and deception, *Blood Simple,* made the duo the darlings of the arthouse scene.

With their second feature, *Raising Arizona,* they crossed over into the mainstream—or at least the fringes of the mainstream—but with their doggedly distinctive style intact. Each of their subsequent films (*Miller's Crossing, Barton Fink, The Hudsucker Proxy*) have defied categorization, but each has been tinged with twisted humor. The Coens' bizarre sense of humor, which fueled *Raising Arizona,* again reached full expression in 1996's *Fargo,* which won Oscars for best original screenplay and for Frances McDormand's blisteringly funny performance as a pregnant police officer trying to crack a multiple murder case in Minnesota. (McDormand, a tough-minded actress who is mar-

BABY BOOM   Holly Hunter and Nicholas Cage proudly admiring the latest addition to their family in the Coen Brothers' *Raising Arizona* (1987), a bizarre, frenetic comedy that often feels like a live-action Road Runner cartoon. Cinematographer Barry Sonnenfeld went on to direct *Get Shorty* and *Men in Black*.

ried to Joel Coen, starred in *Blood Simple* and has a small role in *Raising Arizona*.)

Holly Hunter also plays a police officer in *Raising Arizona*, which is just as disarming and demented a comedy as *Fargo*, but lighter and slightly less gruesome and disturbing. Hunter plays Edwina, who meets H. I. McDonnough (Nicolas Cage) on his frequent trips through the police station, where she takes his mug shot before he's sent to jail for robbing convenience stores. Hi, who never loads the gun he uses in his armed robberies, keeps getting paroled but just can't stay away from the temptation of a 7-Eleven. During his third fingerprinting, Hi slips an engagement ring on Edwina's finger. When he gets out of prison he vows to go straight, and the unlikely couple weds.

They settle into blissful domesticity in a trailer in the Arizona desert and prepare to start a family. "There was too much love and beauty for the two of us, and every day we kept a child out of the world was a day he would regret having missed," Hi says to explain the ticking of Ed's biological clock. Ed, however, discovers she is barren. "Her insides were a rocky place where my seed could find no purchase," Hi informs the audience in his voice-over narration, written with an elegance that contrasts with his flaky, working-class appearance and flatly delivered in a natural voice that makes it sound all the more loopy.

No adoption agency will consider giving a baby to a convicted felon, so, with "biology and prejudice conspiring against us," Ed hits upon a plan to kidnap one of the Arizona quints. Reasoning that unpainted furniture magnate Nathan Arizona (Trey Wilson) and his wife have more than they can handle, Ed and Hi decide it's not fair for one family to have five babies when they have none. In one of the movie's merriest scenes, Hi, trying to make his selection, madly chases five crawling kids moving in all directions around the Arizona mansion. Unable to determine which baby is the best, Hi emerges empty-handed, only to have Ed scold him, "You go right back up there and get me a toddler." When he comes back out, he hands her little Nathan junior and says, "Here's the instructions," tossing a pilfered copy of *Dr. Spock* on the seat.

The proud parents bring Nathan Jr. back home and begin to enjoy life as "a family unit," although Hi is the first to admit, "It ain't *Ozzie and Harriet*." Crime does not pay, however, even in the Coens' topsy-turvy universe. Nathan senior wants his boy back. The Lone Biker of the Apocalypse (Randall "Tex" Cobb)—a motorcycle-riding, diabolical demon summoned, perhaps, from Hi's feverish imagination—is hot on their trail. Hi's no-class boss (Sam McMurray) discovers the truth and demands Hi hand over the ill-gotten baby to his own wife (McDormand), whose own brood of monstrous home demolishers no longer contains a child small enough to cuddle. Then two buddies who just busted out of the slammer (John Goodman and William Forsythe) show up and use Hi's home as a hideout. When Ed kicks them out they decide to steal the stolen baby and collect the reward.

The comedy climaxes in a delirious chase through the cement wasteland of Tempe, a town depicted as the tacky epitome of bad taste. Cinematographer Barry Sonnenfeld (a chum of the Coens who went on to direct the monster hit *Men in Black*) has a field day filming the action-packed finale, one of the screen's most frenetic and funniest chases. Sonnenfeld uses every trick in the book, from point-of-view shots to incredibly fast tracking shots, in order to establish the visual intensity for which the Coens' films are known.

Although sometimes accused of being smart-ass show-offs who make technically dazzling but hollow, condescending, and self-consciously weird films, the Coens have also attracted a fair share of critical acclaim for their startlingly original vision, which is admittedly cool and detached. *Raising Arizona* had its detractors, such as Roger Ebert. Leonard Maltin hits the nail on the head with his assessment that the "aggressively wacked-out sense of humor may not be for all tastes, but if you're attuned to it, it's a scream." The *Village Voice* also astutely deemed *Raising Arizona* "juvenilia for grown-ups," adding, "To argue that its auteurs value style—and ersatz style at that—over substance is to miss the joke: their characters live in an ersatz culture."

The characters in *Raising Arizona* are indeed cartoon figures who exist in an out-of-proportion landscape drawn by their live-action animators, an alternate universe that is both frightening and funny. Hi has Woody Woodpecker tattooed on his arm (so does the lone biker), a direct reference to the cartoon nature of the comedy.

It takes actors able to pitch their performances at this cartoon scale without losing a sense of believable human emotion to make a movie like *Raising Arizona* work. The Coens wrote the role of Edwina, a prickly desert flower, with Hunter in mind, and with her bull terrier determination and her naked vulnerability, Hunter is more than up to the challenge. A crackerjack comedienne, Hunter scored a double success in 1987, earning acclaim for her performance as the professionally competent news producer whose personal life is a mess in James Brooks's witty and incisive *Broadcast News.*

Cage, an actor known for his intensity and crazy edge, is sweetly earnest as the goofy Hi. Sexy, stupid, sincere, and inept, his Hi is somehow both appalling and appealing. Fresh from his success in *Peggy Sue Got Married,* Cage also hit a comedy doubleheader in 1987, costarring with Cher as the eccentric romantic hero of *Moonstruck.* Cage has since tended to star in heavy dramas, where his commanding presence is put to good use, but he successfully returned to comedy in *Honeymoon in Vegas* (1992). His 1993 comedy, *Amos & Andrew,* bombed, however, and Cage went on win a best actor Oscar for his role as a hopeless alcoholic in *Leaving Las Vegas* and to become an action hero in *The Rock* and *Con Air.*

The late Trey Wilson was also an able farceur who could find a layer of truth within a caricature, in this case the crass mogul modeled loosely on Crazy Eddie. Goodman, an oversize actor, is adept at comic exaggeration. Goodman—who did his best comic work in the Coens' 1998 engaging shaggy dog comedy, *The Big Lebowski*—is also well cast as the two-faced con who worms his way into Hi and Edwina's life. Gloriously crude, Goodman's jailbird uses expression such as "If a frog had wings, it wouldn't bump its ass a-hoppin'." Goodman went on to costar in the Coens' *Barton Fink,* a mordantly funny, hyperexpressionistic story about a pretentious playwright (John Turturro) lured to Hollywood in the 1930s.

It is not only the characters that are larger than life in the Coen brothers' movies. The Coens also love to satirize subcultures: the South in *Blood Simple,* the gangster culture in *Miller's Crossing,* old Hollywood in *Barton Fink,* bowling in *The Big Lebowski,* and the suburban wilderness of western America in *Raising Arizona.*

As much as *Raising Arizona* can be said to be about anything, it is a sly meditation on materialism, the American dream, the family, and love. It's just that by the time the Coen brothers are through having fun with these subjects, we hardly recognize them.

27

My Little Chickadee

Universal (1940)
CAST: Mae West, W. C. Fields, Margaret Hamilton
DIRECTED BY: Edward Cline
83 minutes [Not rated]

My Little Chickadee is responsible for one of the oddest and most inspired pairings in screen comedy—sultry sex goddess Mae West pitted against boozing bungler W. C. Fields. Egads, who will get the most laughs, the naughty, haughty dame or the dyspeptic geezer? More of a competition than a collaboration, *My Little Chickadee* was cowritten by West and Fields. That is, they both wrote scripts separately and then merged them into an improbable creature—half siren, half gargoyle—that has since entered movie mythology.

Where West was languorously seductive, Fields was sputteringly caustic. Where West projected bawdy sexual magnetism, Fields was an asexual misogynist. West was all honey, while Fields was pure vinegar. Despite the differences in their comic styles and personas, West and Fields shared some vital similarities that unify *My Little Chickadee* into a satisfying, cynical comedy. United in utter contempt for respectability and propriety, both the unapologetic sensualist and the unrepentant misanthrope continually expressed their scorn for bourgeois society.

In their distinct ways, West and Fields were equally unconventional—and were certainly equally funny in their own right. Together they set comic fire to the myth of the American West, here depicted as moralistic and hypocritical. This barbed parody of the movie western is an obvious precursor to *Cat Ballou, Blazing Saddles,* and other, much later satires of small-mindedness in the Old West. Margaret Hamilton—fresh from her stint as the Wicked Witch of the West in *The Wizard of Oz*—is cast as a puritanical busybody, representing everything West and Fields detested.

Their openly defiant screen personas were also both always out for themselves, high livers looking for easy pickings, forever on the make or on the take. The title of Fields's *Never Give a Sucker an Even Break,* released a year after *My Little Chickadee,* says it best. The question in *My Little Chickadee* is which of the two consummate opportunists is going to get the upper hand.

103

West and Fields, who had worked their way up through vaudeville and Broadway, were also well matched in abilities. Both known for their distinctive use of language—and body language—they were at home with physical pantomime as well as verbal repartee. West was the mistress of the double entendre. Fields employed antiquated, high-flown verbiage in his satire of pretentious affectation.

Both West and Fields had been major movie stars in the 1930s. West established a reputation as the greatest female comedienne of the early sound era with hits such as *She Done Him Wrong* (1933), *I'm No Angel* (1934, costarring Cary Grant), and *Belle of the Nineties* (1934). By 1935 West was the highest-paid woman in America. In that same year Fields, already a famed comic actor, took his first role in a serious film, playing Mr. Micawber in *David Copperfield,* and appeared in one of his funniest films, *The Man on the Flying Trapeze.* Fields, who was portrayed by Rod Steiger in the even-handed 1976 screen biography, *W. C. Fields and Me,* had gathered a cult following beginning with 1934's *It's a Gift* and solidified his status with such classics as *You Can't Cheat an Honest Man* and *The Bank Dick.*

By 1940 West's popularity was beginning to wane, and Fields was considered something of a liability due to his failing health, drinking, and prickly temperament; in a calculated attempt to bolster their careers, Universal decided to pair them in a vehicle built for two. The ploy worked, although West never had another hit and Fields faltered a few short years later. In 1925, *Vanity Fair* asked Fields what he wanted inscribed on his tombstone, and upon his death in 1946, the comedian's wry utterance became immortalized in granite: "On the whole, I'd rather be in Philadelphia." West spent the forties and fifties on Broadway, on tour or in nightclubs, then went into seclusion, returning to the screen at the age of seventy-eight in 1970 in *Myra Breckinridge.* Her final film fling came in 1978 with *Sextette,* a movie based on one of her plays that is best remembered as a curiosity piece featuring an eighty-five-year-old sex symbol.

My Little Chickadee, a profitable and popular showcase for the two beloved caricatures of decadence, begins with West, as Flowerbelle Lee, blithely buffing her nails aboard a stagecoach, which is robbed by a masked bandit. "He's just another man to me," Flowerbelle scoffs just before she's kidnapped by the mysterious man in black. Returning home later unharmed, and with some of the bandit's stolen gold, Flowerbelle has clearly worked her feminine wiles on the outlaw. When he shows up for a midnight tryst with the irresistible temptress, the townsfolk ride Flowerbelle out of town.

On the train, Flowerbelle meets the oafish and effusive J. Cuthbert Twillie (Fields), who is carrying what appears to be a bag of bills. When Twillie introduces himself as the purveyor of novelties and notions, Flowerbelle smirks, "What kind of notions you got?" Since Flowerbelle needs a husband to confer respectability on her, she agrees to marry the old fool and enlists a cardsharp to pose as a preacher. "Will you take me?" Twillie proposes. "I'll take you, and how," she replies in a play on words that is typical of both Fields and West.

Arriving in town, Twillie is chagrined to find that Flowerbelle has no intention of consummating this marriage of convenience, and he heads for the local saloon to hustle a card game. "Is this a game of chance?" one novice asks him. "Not the way I play it, no," Twillie replies.

When Flowerbelle arrives at the tavern, she makes a few conquests of her own, attracting the attentions of both the dastardly saloon owner and the upstanding newspaperman. Meanwhile Twillie's tall tales of heroism result in an offer to become sheriff of

TRUE WEST   "A plumber's idea of Cleopatra" is how costar W. C. Fields described the legendary Mae West when they costarred in *My Little Chickadee*. There was little love lost between West and Fields during production of the picture; their scenes were filmed separately.

the lawless town, an honor that is sure to lead to his untimely death. It is, however, a subsequent charade that almost proves his undoing. After dressing up as the masked bandit to steal his own wife's affections, he is apprehended and almost hung, but Flowerbelle again uses her wiles to save the day and his skin.

The two part company amiably, as Twillie leaves town to seek his fortune in oil wells—hair oil, that is. Fields gets the last word, reciting one of West's catch phrases, "Come up and see me sometime." But West gets the last shot: the camera lingers on her swiveling bottom as she sashays up the stairs.

Although both Fields and West were accustomed to working with a straight man, here they take turns setting up each other's jokes. The problem of pitting two larger-than-life personalities was also overcome by limiting their shared screen time. Both actors are allowed to take center stage in their scenes with other characters. The two stars reportedly got along well on the set and established an easy rapport on screen.

My Little Chickadee may not be the best film West or Fields made, but they are both at their best in this two-for-the-price-of-one comedy bargain.

28

The Full Monty

Twentieth Century-Fox/Searchlight (1997)
CAST: Robert Carlyle, Tom Wilkinson, Mark Addy
DIRECTED BY: Peter Cattaneo
95 minutes [Rated R]

A surprise hit from England, *The Full Monty* is funny from top to bottom, a bold, bracing, and revealing look at the lengths to which men will go to preserve their dignity—even if it means standing stark naked in front of a crowd of screaming women. An affecting tribute to self-preservation, this invigorating comic tale of redemption was nominated for four Academy Awards, including best picture, director, original screenplay, and score. The rousing story of scrappy, scruffy underdogs was made for $3 million and grossed more than $200 million, making it Britain's all-time box office champ.

Naughty, cheeky, and loaded with empathy for its colorful characters, *The Full Monty* earns its plentiful laughs honestly as it celebrates inventiveness born of adversity. Desperate times call for desperate measures, and things couldn't be much more desperate for the unemployed steel workers in Sheffield. With no prospects for work in sight, the men are humiliated by their inability to support their families. Those who rely on their wives' incomes and live off the dole feel emasculated. Despair has descended on this once thriving Yorkshire steel town, and the men have given up hope. The stage is thus set for an uplifting comedy—for while desperation itself is not funny, the crazy things people will do because they are desperate has been a staple of comedy since time immemorial.

Gaz (Robert Carlyle), a divorced dad who has fallen behind in his child support payments, is not quite ready to admit defeat. When the famed Chippendale revue comes to town, Gaz is at first offended that "some poof is waving his tackle at my wife." He is also astounded to see the local bar filled to overflowing with howling, cheering women and quickly calculates the huge profit male strip shows make.

Still, when he suggests to his best mate, Dave (Mark Addy), that they put on their own show, the idea seems absurd. For starters, they can't dance. As Gerald, their former foreman, informs Gaz and Dave, "You're skinny, you're fat, and you're both ugly." Undaunted, the idle mill workers reluctantly agree to solve their financial woes with a Yorkshire-style strip show. But since the paying women have already had a taste of the best, the local lads will somehow have to top the Chippendale act. Goaded into putting up or shutting up, they resolve to go the pros one better with the full monty—full frontal nudity. "We dare to be bare," they boast while privately agonizing over the decision. "Jiggling about in the buff" may seem a strange way for these unlikely beefcakes to regain their pride, but that's the delight of this off-kilter comedy.

Before they can embark on their brazen bid for cash, Gaz and Dave have to persuade Gerald (Tom Wilkinson), an accomplished ballroom dancer, to join them as choreographer and performer. At first he resists. "Dancing takes coordination, fitness, skill, timing, and grace," he tells them, pointing out that they have none of these qualities. But the lure of easy money proves greater than his fear of embarrassment, and stuffy, middle-aged Gerald signs on.

They then set up auditions, netting an aging black man promisingly nicknamed Horse (Paul Barber), who is a bit rusty but still has some moves, including the funky chicken. In one of the film's many fall-down funny moments, they discover a candidate whose lack of dancing ability is more than offset by his impressive anatomical endowments. "Gentlemen, the lunch box has landed," Gaz says when Guy (Hugo Speer) drops his drawers.

Along the way they befriend Lomper (Steve Huison), a suicidal, sad-faced fellow who is beyond caring if he makes a fool out of himself. Although Gerald sneers that he's a "pigeon-chested little tosser," Lomper is embraced by the boys, who know all too well how it feels to be useless. Dave, however, has serious reservations about "making the biggest arses of ourselves in the known universe." A husky fellow, he's self-conscious about his weight, and his anxiety leads to an experience of impotence that further shakes his confidence. Gerald, on the other hand, worries about getting a "stiffy" on stage.

Gaz's seemingly boundless enthusiasm also wavers at the last moment, but in the end he gives it his all by baring all. To earn the respect of his son (William Snape), Gaz has to make good on his promise, no matter how foolhardy or outrageous.

Some of the film's funniest moments take place during the rehearsals, as the hopelessly incompetent dancers start to practice their routine—after watching *Flashdance* on video and critiquing not only Jennifer Beals's moves, but her welding. As they begin to work on their bump and grind act, the klutzes step on each other's toes, hit each other as they whip off their belts, and hop about trying to get their pants off. One of the joys of the film is that, unlike a Hollywood movie, there is no radical transformation from novices into studs who strut their stuff with professional polish. But by the end they aren't half-

TAKING IT ALL OFF   The cast of the 1997 smash British comedy *The Full Monty*. Made for a mere $3 million, *Monty* grossed $200 million worldwide and was nominated for four Academy Awards.

bad, either, as they begin to find the magic locked in their less than perfect bodies. In one knockout scene the men are standing in the unemployment line when Donna Summers's "Hot Stuff" starts playing and they can't resist responding, in unison, to the beat with some sexy moves.

In its theme of dance as a liberating personal force, *The Full Monty* echoes the engaging romantic drama *Dirty Dancing* (1987), the Australian delight *Strictly Ballrooom* (1992), and the disarming 1997 Japanese comedy *Shall We Dance?*. Its theme of recovered pride among the English unemployed was uncannily echoed in another delightful 1997 British comedy, *Brassed Off*, in which laid-off miners score a musical triumph playing in a brass band.

Although *The Full Monty* is heartily funny, Simon Beaufoy's deliriously wacky script also touches on serious themes, including the emotional toll of economic hardship and the shifting dynamics between men and women that takes place when they change financial roles. It also deals with another aspect of sexual politics, as the men begin to realize that women will be sizing them up in the harsh way they have always appraised women. Unfamiliar feelings of inadequacy and vulnerability grip the men as they engage in a bit of role reversal.

One reason this low-budget British comedy became such a sensation is that the largely unknown actors give such natural, unaffected performances. Robert Carlyle, who played the psycho Begbie in *Trainspotting*, is especially engaging as Gaz, an easygoing sort struggling to take responsibility for his life.

First-time director Peter Cattaneo is able to balance humor and honesty, depth of feeling with broad humor. Tastefully shot but filled with sexual frankness, *The Full Monty* is a deeply affectionate story of male bonding. In the end, the blue-collar lads bare their souls as well as their bodies.

29

National Lampoon's Animal House

Universal (1978)
CAST: John Belushi, Peter Riegert, Tim Matheson, Tom Hulce,
Donald Sutherland, Karen Allen
DIRECTED BY: John Landis
109 minutes [Rated R]

A critic crowing about the Farrelly brothers' ribald 1998 comedy, *There's Something About Mary,* referred to it as "the *Animal House* of the '90s." Clearly the complimentary comparison suggests that both gross-out comedies share an anything-goes, over-the-top style of unrefined humor. The association with the bawdy 1978 classic also carried a prediction that the new comedy will become a monster hit. Most obviously, however, the reference to *National Lampoon's Animal House* is shorthand for "a film that defines a generation."

Time will tell if the gloriously crude, uneven, but very funny *There's Something About Mary* will go down in screen history as the quintessential youth culture comedy of the 1990s. The boisterously funny *Animal House,* however, may not have been the best comedy of its time, but it so perfectly embodied the sentiments of the era's youth subculture, it became a milestone in movie history. A riotous comedy that is synonymous with anarchy, *Animal House* took antiauthoritarianism to new heights, simultaneously pushing the limits of taste to new lows.

Animal House was one of the screen's first major hit comedies targeted directly at the eighteen- to twenty two-year-old age group. Set in 1962, the story of a fraternity that runs amok at fictitious Faber College—whose motto is "Knowledge is good"— glorified the rebellion of youth against the conservative academic establishment that seeks to destroy it and spoil their fun. One of the biggest box office hits in movie history and the first $100 million hit comedy, *Animal House* paved the way for a seemingly endless succession of tasteless comedies aimed at the youth market, forever changing the demographics that dictate Hollywood policy.

Animal House, National Lampoon's first foray into film, was cowritten by Harold Ramis, who had appeared on stage with John Belushi, Gilda Radner, and Bill Murray in *The National Lampoon Show* and was a head writer and performer on *SCTV*. The breakthrough comedy brought to film the kind of crude, rudely irreverent humor previously found in improv comedy troupes and TV sketch comedy then popular with young audiences. The heroes of the splendidly messy movie are a group of misfits who refuse to take college seriously or to respect the repressive forces that conspire to make them conform to the ideals of college life. Inveterate party animals, the Delta frat brothers know how to have a good time, however, and prefer to put their creative energies into pranks that undermine the authority of their prissy, uptight, all-American rivals at the Omega House.

Their neighboring fraternity brothers are short-haired, clean-cut WASPs who wear letter sweaters, belong to the ROTC, and date bubble-headed blondes named Babs and Mandy. The Omegas are in cahoots with the dean to rid the college of this foul stain upon its upstanding character, and the film's loose plot revolves around their rivalry. Much of the humor comes from the contrast between the nasty straight-arrows and the essentially decent goof-ups. This "losers of the world unite" theme would find expression in countless future youth culture comedies championing geeks, most notably *Revenge of the Nerds, Weird Science, The Breakfast Club,* and *Pretty in Pink.*

Delta's most flagrant screw-up is played by John Belushi, who had already won an Emmy for his crazed caricatures on TV's *Saturday Night Live* when he was typecast as the beer-bellied Bluto in his first feature film. As the resident pig in the fraternity known as the animal house, Belushi's Bluto Blutarksy is a perpetually inebriated cretin who loves to gross people out with his impression of a zit. The food fight is his métier, the toga party his true calling. Foul, lewd, and apparently stupid, Bluto crushes beer cans on his forehead and downs a bottle of Jack Daniel's without pausing for breath. His prospects for the future may look glum, but *Animal House* reminds us that plenty of kids who goof off in college nevertheless manage to succeed. In the closing credits, as each character's future destiny is flashed on the screen, we discover that Bluto—who is dressed as a pirate and has just stolen a car and kidnapped Mandy (or is it Babs?)—will become a senator.

The future is similarly bright for most of the Delta House renegades, who, having been expelled from school by the closed-minded Dean Wormer (John Vernon), execute their revenge by sabotaging the homecoming parade, leaving the town in shambles. Although the boys themselves admit they are making a "stupid and futile gesture," the wanton destruction of property is here equated with the rejection of the materialistic values of an oppressive and bigoted society.

Animal House introduced the bright young faces of a number of actors who would go on to make their mark in film. Tom Hulce (*Amadeus*) plays freshman Larry Kroger, who pledges with Delta after being herded into a corner with other rejects—including an Arab, an Indian, a Jew, and a blind guy—at an Omega rush party, along with his fat, dorky roommate, Kent Dorfman (Stephen Furst). A decent, normal guy, Larry serves as the recruit who learns to appreciate the freewheeling fun and camaraderie at Delta. Larry will go on to become an editor at *The National Lampoon.* In fact, he may write the movie we are now watching.

Tim Matheson stars as the good-looking Romeo of Delta House, a smooth operator named Otter who will become a Beverly Hills gynecologist. In real life Matheson went on to roles in Mel Brooks's *To Be or Not to Be* and *Fletch* and eventually bought the National Lampoon company and became its chairman and chief executive officer in 1989.

Peter Riegert made his screen debut in *Animal House,* playing Boone, the resident nice guy. Boone is having romantic trouble with his girlfriend, Katie (Karen Allen), who thinks it's time for him to grow up and spend less time

FOOD FIGHT, ANYONE?   The late John Belushi in the climactic scenes of the 1978 groundbreaking comedy *National Lampoon's Animal House.* Audiences the world over loved the "losers triumph over the Establishment" theme and the crude, gross-out humor, making *Animal House* a box office biggie.

guzzling brew with the boys. Riegert went on to do fine work in the comedies *Local Hero* and *Crossing Delancey*. Allen, who enjoyed future success in *Raiders of the Lost Ark* and the very funny *Starman*, plays a young woman flirting with a different kind of rebellion that is about to blossom into the 1960s' flower power. Katie has a fling with her cool, pot-smoking professor, drolly played by Donald Sutherland, who flashes his derriere in one of the movie's many naughty little moments. Sutherland's renegade professor serves as an indication that the emerging anti-Establishment attitudes were not confined to the student population.

Although *Animal House* struck a chord with audiences apparently eager for comic chaos and mayhem with a modern spin, the crude comedy caught the fancy of a number of critics as well. Roger Ebert gave it four stars. While acknowledging it was "vulgar, raunchy, ribald, and occasionally scatological," Ebert deemed it "the funniest comedy since Mel Brooks made *The Producers.*"

Having struck comedy gold, National Lampoon went on to make a series of comedies, none nearly as funny as *Animal House*. *National Lampoon's Vacation* (1983) was popular enough to spawn two sequels and to inspire a series of mediocre Chevy Chase comedies, the best of which are *Fletch* and *The Three Amigos*. Encouraged by Belushi's success in *Animal House,* *National Lampoon Show* veterans and *Saturday Night Live* alums Gilda Radner, Dan Aykroyd, and Bill Murray all successfully made the transition to film comedy. Most notably, Murray, Ramis, and Aykroyd teamed up for *Ghostbusters* (1984), the first multimillion-dollar scare comedy.

Belushi went on to make what many fans consider his best comedy, *The Blues Brothers,* with Aykroyd, in 1980, based on a musical act the pair had created for *Saturday Night Live*. Landis scored big with Aykroyd and another *Saturday Night Live* veteran, Eddie Murphy, in *Trading Places* (1984), the story of a have and a have-not whose fortunes are switched in an heredity-versus-environment experiment.

Although *Animal House* draws on a long tradition of college humor—most notably the Marx Brothers' satirical *Horse Feathers* as well as Harold Lloyd's *The Freshman,* Buster Keaton's *College,* Jerry Lewis's *The Nutty Professor,* and the Henry Fonda comedy *The Male Animal*—it was the first to make a complete mockery of the educational establishment. It also launched a spate of youth comedies—from *Bill and Ted's Excellent Adventure* to *Porky's* to *Dumb and Dumber*—that owe a debt of gratitude to the liberating, bawdy excess of *Animal House,* which ushered in the age of adolescent anarchy and changed the face of comedy forever.

30

The Court Jester

Paramount (1956)
CAST: Danny Kaye, Glynis Johns, Angela Lansbury,
Basil Rathbone, Cecil Parker, Mildred Natwick
DIRECTED BY: Norman Panama, Melvin Frank
101 minutes [Not rated]

Among the all-time great comedy routines, Danny Kaye's dazzling rendition of "the vessel with the pestle and the chalice from the palace" from *The Court Jester* ranks alongside Abbott and Costello's "Who's on first?" as the funniest ever recorded on film.

A spoof of swashbucklers set in medieval England, *The Court Jester* is filled with inspired jesting and jousting and brilliant wordplay coupled with comic swordplay. A complicated story of mistaken identity and characters working at cross-purposes, the film ably pokes fun at the Douglas Fairbanks–style costume drama, predating Mel Brooks's *Robin Hood: Men in Tights* by almost forty years.

The Court Jester is Kaye's most tightly written, liveliest, and most clever comic vehicle. Kaye's best film is also, not coincidentally, the only one to make full use of the comedian's versatility. In this tour-de-force comedy, Kaye—an agile actor equally adept at broad clowning and bright banter—is called upon to handle literate dialogue as well as vaudeville-style slapstick. Armed with an arsenal of tongue twisters and humorous songs in a vehicle designed specifically to demonstrate his vocal and physical virtuosity, the legendary entertainer attacks the role with obvious glee. His talent for mimicry and his ability to wrap his lips around a script peppered with alliteration, rhymes, and fast-paced poetic patter are highlighted throughout the film. "Get it? Got it. Good!" is one running refrain. Kaye also demonstrates his verbal flair when, as a supposed "master of many tongues," he speaks gibberish in several languages.

The forty-two-year-old actor also leaps, cavorts, and athletically engages in robust buffoonery. The final duel—imitated by Mandy Patinkin in *The Princess Bride*—is a physical comedy masterpiece. Although Kaye displays an almost manic energy, he is in complete control of every gesture, word, and expression. The story centers around a circus performer (Kaye) who agrees to double as a

SURELY YOU JEST "A jester unemployed," Danny Kaye sings in the title role, "is nobody's fool." Leonard Maltin called *The Court Jester* (1956) "one of the funniest comedies ever made."

renowned court jester who has been deliberately waylaid en route to an engagement at the castle. The famed Giacomo—every name begins with "G" in the film—is "king of jesters and jester of kings," an entertainer whose celebrity gains him entree to the private domains of the rich and powerful at court. Kaye's humble carnival performer gamely takes Giacomo's place in order to foil an evil plan and restore the rightful heir to the throne, an infant whose bottom is marked by the royal purple pimpernel beauty mark. "I made a fool of myself" is how the jester explains his situation.

At the castle, the phony jester quickly establishes himself as an intimate of the king and becomes embroiled in court intrigue. Unknown to the fake jester, however, the real Giacomo is actually an assassin in league with the king's wicked minister. This confusion is compounded when our impostor catches the eye of Princess Gwendolyn (Lansbury), who has refused to obey the king's orders to marry the "grim, grizzly, gruesome Griswold." Seeing the princess's interest in the jester, the ambitious court witch Griselda (Mildred Natwick) casts a spell on the hapless jester to endow him with the derring-do he needs to fulfill the prophecy of a handsome "true love" she has manufactured and ceaselessly reinforced in Gwendolyn's mind. Unfortunately, since the spell can be undone, and reinstated, with a snap of the fingers, the jester continually—and hilariously—vacillates between courage and cowardice.

Kaye, who enjoyed great popularity in England, was fresh from a stint at London's Palladium when he took on what was to become his signature role. *The Court Jester,* which was set in Merry Olde England, featured stage-trained British stars Mildred Natwick, Angela Lansbury, Cecil Parker, and Basil Rathbone, all accomplished farceurs. Smart and stylish, the Robin Hood satire was nimbly played by an ensemble that, in Lansbury's words, "danced around" the star.

A singer, dancer, actor, and veteran of the Borscht Belt circuit and Broadway, Kaye began appearing in films with 1943's *Up in Arms,* the first in a series of popular comedies he made for producer Samuel Goldwyn. In 1947 Kaye appeared in *The Secret Life of Walter Mitty,* based on a short story by James Thurber about a chronic daydreamer. The indelible hit comedy, which was greeted as an international event, allowed Kaye to play a variety of roles, including a swishy fashion designer, a surgeon, a debonair riverboat gambler, and an RAF officer.

Kaye's wife and lifelong collaborator, Sylvia Fine, who had long composed Kaye's trademark tongue-twisting songs, wrote the songs for *The Secret Life of Walter Mitty* and again provided the musical numbers for *The Court Jester,* including "They'll Never Outfox the Fox" and "The Maladjusted Jester." Fine, a witty lyricist, is often credited with being the true brains behind Kaye's success. While her influence over the scripts he chose and the material she wrote for him no doubt contributed to his success, it was Kaye who impressed audiences with his ability to do the work justice. Who else could name fifty-four Russian composers, fictitious and real, in thirty-eight seconds as Kaye did in his famed song "Tchaikovsky"?

Kaye, who earned an honorary Oscar in 1954 for "his unique talents," was at a pivotal point in his career when he made *The Court Jester.* The most expensive comedy to date upon its release in 1956, *The Court Jester* cost $4 million and made only $2.2 million. Despite its poor showing at the box office, it earned wide acclaim and continues to be held in high regard. "Filled with more color, more song and more funny lines than any three comedies put together, this is Kaye's best performance," reads the description in *The Videohound's Golden Movie Retriever.* Leonard Maltin deems it "one of the best comedies ever made."

Kaye's popularity began to wane in the late 1950s, and he made few films during the 1960s, when he turned to television as the host of the Emmy and Peabody Award–winning program *The Danny Kaye Show.* In 1981 he made a rare TV appearance in a dramatic role in *Skokie,* playing a Holocaust survivor. He was honored by the Motion Picture Academy of Arts and Sciences for his humanitarian efforts, most notably on behalf of UNICEF, in 1982.

The screen work for which he is most fondly remembered, however, is *The Court Jester,* which showcased his indubitably inimitable gifts as no other film had.

31

King of Hearts

United Artists (1966)
CAST: Alan Bates, Pierre Brasseur, Jean-Claude Brialy,
Genevieve Bujold, Michel Serrault
DIRECTED BY: Philippe De Broca
102 minutes [Not rated]

King of Hearts played for years at a Boston theater, where audiences never seemed to tire of the French comedy's insouciant charm. Directed by Philippe De Broca, the enchanting metaphorical film depicts a community created by the escaped inmates from an insane asylum as a haven of sanity amid the madness of war.

In this cult classic, which continues to be shown around the world, Alan Bates plays a Scottish soldier sent to rescue a small French town during the waning days of World War I. The Germans have booby-trapped the munitions dump, which is set to explode at the stroke of midnight, when a mechanical knight emerges from the clock in the town square to toll the fatal bell. Private Charles Plumpick (Bates) has no experience with explosives and is sure he is not the right man for the job. But he speaks French, and his buffoonish superior officer, Colonel Alexander MacBibenbrook (Adolfo Celi)—who calls him Pumpernickel—is adamant that he go, proving the old axiom about "army intelligence" being an oxymoron.

When Charles arrives, the town's citizens have already been warned by the Resistance and have evacuated their fair city. Charles is spotted by the enemy and escapes into the local loony bin, where he masquerades as one of the inmates. Taking his cue from his card-playing crony, the Duke, he calls himself the King of Hearts. Apparently the inmates have been expecting this mysterious majesty to appear, and they greet him with reverence. After the Germans abandon the doomed city, the inmates wander out into the town and quickly adopt the professions of their choice, creating a convivial community that approximates the real one but is marked by unusual gaiety.

The Duke (Jean-Claude Brialy) becomes a real duke, with his wife (Francoise Christophe) as duchess. Michel Serrault (who played Albin in the 1978 French hit comedy *La Cage Aux Folles,* remade in English in 1996 as *The Bird-*

KING FOR A DAY Alan Bates in *King of Hearts* (1966). This cult movie played for two years straight at a movie theater in Boston; it still pops up at midnight showings around the world.

cage) becomes an effeminate barber who pays his customers. "That's why business is so good," he explains cheerfully. Julien Guimoar becomes a bishop, Pierre Brasseur becomes a general, and Micheline Presle becomes the magnanimous madam of a whorehouse. The beguiling Coquelicot (Genevieve Bujold) undertakes the role of virginal prostitute and tightrope walker, whom Charles finds alluring.

Soon the town is flourishing under the guise of normalcy, even though the inhabitants are complete crackpots. Charles goes along with the charade—what's the point of resisting?—as he tries to decode the mysterious message "The knight strikes at midnight." Baffled by the cryptic clue to the bombs' detonation, Charles gets little help from the residents, whose own logic is enigmatic. When Charles despairs of defusing the bombs, he attempts to lead his subjects out of the town. But they refuse to follow, fearful of what awaits in the outside world and unable to comprehend the danger of their situation. Living so completely in the moment in a community of their own creation, they don't care what awaits them. "I care!" Charles shouts, but his words fall on deaf ears.

Charles slowly succumbs to the town's crazy way of thinking and begins to appreciate the eccentric joie de vivre that governs the lives of the happy oddballs and outcasts. Cast in the role of the king of fools, Charles gradually warms to the part. Following his last minute rescue of the town, his subjects officially anoint Charles the King of Hearts in an elaborate and hilarious ritual, the significance of which only the residents understand. The Duke orders fireworks to celebrate the victory and the coronation, and when the Germans view the display from a distance, they assume the town has been blown up according to plan. The Scottish armies and the German troops converge at the same moment, killing each other off to the last man. "I think they're overacting," the Duchess says as she observes the senseless slaughter.

As the town's real residents return, the "lunatics" retreat to the asylum, casting off the vestiges of their brief return to "normal" life. Charles, who has been hailed by his commander as a hero, is about to pull out with his troops. In the film's final fleeting shot—one of the most famous in film history— Charles stands stark naked, holding a birdcage, in front of the asylum's gates, ready to rejoin the benign lunacy of a society that seems more sane than his regiment.

Bates, an English actor who was just beginning to establish his reputation in films such as *The Entertainer* and *Georgy Girl,* is at his winsome best as Charles, a decent bloke whose reactions are as funny as what's going on around him. Bates, who won an Oscar two years later for *The Fixer,* has tended to play serious roles but has also done fine comic work in films such as Harold Pinter's *Butley* and John Schlesinger's *An Englishman Abroad.*

The "lunatics run the asylum" premise of *King of Hearts* was later echoed in *One Flew Over the Cuckoo's Nest* (1975), a great comic drama based on Ken Kesey's novel about a crook (Jack Nicholson) who also becomes the king of fools when he pleads insanity and ends up in a mental hospital, where he liberates the troubled souls he finds imprisoned in a heartless institution. Although both films on some level romanticize insanity, a common cinematic tradition in which craziness is associated with defiance of convention or superior emotional sensitivity, they do not exploit the colorful characters. Less hard-hitting and realistic than *One Flew Over the Cuckoo's Nest, King of Hearts* is sympathetic in its treatment of the lovable loonies, whose primary function is as a foil for the insanity of war.

Far gentler and more lighthearted in making its case against war than comic relatives such as *Catch-22, M*A*S*H,* and *Dr. Strangelove,* Daniel Boulanger's script is more concerned with celebrating compassion, eccentricity, and the buoyancy of the human spirit. And De Broca, in crafting a delicate and whimsical comedy doubling as a morality play, added a serious edge to the frivolity for which he was known in films such as *That Man from Rio,* a Bond spoof starring Jean-Paul Belmondo. De Broca, a product of the French New Wave, moved in a more comic direction than his contemporaries, Truffaut, Chabrol, and Godard.

Although most films that deal with insanity are serious dramas, the comic tradition has its share of nutty characters. Mentally disturbed figures of fun are found in comedies ranging from *The Couch Trip* to *What About Bob?* to *As Good as It Gets.* But *King of Hearts* stands as the most beguiling comedy of lunacy, the story of a man who makes the sensible decision to seek asylum from the insanity of the real world.

32

Prizzi's Honor

ABC Films (1985)
CAST: Jack Nicholson, Anjelica Huston, Kathleen Turner, Robert Loggia,
William Hickey, John Randolph, Lee Richardson
DIRECTED BY: John Huston
129 minutes [Rated R]

Until the day Jack Nicholson reported for work on *Prizzi's Honor,* he did not realize he had been cast in a comedy. Although he thought he'd signed on for another *Godfather* rather than a send-up of it, he suddenly grasped that he was starring in a trenchant comic variation on the sensational inside story of a Mafia family. Only when he heard the lines read out loud did he appreciate how mordantly funny the script was.

Director John Huston had experienced a similar problem when he tried to find backing for the deviously ironic script, based on the novel by Richard Condon. "Not even Jack Nicholson, say they, could make lovable a man who would kill his wife for money," Huston wrote to Janet Roach, who cowrote the malicious, delicious screenplay with Condon. "All of which demonstrates to what low depths the intelligentsia of the present masters of our great industry have fallen. They all miss the point, of course, that this picture is a comedy, a fact very hard to get over. Have you ever tried to explain a joke to someone?" Audiences, however, did not require any explanations, nor were they troubled by the amoral characters. The joke was abundantly clear in the blistering black comedy, a vicious tale of greed and honor, authentically rendered, albeit with a satirical edge. *Prizzi's Honor* is also a wryly funny love story, although hardly a romantic comedy in the traditional sense.

Nicholson plays Charley Partanna, a trusted member of the close-knit "family" dominated by the devilish and wizened Don Carrado Prizzi, wickedly played by William Hickey, who had appeared in Huston's *Wise Blood*. At a family wedding scene that opens the film—mirroring *The Godfather*'s opening—Charley spots a beautiful blonde in the balcony who stands out among the dark Italians. "How come I met you at a Prizzi wedding and you ain't no wop?" Charley asks Irene, who claims to be a tax consultant. As it turns out, although she's "a Polack," Irene (Kathleen Turner) has quite a bit in common

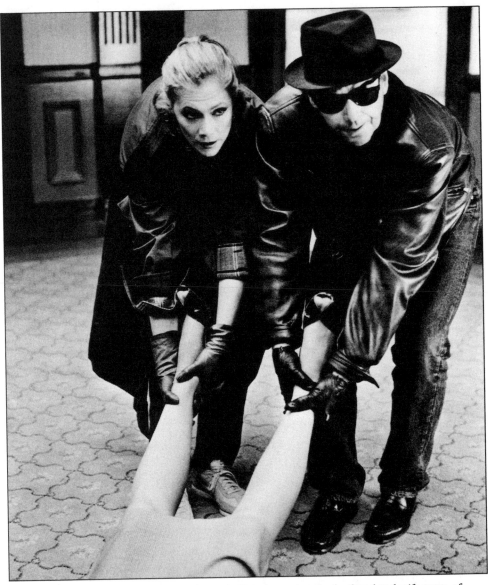

ISN'T IT ROMANTIC?   Kathleen Turner and Jack Nicholson played a husband-and-wife team of Syndicate hired killers in John Huston's *Prizzi's Honor* (1985). Huston's daughter, Anjelica, copped a best supporting actress Oscar for her role as Nicholson's jilted lover. Art imitating life?

with Charley. In fact, she's a hit woman, "the outside talent" the Prizzis brought in to do a job for them.

It's love at first sight for the cold-blooded killers, although there are a few matters to be cleared up, like some money Irene has stolen from the Mob with her husband, Moxie Heller, who is conveniently killed for his part in the Vegas scam. As for Irene's transgression, Charley wonders, "Do I ice her, do I marry her, which of these do I do?" Charley decides on the latter and convinces his father (John Randolph) to allow him to marry outside the family. Charley and Irene form a partnership based not so much on trust as on mutual avarice. Venal and unscrupulous, bound by the same criminal code of ethics, they are a match made in heaven.

Even his cousin Maerose, whom Charley jilted and shamed, causing her to be exiled from the family, encourages Charley to pursue Irene. "Even though she's a hitter and a thief, that doesn't mean she's not a good woman in other departments," reasons Maerose, the black sheep of the family. Maerose is played with malevolent wit by Anjelica Huston—the daughter of the director and the longtime lover of the star. Anjelica Huston won a supporting actress Oscar for her performance as "a grand grotesque," according to *People* magazine, which described her as "Lucrezia Borgia with a Brooklyn accent, Iago in high heels." Huston's first major role launched her richly varied career, which has included high camp comic performances in *The Witches* and *The Addams Family.*

Nicholson, already well-known for playing liberated nonconformists, underwent a dramatic transformation in the opposite direction as Charley Partanna, the dutiful, dim-witted button man who isn't smart enough to realize he and Irene are clearly headed for disaster. Indeed, the reliable, respectable "family" man is eventually forced to choose between his blood ties—and the only world he knows—and his sexy but sinister wife.

Huston had to convince Nicholson that in order for the film to work, Charley had to be a loyal but stupid guy. "Everything you've done is informed by intelligence," Huston told Nicholson, "and you can't have that with this film. It's got to be dumb, very dumb." Nicholson obliged by putting tissue paper under his upper lip, as Brando had done in *The Godfather,* then adopting a squat stance and a lumbering walk. "The eyes I took from the eyes of my dog when he killed another dog," Nicholson reports. In playing the part of the dull and dogged killer, Nicholson gave up his trademark smirk, his quixotic charm, and his aura of sexual magnetism, replacing them with an earnest, pugnacious, dense demeanor that was deadly funny. Actress Julia Bovasso (*Moonstruck, Saturday Night Fever*) was hired as dialect coach to help Nicholson and his Mafioso cohorts perfect their Brooklynese.

Prizzi's Honor was a rare foray into comedy for Huston, although he did direct the 1954 cult classic, *Beat the Devil,* a very funny satire of his own definitive detective picture, *The Maltese Falcon.* But Huston is largely known for such dramatic gems as *The Maltese Falcon* as well as the wildly successful, multi-Oscar-winning *The Treasure of the Sierra Madre,* the big-city crime drama masterpiece *Asphalt Jungle,* and the classics *The African Queen* and *The Man Who Would Be King.* In 1982 the larger-than-life director of masculine, muscular movies made an abrupt change of pace with his adaptation of the musical *Annie.*

But his late-life triumph, made at the age of seventy-nine and in failing health, was *Prizzi's Honor.* (He made only one more film, *The Dead,* before his death in 1987.) A rugged, combative individualist and astute stylist, Huston proved as tough-minded, energetic, and inventive when it came to comedy as he had been with his earlier manly tales of violence, greed, desperation, and devious deeds. Hailed as a comic treasure, the $15 million *Prizzi's Honor* was nominated for best picture, best director, best supporting actor (Hickey), and best adapted screenplay. The Writers Guild also bestowed its award for adapted screenplay on the script. The New York Film Critics named *Prizzi's Honor* best film, Nicholson best actor, Huston best director, and Anjelica Huston best supporting actress. John Huston earned the Golden Globe for best director, and the film was voted best musical/comedy.

It also drew rave reviews. Pauline Kael wrote, "If John Huston's name were not on *Prizzi's Honor,* I'd have thought a fresh, new talent had burst on the scene and he'd certainly be the hottest new director in Hollywood." Roger Ebert gave it four stars, calling it "a movie so dark, so cynical and so funny that perhaps only Jack Nicholson and Kathleen Turner could have kept straight faces during the love scenes."

Nicholson earned an Academy Award nomination and a Golden Globe Award for his role as the lovestruck hit man, one of his best comic performances. Although Nicholson has often tinged his eccentric characterizations with humor—he was particularly amusing in *Easy Rider* and *One Flew Over the Cuckoo's Nest*—his most overtly comic roles have been as the Joker in *Batman* (1989) and his recent success in *As Good as It Gets.*

Although Anjelica Huston steals every scene she's in, and Nicholson and Turner are pure magic together, director Huston also elicits excellent performances from his supporting cast. John Randolph stands out as Charley's father, and Hickey is nothing short of brilliant as the cunning, conniving don.

With its Machiavellian script, ornate style, and operatic score by Alex North, *Prizzi's Honor* replicates the brilliance of *The Godfather,* at the same time satirizing the absurdly amoral nature of a criminal subculture. The diabolic comedy is also a subtle morality tale. "Whatever is good for the family materialistically speaking is morally justifiable according to the Prizzis," Huston wrote. "This is a trait that might well describe society at large at the present moment."

33

The Gods Must Be Crazy

New Realm (1981)
CAST: N!xau, Marius Weyers, Sandra Prinsloo, Louw Verwey
DIRECTED BY: Jamie Uys
109 minutes [Rated PG]

The biggest foreign box office hit in history, *The Gods Must Be Crazy* put Botswana on the world cinema map and established director, writer, producer, and actor Jamie Uys as South Africa's first—and only—internationally celebrated filmmaker.

Uys's disarmingly humble comedy about a bushman trying to return a Coke bottle to the gods was made on the cheap in 1981 and not given an American release until 1984, after it broke box office records in Japan, South America, and Europe. Irresistible and unassuming, the ingenuous and ingenious comedy captivated audiences with its combination of slapstick humor and cultural commentary. *The Gods Must Be Crazy* offered up an anthropology lesson that both charmed viewers and induced gales of laughter, a "collision of cultures" comedy that takes steady satiric aim at so-called civilization.

The guileless star of the improbable hit is a bushman named N!xau, who plays a character called Xi, a member of a tribe known as "the little people" of the Kalahari desert. Xi is an enchanting figure, the ultimate innocent and a symbol of living in harmony with nature. The film begins as a sort of *Wild Kingdom* nature documentary focusing on the peaceful, playful lives of the Xhosa bushmen. Living in what appears an inhospitable environment, the bushmen have adapted remarkably well to the arid climate—unlike "civilized" society, which adapts the environment to suit its needs.

The bushmen—also unlike their "civilized" counterparts—are a contented people, the narrator informs us. They have no police, no rulers, no bosses. They have no concept of ownership, time, or money. Living in total isolation, they also have no concept of evil. Everything, by definition, is good. Why else would it exist?

One day, as Xi is walking, a pilot flying in a plane high above throws his empty Coke bottle out the window. The careless act of littering displays his disregard for the land below, which he apparently regards as a worthless

A Coke and a Smile Xi, the Kalahari bushman, returns the empty Coke bottle from whence it came in *The Gods Must Be Crazy,* which was a huge international hit and put Botswana on the world cinema map.

wasteland. When Xi finds the peculiar glass object—made of a material he has never seen—he concludes that it must be a gift from the gods. He brings the strange utensil home to his people, who quickly find many uses for the hard, cylindrical object. Soon everyone wants it, and anger, jealousy, and greed appear for the first time in the tribe. Deciding to return this thing that has made everyone unhappy—a symbol for material possessions—Xi sets off to find the edge of the world, so he can throw the bottle back. On his journey he encounters a microbiologist, Andrew (Marius Weyers), whose assistant, Mpudi (Michael Thys), happens to speak Xi's language, which consists of odd sounds interspersed with many clicks.

The film's romantic subplot is set in motion when Andrew is asked to pick up the new schoolteacher just as his jeep is acting up. A horse pulls his jeep to get it running, he has no brakes, and he must leave the car running because he won't be able to start the engine again if it stops. A total klutz around women, Andrew does not make a good first impression on Kate (Sandra Prinsloo), especially when a rhino comes and stamps out their camp-fire and the jeep's winch pulls the vehicle to the top of a tree.

Meanwhile a band of militant guerrillas is staging a revolution, and their paths eventually cross with the lovely schoolteacher, the clumsy scientist, and the resourceful bushman. Naturally Xi saves the day, Kate and Andrew fall in love, and Xi finds the end of the world—a huge cliff above the clouds—from which he casts the offending object and returns to his happy family.

In this broad comedy, the revolutionaries, led by swarthy insurgent Sam

Boga (Louw Verwey), are cartoon villains. Andrew is the biggest stumblebum since Jerry Lewis. Andrew's romantic competition is suave safari guide Jack Hind (Nic de Jager), a cad who tries to grab the glory for the rescue of Kate and her schoolchildren from the clutches of the desperadoes. The physical humor consists of many inspired sight gags, some involving wildlife such as the fire-stomping rhino and a marauding lion. Others involve technology run amok. In one of the funniest scenes, Xi, who has just been taught to drive but has not yet mastered shifting gears, rides to the rescue with the jeep in reverse, gamely jumping onto the dashboard to steer.

But beyond the belly laughs, *The Gods Must Be Crazy* has a sweet side. When Xi, who has no notions of ownership and therefore theft, is arrested for poaching after eating a lamb because he was hungry, he languishes in prison, the innocent victim of a society whose rules he cannot comprehend. Andrew rescues him by agreeing to take him into work custody, but when he tries to pay him for his tracking services, the money (another thing Xi doesn't need or understand) is scattered in the desert wind.

The Gods Must Be Crazy questions the benefits of technology and the values of modern culture. Although this is a loving, happy, carefree film without a mean bone in its graceful body, it does make an argument for the simple pleasures as it contrasts modernity with tradition. *The Gods Must Be Crazy* echoes a theme commonly found in films made in Africa—rarely seen in the United States—many of which deal with the conflicts between Western and indigenous traditions. Although the film can be accused of being naive or even condescending in its depiction of the blissful little bushman, it never has fun at Xi's expense. In its reverence for "primitive" culture, the film resembles *Walkabout,* the 1971 Australian cult favorite about an aborigine who comes to the rescue of two lost youngsters.

Of course, the way Xi sees our world is funny. "There are people things down there," Mpudi reports, translating Xi's words as he is the first to spot Sam Boga's army. Mpudi, too, has an amusing way with words. "Ay yay yay yay yay" is his favorite expression. When Andrew nervously rehearses what he will say to Kate, he becomes stiff and formal. "Was that too erudite?" he asks. "Ya," Mpudi replies, "whatever that means."

Just a few years after the release of *The Gods Must Be Crazy,* Crocodile Dundee swaggered onto the screen in the huge Aussie hit, continuing the adventure comedy tradition that audiences found so appealing. Uys's 1989 sequel, *The Gods Must Be Crazy II,* again featured N!xau as Xi. The amusing story, in which Xi's two children are kidnapped by poachers and must be rescued by their clever and capable father, is well worth a look, although it is not as fresh and funny and unexpected as the original. But then few films are.

34

Monty Python and the Holy Grail

EMI (1975)

CAST: Graham Chapman, John Cleese, Terry Gilliam,
Eric Idle, Terry Jones, Michael Palin
DIRECTED BY: Terry Gilliam, Terry Jones
90 minutes [Rated PG]

One of the widest-ranging satires in screen comedy history, *Monty Python and the Holy Grail* lays siege to such diverse topics as religion, war, history, mythology, medieval action epics, ornithology, the Arthurian legend, chivalry, ignorance, communism, obsession, the French, and *Camelot. Monty Python and the Holy Grail,* best described as intelligent nonsense, is by turns sophomoric and sophisticated, surrealistic and stupid, goofy and gross, clever and crude—in short, the impudent bad boys of British comedy at their wickedly irreverent best.

Although critical opinion varies on which of Monty Python's five big-screen outings is the best, aficionados tend to favor their second dauntless assault on all that society holds sacred, *Monty Python and the Holy Grail.* However, their third comedy, *The Life of Brian* (1989), a religious parable parody about a man whose life parallels Christ's, is considered by some critics to be their most outrageously offensive and hence their masterpiece. *Monty Python Live at the Hollywood Bowl* (1982), which features the masters of the skit plying their trade in Los Angeles, is a must for fans. Their final film, *Monty Python's The Meaning of Life* (1983), is more scattered although just as inventive and scandalously funny. All the Monty Python films shatter conventions and glory in excess, inspiring an admiration that borders on worship among their devoted fans. To their credit, their comedy style is so distinctive, it is virtually inimitable.

Monty Python, the collective nom de plume for six wacky writers and uninhibited comedians, burst onto the British comedy scene in 1969 with their wildly popular BBC series *Monty Python's Flying Circus.* The brainchild of Graham Chapman, who died of spinal cancer in 1989, and his Cambridge classmate John Cleese, *Monty Python's Flying Circus* also featured the talents of fellow Cambridge alum Eric Idle, Welshman Terry Jones, Oxford grad Michael Palin, and Terry Gilliam, the sole American.

SHE TURNED ME INTO A NEWT   Graham Chapman, front, accompanied by Terry Jones, far left, John Cleese, behind Chapman, and Eric Idle, right, in *Monty Python and the Holy Grail*. The British bad boys of comedy twisted Arthurian legends like a pretzel in this box office bonanza.

In 1972 the improbable comedy megastars compiled their best skits into a feature-length film, *And Now for Something Completely Different,* which includes such classic Monty Python routines as "The Upper Class Twit of the Year Race," "Hell's Grannies," and "The Townswomen's Guild Reconstruction of Pearl Harbor." Encouraged by the success of the compilation comedy and the continued popularity of their TV show in Britain and America, Monty Python decided to produce a comedy with some semblance of a plot.

The idea for their first attempt at a sustained narrative, hatched by the veteran sketch writers but first-time screenwriters, was simplicity itself: King Arthur and the fabled Knights of the Round Table go on a comic quest for the Holy Grail, encountering all sorts of obstacles, oddballs, and distractions. The writers could thus string together a series of thematically linked sketches, which could go in almost any direction their febrile brains took them.

The idea was also gloriously inexpensive. The low-tech production could be filmed outdoors in the English countryside. They just needed to find a few castle ruins and rent some armor, and they were in business. They could even avoid the expense and complication of using horses by having the actors playing the knights pretend to ride mighty steeds while their servants clapped coconut shells together to create the sound of hoofbeats—which was much funnier anyway.

Indeed, we catch our first glimpse of the valiant and virtuous King Arthur in the opening scene as he comes into sight galloping over a hill. The image of this legendary hero of the court of Camelot in a white tunic and chain mail prancing along astride an imaginary stallion like an escapee from a loony bin sets the cheery comedy's gleefully demented tone and establishes its myth-deflating agenda. The running gag—pardon the pun—also sets audience expectation for the barrage of absurd visual gags that follows.

Nothing, however, quite prepares us for the audaciously amusing, albeit grotesque, scene in which Arthur does battle with a knight who refuses to concede defeat as his limbs are dispatched, one by one, until he is nothing but a head and torso on the ground, yelling at the departing Arthur to stay and fight like a man. The gore does not stop here, however. Later, Lancelot (Cleese) slaughters an entire wedding party as he attempts to rescue a damsel in distress, who turns out to be no lady. Still later, the knights do bloody battle with a killer rabbit.

Excrement is another bodily fluid that is featured prominently in the scatalogical comedy. The snooty French guards who have unaccountably assumed control of an English castle hurl insults as well as human waste upon Arthur's head.

Some of the film's humor is considerably more refined than this vulgar, raunchy stuff. In one cleverly written scene, the king comes upon a Communist farm collective, where the peasants spew political rhetoric at the abashed Arthur, whose explanations of his God-given right to rule (he pulled a sword from a stone, remember?) are greeted with hoots of open derision. This contemporary view of history is again layered onto the satire of the romantic age of chivalry at a witch-burning party. One of the men accusing the obviously innocent "witch" sputters his proof: "She turned me into a newt." Then he pauses guiltily and adds, "But I got better."

Although known for their bawdy material, the satirical sextet is here fairly restrained. One ribald scene finds Sir Gallahad the Chaste at the Castle Anthrax, where "eight score blondes and brunettes between eighteen and twenty-one" amorously attend the knight. Just as he's been ordered to spank the girls and promised oral sex, he's rescued—over his vigorous protestations—by his fellow knights, who save him from certain temptation.

Then it's back to the quest for the Grail, which will lead the lads to the Gorge of Eternal Peril and over the dreaded Bridge of Death. First, however, they must elude the three-headed gorgon and appease the towering knights who say "nee" by bringing them shrubbery. Finally, thunderbolt-hurling Tim the Enchanter guides them on the final leg of their journey, which comes to an abrupt, anachronistic end much like the one that concludes *Blazing Saddles.*

The quest for the Holy Grail did continue, in quite another form, in director Terry Gilliam's *The Fisher King* (1991), a beautiful and darkly funny tale of madness and redemption starring Robin Williams and Jeff Bridges. Although their careers have continued to overlap, the members of Monty Python went their separate ways in the mid-eighties. Gilliam has established a reputation as a director who brings a bold vision to his unusual projects. Gilliam's dazzling futuristic *Brazil* (1985) is a brilliant black comedy, and *The Adventures of Baron Munchausen* is a visually explosive and imaginative family film that never found the audience it deserved.

Cleese made his post-Python mark with the hit comedy *A Fish Called Wanda* (1988), for which he won the British Academy Award for best actor and was nominated for best screenplay. Palin earned the British Academy Award for best supporting actor in *A Fish Called Wanda* and also appeared in Gilliam's *Time Bandits* and *Brazil.* Idle, who wrote a number of Monty Python's books, has made only sporadic screen appearances. Jones undertook the direction of *Eric the Viking* (1989), an attempt to recapture the Monty Python magic, in which he costarred with Cleese. Unfortunately, the film—a satire featuring a legendary hero and set in the mists of the past—could not touch the inspired lunacy of *Monty Python and the Holy Grail.*

Monty Python and the Holy Grail is so packed with visual jokes that fans report they see new things in it every time they watch it. Unlike many great comedies, it grows funnier with repeated viewings. To paraphrase the immortal words of Monty Python's Reginald K. Denktas, "You'll laugh until you stop."

35

The In-Laws

Warner Bros. (1979)
CAST: Alan Arkin, Peter Falk, Richard Libertini, Ed Begley Jr.
DIRECTED BY: Arthur Hiller
103 minutes [Rated PG]

Alan Arkin and Peter Falk were on a roll in 1979 when they were cast opposite each other in *The In-Laws,* the flat-out funniest film in either actor's distinguished comic canon. A sensationally entertaining and deliriously unpredictable comedy, *The In-Laws* pairs two eccentric actors known for their offbeat comic flair and quirky sensibilities.

Arkin and director Arthur Hiller coproduced the wacky, screwball farce about a mild-mannered dentist (Arkin) whose life is turned upside-down when his daughter marries the son of a shady character (Falk) who claims to be working for the CIA. Screenwriter Andrew Bergman, who coauthored *Blazing Saddles* and went on to write and direct *The Freshman* and *Honeymoon in Vegas,* leads his characters on a merry chase as they become embroiled in increasingly dangerous and bizarre high jinks.

The energetic and ingenious comedy begins with the daring armored car robbery of plates for making U.S. currency. Vince Riccardi (Falk) is the customer for whom the crime has been orchestrated, but he needs to come up with $1.5 million by the next day to pay for the plates. To complicate matters, Vince's son is getting married in a few days, and he is headed off the meet the bride's parents for the first time.

Vince does not exactly make a good impression on Sheldon Kornpett (Arkin), a solid citizen who is about to be dragged kicking and screaming into Vince's world of danger and intrigue. Vince claims to be involved in "international consulting" and keeps sneaking off to make mysterious "business" phone calls during dinner. He also tells hilariously tall tales about his exploits, which leave Sheldon flabbergasted and outraged. Sheldon, a rational man with a suspicious nature, is alarmed by the dubious sanity and stability of a man who tells obviously fabricated stories about mammoth tsetse flies carrying off small children in Guatemala.

Sheldon, who is easily shaken, is ready to call off the wedding but decides that since "this is not nineteenth-century Minsk but twentieth-century Manhattan," he cannot prevent his daughter from marrying the son of a lunatic just because "the acorn doesn't fall far from the tree." Matters go from bad to worse, however, when Vince enlists Sheldon in his complicated criminal activity. A respectable, law-abiding citizen, Sheldon is soon dodging bullets and ends up on the lam with his comrade from hell. Vince, who remains cool, calm, and collected throughout the escalating misadventures, has an improbable explanation for everything. Claiming to be a rogue CIA agent, he concocts one story after another with such aplomb, Sheldon no longer knows what to think—and neither does the audience.

Aside from the wildly imaginative plot twists and turns, much of the film's humor lies in the contrast between Vince's seemingly reasonable and unflappable manner and Sheldon's high-pitched hysteria and panic. Sheldon, whose life is in constant jeopardy for much of the movie, does not respond well to danger. Eventually, however, a sort of partnership develops between the audacious, flamboyant Vince and the conservative, unnerved Sheldon.

By turns stupefied and horrified, confounded and astounded, Sheldon reacts to the increasingly absurd situations in which he finds himself much as the audience does. We go along with Sheldon on his wild trip, which ends up in Latin America, where a comically maniacal dictator (played with demented glee by Richard Libertini) is poised to initiate the collapse of the world's monetary system. It's a close shave, but the two men survive their calamities and emerge not only unscathed, but several million dollars richer.

Although not as socially rebellious as other dark comedies of the period, *The In-Laws* does have an anarchistic kick, which was typical of Arkin's films. Although today Arkin is one of the screen's most sadly underused actors generally relegated to supporting performances, at the time he was a reigning star and something of a counterculture hero due to his frequent association with the subversive, absurdist humor of black comedy.

Arkin, recently featured in *The Slums of Beverly Hills,* made his debut in the popular comedy *The Russians Are Coming! The Russians Are Coming!* in 1966 and earned a best actor Oscar nomination for his performance as the Soviet sub commander who accidentally captures a New England town. Arkin then switched gears to play the menacing psycho who terrorized blind Audrey Hepburn in *Wait Until Dark* and the sensitive deaf mute in *The Heart Is a Lonely Hunter,* for which he earned a second Oscar nomination. He returned to comedy in the doomed *Pink Panther* sequel *Inspector Clouseau,* unadvisedly filling in for Peter Sellers. In 1970 he landed the plum role of Yossarian in *Catch-22,* based on Joseph Heller's brilliantly surrealistic satire of the insanity of war. The next year he directed and acted in the screen adaptation of Jules Feiffer's *Little Murders,* a blistering black comedy depicting dysfunctional life in a hellish New York City.

In the years that followed this devastatingly dark cult classic, Arkin played a boisterous cop in *Freebie and the Bean,* Sigmund Freud in *The Seven Percent Solution,* and a Hollywood silent film director in *Hearts of the West.* Arkin's career slowly ran aground, but not before he made one last widely successful film, *The In-Laws.*

Falk was best known for playing the rumpled, deceptively capable police detective in the TV series *Columbo* when he was cast as Vince, also an enigmatic character who is not what he seems. The part was tailor-made for Falk, a master at understated, dry comedy. Falk appeared on the New York stage and on TV in the 1950s, and got his start in film playing thugs and blue-collar types in *Pretty Boy Floyd* (1960) and *Murder, Inc.,* for which he was

I'M A DENTIST—THERE'S NO NEED TO SHOOT!   Mild-mannered New Jersey dentist Sheldon Kornpett (Alan Arkin, left) rests on a bed of tropical fruits. CIA op Vince Riccardi (Peter Falk, right) checks for broken bones in Arthur Hiller's 1979 *The In-Laws,* written by comedy ace Andrew Bergman.

nominated for a best supporting actor Oscar. He received another nomination the following year for *Pocketful of Miracles.*

After appearing alongside a legion of legendary comics in *It's a Mad Mad Mad Mad World* in 1963, Falk became known for his comic talents, which were put to use in *The Great Race, Luv, Murder by Death, The Cheap Detective, The Brink's Job,* and John Cassavetes's seriocomic *Husbands.* Although Detective Columbo, immortalized by Falk on the small screen from 1971 to 1977, was not exactly a comic character, he was always amusing thanks to Falk's sly performance. With his squinty gaze—the result of a childhood accident that left him with a glass eye—and unassuming manner, Falk established a likable but shrewd and crafty identity that has served him well in a variety of parts. Like Arkin, Falk began to play smaller roles in the eighties and nineties, although when he did pop up in a featured role—as in 1989's *Cookie* and the underrated 1990 comedy *Tune in Tomorrow*—he was in top form.

Falk and Arkin are both steadfastly eccentric actors, and their off-center, aberrant quality is put to effective use by director Hiller in *The In-Laws.* Perhaps best known for *Love Story* and *Hospital,* Hiller is a capable craftsman who has made his share of competent comedies. The barbed humor of 1967's *The Tiger Makes Out* was acutely attuned to the times. He did a fine job adapting Neil Simon's *Plaza Suite* in 1971. He was fresh from his inspired pairing of Gene Wilder and Richard Pryor in *Silver Streak* when he hit on the equally felicitous coupling of Arkin and Falk in *The In-Laws.* He went on to make the underappreciated comic study of modern alienation, *The Lonely Guy,* and the popular female odd couple comedy *Outrageous Fortune,* which paired Bette Midler and Shelley Long.

Outlandish and unconventional, *The In-Laws* was not the first comedy to center on a crime caper, but it did pioneer a renegade morality that informed future comedies such as Henry Jaglom's very funny *Sitting Ducks* (1980).

It's a shame that Arkin and Falk are no longer considered bankable stars and are rarely assigned leading comedy roles. Perhaps one day directors will again find use for their formidable comic abilities. Until then, we'll always have *The In-Laws.*

36

When Harry Met Sally . . .

Castle Rock (1989)
CAST: Billy Crystal, Meg Ryan, Carrie Fisher, Bruno Kirby
DIRECTED BY: Rob Reiner
96 minutes [Rated R]

Romantic comedy has not fared well in the age of cynicism. Audiences are less inclined to buy the idea of love at first sight or many of the other silly notions about l'amour that infused romantic comedy in earlier, more innocent times. In 1977 *Annie Hall,* which did not even end happily, began to change the smiling face of romantic comedy, replacing sunny idealism with a more rueful realism.

Then along came *When Harry Met Sally . . .,* a romantic comedy that reflected contemporary reality and still found a way to warm our suspicious, discouraged hearts. This delightfully honest story throws the old notion of love at first sight right out the window. Sally initially detests Harry, and although he's attracted to her, he disagrees with everything she says and challenges how she thinks. Never has a screen couple's tumble been slower as they gradually create a respectful relationship. They finally fall in love only after first becoming good friends. Love founded on a solid friendship was a fairly radical concept in 1989, but the notion that forming a lasting relationship was hard work was no doubt reassuring to audiences. Viewers were apparently comforted by the acknowledgment that—contrary to cinematic tradition—happily ever after isn't something that happens automatically.

An optimistically old-fashioned love story retooled for relationship-savvy modern audiences, *When Harry Met Sally . . .* takes its musical cue from the soundtrack by Harry Connick Jr., who sounds like Frank Sinatra but is much more hip and ironic. The familiar but revitalized music sets the tone for a comedy that dusts off romantic clichés and makes them seem new again. Similarly, the film makes direct reference to the changing notions of romance when, early in the film, Harry and Sally argue over the ending of *Casablanca* and then, later, savor the prophetic closing line, "This could be the beginning of a beautiful friendship."

When Harry Met Sally . . . capitalizes on a wise and witty Oscar-nominated script from Nora Ephron, deft comic direction by Rob Reiner, and winsome

PASTRAMI ON WRY   The prelude to the now classic orgasm scene in Rob Reiner's 1989 *When Harry Met Sally,* with Meg Ryan, left, and Billy Crystal, right. The setting is New York City's legendary Katz's Delicatessen.

yet acerbic performances by Billy Crystal and Meg Ryan to offer a bracing look at the travails of finding true love. Also a devastatingly incisive portrait of the upscale singles scenes, the story originated when Reiner, divorced from Penny Marshall, told Ephron, who had humorously recorded the details of *her* painful divorce in *Heartburn,* that he wanted to make a comedy "about two people who become friends and are really happy they become friends because they realize that if they had sex, it would ruin everything. And then they have sex and ruin everything."

The lively love story Reiner and Ephron devised, based in part on personal experience, begins with the first of six pseudodocumentary short scenes interspersed throughout the comedy. Each "interview" features an elderly couple describing the sometimes rocky road that has led to their long-standing union. It's a wonderful device that establishes the film's central question—one that its young audience surely wanted answered: How do you get to be an old, happily married couple?

Harry Burns and Sally Albright hardly seem destined for such a blissful domestic fate when they meet for the first time at the University of Chicago in 1977. Harry is dating Sally's friend, who has arranged for Harry to share a ride to New York City with Sally. The two are complete opposites. She's neat, fussy, organized, methodical, cheerful, and practical. He's sloppy, crude, casual, outspoken, moody, and deliberately provocative. They spend a good portion of the eighteen-hour trip staring at each other in disbelief. Although they rub each other the wrong way, Harry comes on to Sally, who rejects his advances and suggests they just be friends. Men and women can never really be friends, Harry argues, "because the sex part always gets in the way."

Five years later Harry and Sally meet again at the airport and once again find themselves in uncomfortably close quarters as traveling companions. Harry is engaged to be married, Sally is in love with blond dreamboat Joe (Gerald Ford's son Steve). Sally still can't stand Harry's pessimism and the abrasive way he expresses his thoughts and feelings, and they again part in a huff.

The third time they meet, Sally has broken up with Joe, who wasn't ready to get married, and Harry is divorced from his wife, who has left him for another man. They meet by chance in a bookstore, where Sally is thumbing through *Smart Women/Foolish Choices*. "Someone is staring at you in Personal Growth," Sally's single friend Marie (Carrie Fisher) tells her before slipping off discreetly. Products of the "personal growth" generation, Harry and Sally indeed are struggling to make mature choices in the increasingly complicated dating game.

United in failed-relationship misery, Harry and Sally begin to prove false Harry's assertion that men and women can't be friends. They go for walks, chat on the phone, share the details of their disastrous dates, and spend New Year's Eve together, promising to do the same the next year if they don't have real dates. Best of all, Harry and Sally do something most screen couples rarely do. They have conversations and disagreements, mostly about the different way men and women tend to view the world.

The film's funniest moment—one of the most memorable in any comedy of the last ten years—comes as Harry and Sally are eating in New York City's legendary Katz's Deli. Harry insists that although he bolts out the door immediately after sex, he knows he leaves his dates well satisfied. When Sally protests that most women occasionally fake orgasms, Harry insists he could never be fooled. Sally proceeds to demonstrate the fine art of the fake orgasm with such conviction, she leaves Harry flabbergasted—and uncharacteristically speechless. The woman at the next table (played by Reiner's mother, Estelle) gets the last laugh when she tells the waiter, "I'll have what she's having." (This cap to the explosively funny moment was reportedly Crystal's suggestion.)

In an attempt to remain platonic friends and resist the attraction that is developing between them, Harry and Sally even try to fix each other up with their best friends, Marie (Fisher) and Jess (Bruno Kirby), but the plan backfires when Marie and Jess fall in love with each other instead.

In another of the film's funniest scenes, Harry gets a desperate late night phone call from Sally, who needs company because she has just found out Joe is getting married. Weeping and wailing and tossing tissues about, Sally is devastated by the realization that although she always thought Joe didn't want to get married, she now knows he just didn't want to marry her. Harry's attempt to comfort Sally leads to sex, which Harry, who has something of a problem with intimacy, immediately regrets. Stung by his refusal to acknowledge the change that has taken place in their relationship, Sally refuses to see Harry, who begins to miss Sally and to realize how much she means to him. On New Year's Eve he finds himself running through the streets of Manhattan (just like Woody Allen in *Manhattan*) to declare his love for Sally: "When you realize you want to spend the rest of your life with someone, you want the rest of your life to start as soon as possible."

Ephron and Reiner's film owes a great deal to Woody Allen's romantic comedies, with their gabby, sophisticated, self-scrutinizing characters agonizing over the impossibility of permanent love in picturesque Manhattan locations while Gershwin plays on the soundtrack. With his Jewish cynicism and deprecating wit, Harry plays Allen's neurotic nudge Alvy Singer to Ryan's gay, dithering Annie Hall. Reiner, however, puts his own bright stamp on the crackling comedy, which is brimming with empathy for its characters and is more hopeful than Allen's very funny angst fests.

When Harry Met Sally . . ., which led to further collaborations between the principals, was greeted with raves from the critics. *Newsday* praised the "story of a friendship that ripens into love, vibrates with truth and humor, managing to be both emotionally involving and a four-star howler." The *New York Post* noted that the comedy "sends up every aspect of today's dating game so affectionately and hilariously you forget it's been done a zillion times." The *Los Angeles Times* praised the "uncorseted, unqualified delight" for its "splendid, risible exchanges that fly by with the speed and delicacy of a great badminton game."

Reiner established himself as an A-list director with this felicitous follow-up to the devastatingly deadpan comic rockumentary *This Is Spinal Tap, The Sure Thing, Stand by Me,* and the underrated comic fairy tale, *The Princess Bride,* which featured Crystal in a cameo role. Although as a director Reiner scored with hit dramas such as *Misery* and *A Few Good Men,* he also has made comic appearances in films such as *Postcards from the Edge,* based on Carrie Fisher's screenplay, and *Sleepless in Seattle,* directed by Ephron and starring Ryan.

Crystal had already appeared in *Running Scared, Throw Momma from the Train,* and *Memories of Me* when he was cast as the romantic lead by his longtime friend and collaborator. The success of *When Harry Met Sally . . .,* which proved Crystal's popularity as a comic actor, led to *City Slickers,* a megahit costarring Kirby that Crystal produced before writing, directing, producing, and starring in *Mr. Saturday Night,* a viciously funny although overly sentimental comedy.

Perky and quirky, Ryan has divided her time between drama and comedy, making memorable comic appearances as Einstein's niece in *IQ,* the girl of Tom Hanks's dreams in *Sleepless in Seattle* and *You've Got Mail,* and the object of Kevin Kline's affection in *French Kiss.*

The product of a true collaboration, in which Crystal contributed comic ideas and lines to Ephron's script, *When Harry Met Sally . . .* is an example of the magic that sometimes happens when a group of creative people who think alike pool their talents and address a subject they actually know something about.

37

Soapdish

Paramount (1991)
CAST: Sally Field, Kevin Kline, Elisabeth Shue, Whoopi Goldberg,
Cathy Moriarty, Robert Downey Jr., Carrie Fisher, Kathy Najimy
DIRECTED BY: Michael Hoffman
95 minutes [Rated PG-13]

A bubbly comedy that dishes soap operas, the aptly titled *Soapdish* magically makes a silk purse from those old sows that life not only imitates art, but sometimes surpasses it and that truth is sometimes stranger and more fascinating than fiction. *Soapdish* works up a comic lather as it takes us behind the scenes of a daytime television show, where the torrid lives of its stars rivals the sensationalistic story concocted by the soap opera's writers.

Played at fever pitch by a cast adept at farce, *Soapdish* is an inconsequential and obvious comedy that is much funnier than it has any right to be, thanks both to the flashy performances and to the snappy script cowritten by Andrew Bergman (*Blazing Saddles, The In-Laws, The Freshman*) and Robert Harling, who had given Fields a gloriously funny role in 1989's *Steel Magnolias.*

Soapdish has all the absurd high drama of daytime TV. Peopled by vain, ruthless, petty, selfish characters—on screen and off—and filled with dark secrets, devious plottings, and sexual intrigue, *Soapdish* also has something sorely lacking from daytime television: a sense of humor. And what a wicked, lubricious sense of humor it has, a cunning and canny wit that extends right down to the casting.

Two-time Oscar winner Sally Fields is a gifted comedienne and an often irritating actress, which makes her perfect for the part of the galling, over-the-hill prima donna Celeste Talbert. Known as America's Sweetheart, the beloved star of *The Sun Also Rises* is a catty, shallow, insecure, ill-tempered diva whose inflated ego constantly needs to be pumped with hot air. Fields's full-throttle performance lampoons her own annoying "you really like me" image, and the result—a viciously funny send-up of a tempestuous star who desperately wants to be loved just a little longer—is right on the money.

Celeste may throw a tantrum when the new costumer (Kathy Najimy) makes her wear a turban—"I feel like Gloria fucking Swanson!" she screams—

IN A LATHER   The cast of 1991's *Soapdish*, from left: Whoopi Goldberg, Teri Hatcher, Kevin Kline, Sally Field, Elisabeth Shue, Robert Downey Jr., and Cathy Moriarty. Another comedy grand slam from writer Andrew Bergman.

but she is not the bitchiest star on the show. That dubious distinction—and comic opportunity—belongs to ambitious actress Montana Moorehead, a venomous viper played with humorous fury by Cathy Moriarity. A husky-voiced blonde, Montana is plotting to usurp Celeste, and to solicit assistance she has bribed the show's libidinous producer, David (Robert Downey Jr.), with the promise of sexual favors. "Get rid of her, and Mr. Fuzzy is yours," she growls with seductive rage. "Gosh, she's cheap," David responds with lustful admiration. He does not quite understand his strange attraction to the flagrantly oversexed, power-hungry Montana, which will be explained by a surprise revelation at the film's zany climax.

Like *Tootsie*, *Soapdish* ends with a live taping of the show in which the actors ad-lib, using lines from the script of their own lives. As the actors cross the line separating illusion and reality, the head of daytime TV (Garry Marshall) watches in awe. Marshall, the creator of TV shows such as *Happy Days* and the director of commercial entertainments such as *Pretty Woman,* is another example of mischievous casting. Marshall is wonderful as the uncouth arbiter of popular taste who tells *The Sun Also Rises* staff that the two words he likes to hear are "peppy and cheap."

As Montana and David conspire to supplant Celeste, they hit upon a two-pronged strategy. First, they bring back Jeffrey Anderson, Celeste's onetime flame, whose firing she had ordered twenty years earlier. Anderson, whose character was decapitated on the show, is brought back from the dead, literally and figuratively. Anderson is rescued from playing dinner theater in Opa-Lacka, Florida, where he is seen, in one of the film's funniest scenes, valiantly but futilely trying to perform *Death of a Salesman* before an audience of inattentive senior citizens. "Don't call me Mr. Loman," he barks when he's summoned from his dressing room, unable to bear being permanently associated with the theater's great symbol of failure.

Kevin Kline, a nimble, stage-trained farceur (*The Pirates of Penzance*) as well as serious actor (*Sophie's Choice, The Big Chill*), is the perfect choice for Jeffrey. Kline's versatility allows him to play a talented actor who is also a vain, self-aggrandizing comic figure. Kline, the star of such exceptional comedies as *A Fish Called Wanda, Dave, French Kiss,* and *In and Out,* plays the bemused, indignant Jeffrey with the kind of comic aplomb few actors could manage.

The second part of the plan to dethrone the queen of the soaps involves finding a way to have Celeste do something so reprehensible on the show that her fans will turn on her. How about having her murder a mute, homeless girl, played by a sweet-faced ingenue (Elisabeth Shue) who also happens to be Celeste's real-life niece? All Montana and David have to do is convince head writer Rose Schwartz, played by—with a name like that, who else?—Whoopi Goldberg. Rose is a smart cookie, perceptive and tough, and is Celeste's oldest friend and ally. When Celeste is in the dumps, Rose takes her to a New Jersey mall, pretends to be a fan, and sets off a frenzy among her admirers. When Rose hears of the proposed murder, she knows this is too inane even for a potboiler like *The Sun Also Rises*. Rose suspects something is up and in the end foils Montana's evil machinations. Rose is a small part but one of Goldberg's best roles, a shrewd professional and loyal friend blessed with a writer's sharp wit.

Soapdish ends with a series of bizarre revelations that are right in keeping with soap opera's glaringly improbable Sturm und Drang plot twists. All the loose ends are neatly tied up with a great big, garish bow that makes the brightly colored package all the more attractive. There may not be anything inside the box, but a movie this funny doesn't have to offer substance as well.

As David Ansen wrote in his glowing review in *Newsweek*, "Any movie with this many belly laughs can be forgiven almost anything." Georgia Brown of the *Village Voice*, who thought *Soapdish* was "a gas," deemed the comedy "indecently funny" and "very classy." David Denby confessed that he "absolutely lost it" during one of Kevin Kline's "moments of genius" as the European doctor, a scene in which the narcissistic actor refuses to wear his glasses and can't read the TelePrompTer. Jami Bernard of the *New York Post* reserved her highest praise for Field, who, she felt, "has found her métier at last."

Although Fields and Kline are indeed at their comic best in *Soapdish*, there are other, equally funny characterizations. Moriarty, who was nominated for a supporting actress Oscar for *Raging Bull*, gives a powerhouse comedy performance as the show's wicked witch. She is demonically funny, hinting ever so slyly at her character's dark secret. Downey, too, does fine work as the weasel who is caught in her trap. Carrie Fisher makes a brief but vivid appearance as the seductive casting director who asks the actors auditioning for the walk-on role of a waiter to take off their shirts so she can better assess their "talent."

Blessed with a superb cast uniquely suited to their parts, *Soapdish* gives the actors plenty of comic material, from slapstick to great zingers. The first-rate dialogue is dripping in sarcasm. "I don't deserve friends like you," Celeste says with phony sincerity, adding with an icy edge, "I'm just so lucky."

Making fun of soap operas may be like shooting fish in a barrel, but *Soapdish* is much more than a parody of the ludicrous excesses of daytime TV, where many fine actors got their starts. It is a genuinely entertaining, high-flying comedy about the travails and egotism of acting—a farcical version of the 1950 classic *All About Eve,* starring Bette Davis as an aging star.

A frothy, frenetic farce like *Soapdish* doesn't come along every day, and when it does it is rarely handled with such consummate skill, style, and delicious, malicious wit.

38

Sons of the Desert

Hal Roach/MGM (1933)
CAST: Stan Laurel, Oliver Hardy, Mae Busch, Charley Chase
DIRECTED BY: William Seiter
73 minutes [Not rated]

The original odd couple, Laurel and Hardy were a study in comic contrasts. Stan Laurel was thin, shy, and dim-witted. Oliver Hardy was fat, overbearing, and short-tempered. Laurel, easily flustered and often bewildered, burst into tears at the slightest provocation. Hardy, given to exasperation, blustered and bellowed and constantly complained to his befuddled companion in comedy, "Here's another fine mess you've gotten us into."

The saucer-eyed Laurel, whose light hair stood on end, and the squinty-eyed Hardy, who slicked his dark hair down, were exact opposites in size, shape, and manner. Their comic personas had but one thing in common: complete and utter incompetence. Whatever the luckless lads put their minds to was bound to fail.

Together Laurel and Hardy worked their special hapless magic act for three decades. The most successful comedy team in movie history, Laurel and Hardy first appeared on screen together in *The Lucky Dog* (filmed in 1917 and released in 1922), while working at the legendary Hal Roach studios. Although they appeared in several films together, they did not begin to work as a team until 1927. Director Leo McCarey (who went on to direct the Marx Brothers in *Duck Soup*) is credited with first recognizing the obvious comic potential of their physical disparity and was charged with developing material for the pair.

Stan Laurel was thirty-seven and Oliver Hardy thirty-five when they began to make a string of winning comedies that blended slapstick with verbal wit. Credited with introducing a slower rhythm to silent comedy, they pioneered the use of long, well-developed gags that involved a series of escalating reactions. After making one hundred silent two-reelers, the popular duo easily made the transition to sound and to full-length films. They starred in numerous feature films, ending their career with an Italian-French coproduction, *Utopia*, in 1950. Such was their devotion to each other that when Hardy died in 1957, Laurel refused to work in film again, although he did continue to write comic material until his death in 1967.

Throughout their tandem career, the twosome relied on the ever-hopeful, always ineffectual personas they developed in their first films. They rarely played characters with names other than their own as they appeared in a series of films that offered endless variations on a basic formula.

Hardy, who hailed from Georgia and weighed fourteen pounds at birth, had often been cast as a bully and brat before uniting with the English-born Laurel. A gifted pantomimist and limber physical clown, Laurel had been an understudy for Charlie Chaplin and made more than sixty short films before teaming with Hardy. In contrast with the passive and submissive role he played on screen, Laurel was the dominant member of the team in life, actively involved with the writing and editing of their films.

Together Laurel and Hardy created a good-natured type of humor. "Well-intentioned muddle-headedness" is how Vincent Canby aptly described the team's combination of naïveté and stupidity. Although they played bumbling buffoons, Mr. Hardy and Mr. Laurel—as they always referred to each other with mock formality on screen—were decent, warm human beings. The anti-heroic characters they played were believable human beings, and the enduring friendship of the oddly mismatched buddies was a large part of their appeal.

In 1933 Laurel and Hardy were teamed in what is widely considered their best written film, *Sons of the Desert*. Rather than a series of routines strung together by a thin plot, it featured a strong storyline yet was close in spirit to their celebrated short subjects.

In this bright but slight comedy, Laurel and Hardy play "two peas in a pot." Assuming their common guise, these seemingly mature men are really overgrown children who are out of their depth in the grown-up world. Laurel sneaks an apple and is so pleased with himself, he doesn't notice it's made of wax. Both men sneak off to play and are caught and punished in *Sons of the Desert*, which has a simple but elegant premise.

Mr. Laurel and Mr. Hardy are members of a fraternal order called Sons of the Desert, an American institution that comes in for some ribbing and also provides the opportunity for plenty of sight gags. Trading their trademark ill-fitting bowlers for even sillier headgear—a fez with a tassel—Laurel and Hardy disrupt the organization's solemn proceedings with their usual clumsiness. When it is announced that 100 percent participation in the annual convention in Chicago is expected from the members of the oldest lodge in the fraternal organization, Stan and Ollie are more than happy to oblige. Getting their wives to agree to let them go is another matter.

"Do you have to ask your wife everything?" Ollie badgers his meek companion, exhorting him to "be a man."

I Never Forget a Fez   Oliver Hardy, left, Charley Chase, center, and Stan Laurel in the 1933 *Sons of the Desert,* widely considered to be their finest full-length feature. It was also one of the top-grossing films of that year and established the boys as bona fide movie stars.

"But if I didn't ask her, I wouldn't know what she wanted me to do," Stan counters innocently.

When they return home to their neighboring apartments, however, it is Ollie who finds his own bossy wife (played by Mae Busch, who appeared in fourteen Laurel and Hardy films) has other plans for her "bad boy." Undeterred, Ollie concocts a plan. He pretends to be ill and hires a veterinarian to pose as a doctor and prescribe a sea voyage. His wife agrees he must go to Hawaii for his health and asks Stan to accompany him, as she can't bear being on a boat.

The ruse gets them to Chicago but soon begins to unravel, as all lame-brained schemes must, when the boys meet an obnoxious conventioneer played by Charley Chase, who was about to come into his own as a Hal Roach comic. The drunken prankster, it turns out, is the long-lost brother of Ollie's wife, and Ollie is almost caught by a phone call home.

When the ship they are supposed to be on sinks, it looks as though they'll be caught for sure. Not knowing that their wives have seen newsreel footage of them cavorting in a Chicago parade, Stan and Ollie devise yet another tall tale to get out of their jam.

"That's our story, and we're stuck with it," Hardy insists stubbornly. His "imposterous" tale is rewarded with a hail of pots and pans bounced off his head. Stan whimpers like a baby, spilling the whole truth to his wife, thus earning her forgiveness.

Sons of the Desert is a deft mixture of physical comedy and verbal wit. The normally simple Laurel humorously skewers his own slow-witted image when he takes a deep breath and compliments Hardy on "the meticulous care you've taken in the finely formulated machinations extricating us from this devastating dilemma."

Sons of the Desert earned positive reviews and was among the top-grossing films of the year. It remains Laurel and Hardy's most popular film, although 1934's fantasy comedy *Babes in Toyland* (titled *March of the Wooden Soldiers* on video) was another big hit. The boys scored another success in 1936's *Way Out West,* which some critics consider their second most consistently funny film.

Despite their popularity with audiences—enhanced by the marketing of their likenesses in an early foray into movie merchandising—Laurel and Hardy's contribution to comedy was not fully appreciated by the critics of the day. Although the duo elevated comic frustration to new heights, the critics did not consider the lowbrow clowns to be in the same league as Chaplin, Keaton, Lloyd, or the Marx Brothers. Unlike these more aggressive and outrageous comedians, who generally went on the comic attack, Laurel and Hardy always played the butt of their own jokes.

Their popularity has endured, however, and today they are revered as a brilliant comedy team. Their reputation does not rest, however, on a single film that can be pointed to as an undisputed work of comic genius. Rather, they are remembered today for the consistency they brought to a body of work, including silent films such as *Wrong Again*.

Legions of Laurel and Hardy fans are still active in a club devoted to the stout, tie-twiddling comedian and his lean, head-scratching cohort. The fan club is called, quite naturally, Sons of the Desert.

39

What's Up, Doc?

Warner Bros. (1972)
CAST: Barbra Streisand, Ryan O'Neal, Madeline Kahn, Kenneth Mars,
Austin Pendleton, Liam Dunn, Randy Quaid
DIRECTED BY: Peter Bogdanovich
94 minutes [Rated G]

A former film critic, Peter Bogdanovich is a true cineast and serious scholar who worships classic Hollywood films. The director is so enamored of screwball farce in particular, he couldn't resist making one himself.

But while imitation may be the sincerest form of flattery, it is also risky business for a director. More often than not, remaking a classic is like trying to capture lightning in a bottle. A rare exception to the "leave well enough alone" rule, *What's Up, Doc?* is both an affectionate homage to the farcical comedies of the 1930s and a giddily entertaining comedy in its own right.

Both referential and reverential, *What's Up, Doc?* is based loosely on *Bringing Up Baby*, Howard Hawks's 1938 definitive screwball comedy starring Katharine Hepburn and Cary Grant. It also contains humorous references to *Casablanca, The Caine Mutiny,* and *Love Story* and to some sparkling screen gems directed by Hollywood legends such as Leo McCarey and Frank Capra. Bogdanovich's pastiche of comic styles also pays tribute to the silent comedies of Mack Sennett, Buster Keaton, and Harold Lloyd.

It's no wonder the *New York Times* calls *What's Up, Doc?* "a one-film comedy retrospective." David Thomson considers it "one of the great farces of the modern era." Judith Crist describes it as "a barrel of carefree laughs." Written by Buck Henry (*The Graduate, Catch-22, Heaven Can Wait*), Robert Benton, and David Newman, the script won the Writers Guild Award for original screenplay.

Enlivened with bright repartee and loaded with slapstick humor, *What's Up, Doc?* was Bogdanovich's third film. It was far removed in style and tone from his previous hit, *The Last Picture Show,* a bouquet to the small-town America of the 1950s. While that highly regarded picture was also steeped in sincere nostalgia for an earlier era and aesthetic, its mood was rueful and melancholic and its effect poignant.

ROAD RAGE   Barbra Streisand and Ryan O'Neal in *What's Up, Doc?*, Peter Bogdanovich's affectionate and hugely entertaining homage to the screwball comedies of the 1930s, most notably Howard Hawks's *Bringing Up Baby.*

What's Up, Doc?, on the other hand, is pure, pixilated delight—although every bit as precise and vital as *The Last Picture Show*. *What's Up, Doc?* rolls merrily along, a fast-paced frolic piling on enough comic set pieces for a dozen comedies. Bogdanovich's most remarkable accomplishment, however, may be the performance he elicits from Streisand, one of the least strident of her career. Shown here at her easygoing, breezy best, Streisand plays the dizzying, determined, uninhibited screwball heroine—Hepburn in flavor, but not manner. Like Hepburn, Streisand is an unconventional, headstrong beauty with a distinctive personality. Still, Streisand wisely does not try to trade her New York Jewishness for Hepburn's well-bred Connecticut WASP affect.

Streisand plays Judy Maxwell, who has been kicked out of colleges across the country but has retained the knowledge gleaned at each one. Judy is sexually aggressive, shrewd, and unstoppable, a force of nature when she sets her sights on something. Like Hepburn's madcap heiress in *Bringing Up Baby*, Judy is a vivacious and capricious creature who resorts to outrageous measures to win her reluctant man, inadvertently landing them both in one comic predicament after another.

The improbable object of Judy's affections is Howard Bannister (Ryan O'Neal), a nerdy musicology professor from Iowa who has developed an obtuse theory about rocks and music. They meet at a hotel in San Francisco, where befuddled Howard has come for a convention with his blitheringly idiotic, domineering, quintessentially midwestern, and impossibly square fiancée Eunice, played by Madeline Kahn in her screen debut. For unknown reasons the free-spirited Judy is smitten by the dull and dopey Howard, who does not return her seemingly misplaced affections. Undeterred by their obvious differences, Judy launches a campaign to woo Howard with her brazen charm.

Staid Howard and wacky Judy have only one thing in common: They both own identical plaid bags. Howard's bag is filled with igneous rocks, Judy's with clothes. There are two more of the exact same bags at the hotel. One belongs to a rich dowager and is filled with jewels, which the bell clerk and the house detective plan to steal. The other contains top-secret documents, which are also the object of a planned theft. The four bags, of course, are accidentally switched any number of times during the course of the comedy. (A bag with a dinosaur bone is a similar source of confusion in *Bringing Up Baby*.)

The plaid bags are not the only "cases" of mistaken identity, however. Judy poses as Howard's dippy fiancée, Eunice, at the musicology convention, where Howard hopes to win a large grant from a man named Larrabee (wonderfully played by Austin Pendleton). Judy charms Larrabee, hoping to ingratiate herself to Howard, who indeed finds he has to sustain the charade if he wants to get the grant.

Howard's main competition is Hugh Simon, a pretentious, petty professor with a hilariously unidentifiable European accent, played by Kenneth Mars (who played the moronic Nazi playwright in *The Producers* in 1967). Simon was reportedly based on Bogdanovich's least favorite critic, John Simon, but is a scathingly funny caricature of pompous nastiness whether or not one gets the reference.

The wittily worded script is graced with quite a few funny lines. Told by Howard that she's "different," Judy responds, "But from now on I'll try to be the same." And at one point Howard protests her crazy driving: "This is a one-way street." She responds, "I'm only going one way."

The emphasis, however, is less on amusing dialogue than on situation and character. Above all, *What's Up, Doc?* is an inventive celebration of physical comedy that makes slapstick seem fresh and new. In one highlight Howard's room is demolished through a series of mounting catastrophes. The film's comic climax begins when the bags and characters all converge in a free-for-all fight at Larrabee's elegant home.

The final ten-minute chase that follows is marvelously sustained and features a great running gag with a large pane of glass (an idea credited to Buck Henry). The *Bullitt*-like chase begins with Judy and Howard careening out of control down the hills of San Francisco on a delivery bicycle—and right into a Chinese dragon during a parade, ending with all concerned landing in the drink in San Francisco Bay. The mass hysteria culminates in court, where Howard tries to explain to an exasperated judge (Liam Dunn) the convoluted events that led to the mayhem.

Although O'Neal is not as deft an actor as Cary Grant, who spoofed his suave and sophisticated image by playing the priggish professor in *Bringing Up Baby,* he is surprisingly effective as the plodding pedant who tries to keep both feet on the ground while his ordered world spins out of control. Streisand, who gives one of her best comedic performances, is suitably odd yet endearing as the footloose and fancy-free—make that *screw*-loose and fancy-free—Judy.

Kahn is a hoot as the dumpy, dominating Eunice. She manages to be utterly, outrageously obnoxious and yet to win our sympathy as indignities are heaped on her bewigged head. Kahn and O'Neal reunited with Bogdanovich the following year in *Paper Moon,* a bittersweet comedy that is in some ways a superior film, although not as funny as *What's Up, Doc?.*

Paper Moon, Bogdanovich's tribute to the films of John Ford and Depression-era America, features O'Neal as Moses Pray, a small-time con man who joins forces with Addie, a little girl who may or may not be his daughter. Addie is played by O'Neal's real-life nine-year-old daughter, Tatum O'Neal, who won a supporting actress Oscar for her tough-minded comic performance. The hustling pair bicker and bargain across the desolate West, reaching an understanding that whether or not they are related, they are two of a kind. Kahn costars as a carnival harem slave girl, Trixie Delight, who almost cons the scam artist into thinking she's a lady.

Paper Moon is touching yet frequently amusing, with an Oscar-nominated script by Alvin Sargent. The well-played exchanges between Moses and his pint-size sidekick, who matches him tit for tat, are the movie's humorous highlights. "I got scruples, too, you know. You know what scruples are?" Moses asks Addie. "No, but if you got 'em, I sure bet they belong to someone else," she shoots back.

After making three superb and quite different films in a row, Bogdanovich's career floundered. *Daisy Miller* and *At Long Last Love* were disappointments, and *Nickelodeon,* an homage to the early days of Hollywood that again starred O'Neal, was a flop. *They All Laughed* (1981) was a financial disaster, although the romantic comedy is not without its quirky charm. Bogdanovich, whose life has been beset by tragedy and controversy, was more successful with *Mask* (1985), and in 1992 he competently returned to comedy with his stylish direction of the Michael Frayn British sex farce, *Noises Off.* Still, *What's Up, Doc?* remains the director's funniest film.

Ironically, although *What's Up, Doc?* approaches but does not surpass *Bringing Up Baby,* Bogdanovich's homage was a huge commercial success, while Hawks's classic was a flop in its own day. Bogdanovich scored a double victory with *What's Up, Doc?.* As a director, Bogdanovich earned recognition for his versatility and talent. Perhaps more important for Bogdanovich the movie buff, however, *What's Up, Doc?* brought serious attention to *Bringing Up Baby,* which was finally appreciated as the ultimate screwball comedy.

Bogdanovich has modestly described the director's job as "someone who presides over accidents." In *What's Up, Doc?,* the accidents were all happy.

40

It's a Mad Mad Mad Mad World

United Artists (1963)
CAST: Spencer Tracy, Edie Adams, Milton Berle, Sid Caesar, Buddy Hackett,
Ethel Merman, Mickey Rooney, Dick Shawn, Phil Silvers,
Jonathan Winters, Peter Falk, Jimmy Durante, Terry-Thomas
DIRECTED BY: Stanley Kramer
154 minutes [Not rated]

More like a comics' convention than a movie, *It's a Mad Mad Mad Mad World* holds the world comedy records for length and cast size. This epic comedy, built on "the more the merrier" premise that bigger is better, is admittedly a test of endurance, but for sheer quantity of humor—not to mention ambition and audacity—it stands unrivaled. It was a motion picture event in its day, the first comedy to open with such fanfare, and it is still considered an all-time comedy classic.

Released in theaters at 154 minutes and on video restored to its original 175-minute length, the gargantuan comedy suffers a bit from excess but makes up for it with novelty, energy, and style. It is an oddity in the annals of comedy: the ultimate comic road film directed by a serious filmmaker and featuring virtually every comedian working in Hollywood at the time.

The cinema's first supercomedy was directed by Stanley Kramer, who optimistically hoped it would be "the funniest comedy anybody had ever seen." Kramer also hoped to establish a new image for himself with the supersilly comedy he aptly describes in his autobiography as "a monument to greed, mayhem and nonsense."

Kramer began his career with a satire, *So This Is New York* (1948), which was a dismal failure, but he quickly established a reputation for serious dramas with important subjects. As a director he had successfully tackled social themes in *The Defiant Ones* (racism), *On the Beach* (nuclear holocaust), *Inherit the Wind* (intolerance and the theory of evolution), and *Judgment at Nuremberg* (the Holocaust) and went on to do so in later films, *Guess Who's Coming to Dinner* (racial prejudice again) and *Ship of Fools* (the impending Holocaust). He also produced such landmarks as *High Noon, The Men, The Caine Mutiny,* and *The Wild One.* His work as producer and director has earned sixteen Oscars and eighty nominations.

151

MAD ABOUT YOU Stanley Kramer's 1963 *It's a Mad Mad Mad Mad World* was a *Who's Who* of great comedians. Pictured here, from left: Buddy Hackett, Mickey Rooney, Eddie "Rochester" Anderson, Peter Falk, Spencer Tracy, Ethel Merman, Jonathan Winters, and Phil Silvers.

In 1963, determined to correct the assumption in Hollywood that he couldn't do comedy, Kramer bought an idea pitched to him by veteran screenwriter William Rose (*The Ladykillers* and *The Russians are Coming! The Russians Are Coming!*). Together they sketched out a story about an elaborate race for buried treasure. Kramer then set about assembling the most impressive group of comedians ever to appear on screen together. In addition to his main cast—Spencer Tracy, Milton Berle, Ethel Merman, Phil Silvers, Sid Caesar, Buddy Hackett, Jonathan Winters, Mickey Rooney, Dick Shawn, and Terry-Thomas—Kramer convinced some of comedy's biggest names to make cameo appearances. Jack Benny, Jerry Lewis, Buster Keaton, Joe E. Brown, Don Knotts, Carl Reiner, Andy Devine, Peter Falk, Jimmy Durante, Zasu Pitts, and the Three Stooges all make fleeting appearances in the uproarious film.

With more comedians on the set than crew members, Kramer recalls that the cast engaged in fierce comic one-upmanship, and that because they were all trying so hard to outdo each other, they hardly required any direction at all. Kramer had enormous respect for the comedy legends in his employ, and he gave the cast quite a bit of creative freedom. The main problem he remembers on the set was getting the actors, who loved to improvise and who added many funny bits to the screenplay, to stick to the already long script.

The Mack Sennett–style slapstick comedy begins, oddly enough, with a fatal car crash. Jimmy Durante drives his car off a cliff in the Mojave desert and lies dying by the wreck when a group of motorists who witnessed the accident arrive to hear his last words. Before literally kicking the bucket, he tells them of $350,000 he has buried under a big "W" in Santa Rosita Park near the Mexico border. The travelers initially agree to cooperate in finding the treasure but argue over how the money should be divided. Soon it's every man for himself. But what begins as a competition to see who will get there first turns into a question of who will face the largest calamity en route to the riches.

Although the chase had long been a staple of comedy—particularly the silent film comedy of Mack Sennett's Keystone Kops—*It's a Mad Mad Mad Mad World* is among a small handful of films to build the entire plot around it.

Comedy writers played by Buddy Hackett and Mickey Rooney find a drunken millionaire (Jim Backus) with a private plane to fly them, but they are left to land the plane themselves when the playboy pilot drinks too many Manhattans and passes out. Dentist Sid Caesar and his wife, played by Edie Adams, survive a trip in the world's oldest, slowest, and most rickety plane, only to get locked into the basement of a hardware store, where everything that can go wrong does.

Milton Berle ditches his impossibly bossy, brassy mother-in-law (Ethel Merman) and wife (Dorothy Provine) and throws in his lot with prickly British botanist Terry-Thomas. The mother-in-law from hell tries to reach her swinging son, Dick Shawn (*The Producers*), who lives near the stashed booty, but he's too busy grooving to answer the phone, and when he does he's too zonked to listen. Swindler Phil Silvers gets into the action after hearing about the treasure secondhand, then gets his comeuppance when he goes off the main road and ends up in the river. Truck driver Jonathan Winters finds himself pedaling a girl's bike across the desert. And so it goes. Chaos rules as the greedy fortune hunters encounter a series of obstacles standing between them and unearned wealth.

Unknown to all of them, their every action is being monitored by the police, who are also very interested in finding the ill-gotten gains. Captain Culpepper (a role created by Kramer for Tracy) is particularly interested in solving the fifteen-year-old case of a tuna factory robbery, but before long the lure of easy money also gets the better of the veteran cop.

It is stretching things a bit to call *It's a Mad Mad Mad Mad World* a satire on greed, but if there's a message to be found amid the cartoonish free-for-all, it is that the desire for money can corrupt and debase anyone. The lesson is reinforced in the film's final scene, which finds all concerned in traction in the hospital, headed for prison.

Although anarchistic in mood, the comedy's theme is conventionally moralistic, coming down squarely on the side of law and order. Frequently, however, comedies dealing with crime take a more socially rebellious view, allowing the criminals to get away with the loot. *The In-Laws* and *Sitting Ducks* are two examples of irreverent comedies in which crime does pay.

It's hard to say which of the comics comes off best in this ensemble comedy of heroic proportions. Winters plays the dumb, volatile trucker with endless invention. Berle does a brilliant slow burn as the long-suffering, henpecked son-in-law. Merman, the film's only comedienne, more than holds her own against the male comics, playing the shrill, shrewish, hot-tempered matron with guts to spare.

Although a few critics of the day expressed reservations about the movie's scope and the confusion that resulted from juggling so many plot lines and characters, the comedy was a box office success and inspired awe in a number of critics. *Variety* proclaimed the film "a spectacular achievement in the cinematic architecture" and "a significant addition to Hollywood film comedy and a potential box office blockbuster." The review went on to note that it was both a throwback to wild and wacky silent film comedy and a modern milestone.

Kramer may not have fulfilled his mission to create the world's greatest comedy, but he did a great service to the legendary comedians whose work he ably showcased and whose careers were advanced by the exposure. Kramer also created an extravagant, one-of-a-kind entertainment and pioneered a new genre, the first big-budget, all-star comedy extravaganza. Never before or since has a film suffered from such an embarrassment of comic riches.

41

Abbott and Costello Meet Frankenstein

Universal International (1948)
Cast: Bud Abbott, Lou Costello, Bela Lugosi, Lon Chaney Jr.
Directed by: Charles Barton
83 minutes [Not rated]

In 1948 Universal decided to conduct a ghoulish experiment, removing the comedy brains from Lou Costello and placing them in the head of Frankenstein's monster. That idea actually forms the plot of *Abbott and Costello Meet Frankenstein,* a fiendishly clever plan by Universal to combine its famed comedy team and its stable of classic horror film stars in one big, bubbling cauldron.

Known for its chilling creature features as well as a string of hits showcasing Bud Abbott and Lou Costello, Universal successfully grafted its prized possessions into a monster hit, a frightful, funny film that for many years remained the definite horror-comedy hybrid.

In this amalgam of chills and chuckles, Abbott and Costello play Chick Young and Wilbur Gray, a pair of stumblebum shipping clerks in Florida who deliver two crates to McDougals' House of Horrors and soon unwittingly unleash their contents. One crate contains the coffin of the presumably deceased Dracula, played by Bela Lugosi, who originated the role and plays the part with his usual malevolent flourish. Still quite "undead," Dracula plans to revive the contents of the second crate, Frankenstein's monster, played by Glenn Strange, who took over the role originated by Boris Karloff in 1931.

Following *Abbott and Costello Meet Frankenstein,* Universal retired the famed monster, although Karloff reappeared in *Abbott and Costello Meet the Killer: Boris Karloff* (1949), in which the actor plays a psychotic posing as a mystic who tries to murder bellboy Costello.

Lon Chaney Jr., the veteran of horror films who originated the role of the Wolfman, which he reprises here, appears in the film's opening shot, peering through the blinds in terror as the moon is about to rise on a foggy night in London. He is trying fanatically to reach Florida and avert the impending disaster by preventing the delivery of the two crates. After a night of hairy horror, he arrives in person to continue his attempt to thwart Dracula's devious plot to revive the monster by giving him a new, simpler, and more submissive brain. The count is assisted by Sandra Mornay (Lenore Aubert), a lovely but evil lady surgeon who has found the perfect mind to transplant.

Pretending to be in love with Wilbur (Costello), the mad scientist plans to harvest the doting fool's malleable brain and place it into the monster, who will then do her evil bidding. Wilbur, the improbable object of affection for such "a classy dish," spends most of the film either mooning over his beloved or being scared even more witless than usual. Wilbur's fool-in-love shtick is one of the film's main sources of humor, second only to the "watch Costello go berserk with terror" scenario.

Abbott's Chick Young is left to bark orders, express his disdain and exasperation, and give his "fraidy-cat" partner a hard time, his usual gruff and impatient straight-man assignment. His constant carping and failure to realize the true danger that they are in provide the perfect foil for Wilbur's blubbering hysterics. In one of the film's highlights, a revolving door in the bowels of the castle keeps putting Wilbur face-to-face with the monsters while Chick is kept in the dark.

Directed by Charles Barton, *Abbott and Costello Meet Frankenstein* is filled with mistaken identities—highlighted by a costume ball at which the monsters mingle freely with the guests. The screenplay is filled with clever wordplay emphasizing the misunderstandings. "That's the bunk," Chick scoffs. "That's what I'm trying to tell you—that's his bunk," Wilbur replies, pointing to Dracula's coffin.

Abbott and Costello Meet Frankenstein was such a huge box office hit, it was followed by a series of sequels that tended to be more dreadful than frightening. In rapid succession Abbott and Costello met not only the killer Boris Karloff, but also the Invisible Man, Dr. Jekyll and Mr. Hyde, and the Mummy. Each one of these formula comedies provided Costello with a reason to act terrified. Because Costello's comic persona was that of a child, he was at his cowardly best wailing, whimpering, sputtering with fright, or falling all over himself and everything else while trying to get away from a creepy creature. The beauty of all these films is that the monsters play it straight, leaving the comedy to the comics.

Although *Abbott and Costello Meet Frankenstein* satirizes the hokey horror film genre, it is not a parody. Rather, with Frank Skinner's suitably creepy score and all the visual trappings of the horror film, the film plunks the clowns down into an authentic chiller. *Abbott and Costello Meet Frankenstein* and the duo's subsequent series of chills-and-chuckles outings did, however, lead to future parodies such as Mel Brooks's *Young Frankenstein*—in which the monsters camp it up along with the comedians. It also influenced such later amalgams as the hugely popular, big-budget fright comedy *Ghostbusters*.

Oh, Chick! Virtually every comedy team in filmdom made what the industry called "a scare picture." The best—and most successful—was 1948's *Abbott and Costello Meet Frankenstein.* Pictured here with Bud and Lou is Glenn Strange, who made a memorable Frankenstein. A recent revival at New York City's Film Forum drew record-breaking crowds.

Abbott and Costello Meet Frankenstein was not the duo's first comedy-horror film, however. *Hold that Ghost,* in which Abbott and Costello inherit a haunted house, was one of their first and very best films. This funny 1941 comedy also features some of the pair's best routines, including the moving candle scene (repeated in *Abbott and Costello Meet Frankenstein*).

Abbott and Costello had met in 1931 in a burlesque showcase in Brooklyn. They played vaudeville and became radio favorites on Kate Smith's popular show in the late 1930s. They first appeared on screen in *One Night in the Tropics* in 1940 and were an instant hit with the public. At the time, with stormclouds gathering on the international horizon, the public was hungry for harmless, innocuous, silly, slapstick comedy. Abbott and Costello offered pure, mindless, unsophisticated escapist entertainment, devoid of irony, sarcasm, or any subversive intent.

During the 1940s the Marx Brothers and Charlie Chaplin faded from favor. Danny Kaye, Red Skelton, Bob Hope and Bing Crosby, and Dean Martin and Jerry Lewis rose to fame. But Abbott and Costello were the most famous and profitable comedy stars of the 1940s. Signed to a long-term contract with Universal in 1940, the team scored a $10 million hit with their first tailor-made feature, *Buck Privates,* which made more money than *Citizen Kane.* The pair made five films in 1941, and by 1942 they were box office champs, outgrossing Clark Gable, Bette Davis, and Betty Grable.

The premier clowns of the 1940s, Abbott and Costello were throwbacks to the earlier comedy traditions of vaudeville and burlesque, and they borrowed freely from Laurel and Hardy. Like Oliver Hardy, Bud Abbott was the dominating partner, forever exasperated by the antics of his dim-witted, infantile partner. Like Stan Laurel, Lou Costello was always getting his surly, superior pal into one fine mess after another.

Abbott and Costello were often dismissed because of the absence of sophistication, and this lack of critical recognition is due, in part, to the fact that they were far from masters of film craft. They are remembered for the memorable characters they created rather than for the vehicles that were designed to showcase their talents. Many of their films were merely a series of routines strung together with a lame romantic subplot and directed with no discernible style. Nevertheless, Abbott and Costello were extremely accomplished and beloved comedians.

Their enduring humor hinged on Costello's consistent failure to understand Abbott or to make himself understood. The pair was forever talking at cross purposes. The comic misunderstanding reached its apex in the classic "Who's on first?" routine, perfected in their early days. This hilarious comedy highlight was often repeated on TV's *Abbott and Costello Show* in the 1950s and endeared them to a new generation of fans. One of the most famously funny routines of all times, it is enshrined on a plaque in the Baseball Hall of Fame.

During their lifetime, Abbott and Costello never had a joint written contract, although Costello always got 60 percent of the take. Their partnership, which had its ups and downs and ended in 1957, was chronicled in *Bud and Lou,* a biography by Bob Thomas that was subsequently adapted into a respectable 1978 TV movie starring Buddy Hackett and Harvey Korman.

Abbott and Costello may not have been great artists, and they certainly were not auteurs, but they were consistently funny. The bumbling, fumbling figures, ever pathetic, ever in over their heads, did their best work in the horror-comedy form they pioneered. While the Wolfman howled at the moon, Abbott and Costello made audiences howl with laughter.

42

Cat Ballou

Columbia (1965)
CAST: Jane Fonda, Lee Marvin, Michael Callan, Dwayne Hickman
DIRECTED BY: Elliot Silverstein
96 minutes [Not rated]

As long as there have been westerns, there have been western comedies, from Buster Keaton's *Go West* and Laurel and Hardy's *Way Out West* to Bob Hope's *Paleface* and *Son of Paleface*. The year 1939 produced one of the all-time best comic westerns, *Destry Rides Again,* starring Marlene Dietrich singing "See What the Boys in the Back Room Will Have."

Cat Ballou, one of the best western comedies ever made, is also the first true parody of the contemporary cinema and one of the best sustained. Although during the silent film era the practice of spoofing genres and specific hit movies enjoyed considerable popularity, it faded from favor until the 1970s, when it once again became the comic rage. In historical discussions of the parody renaissance, however, *Cat Ballou* is frequently overlooked.

A wild ride through the Wild West, *Cat Ballou* predates Mel Brooks's western burlesque *Blazing Saddles,* which is widely credited with inaugurating the parody revival, by nine years. It also predates Woody Allen's send-up of the Japanese spy thriller, *What's Up, Tiger Lily?,* by one year. And it predates *Airplane!,* which fifteen years later launched a spate of popular parodies that continues unabated today.

Unlike the parodies that came after it, however, *Cat Ballou* is first and foremost a comedy and is not dedicated solely to feeding off of earlier movies. It travesties the clichés of the western but never takes cheap pot shots. It gleefully skewers the romantic myth of the old West but also creates real characters, real suspense, and real human emotion. It's high-spirited but never mean-spirited. Because it has a strong story and is not just about movies, it is fun from beginning to end, which is more than can be said of many parodies.

In the title role, Jane Fonda shines as a schoolmarm turned outlaw. We are introduced to Cat—short for Catherine—by two strolling minstrels played by Stubby Kaye and Nat King Cole. The balladeers sing a series of songs that comment on the action and characters, serving as a comic Greek chorus. The

159

STUMBLING TUMBLEWEEDS Lee Marvin in his Oscar- and Golden Globe–winning portrayal of drunken gunfighter Kid Shelleen in the 1965 *Cat Ballou.* Marvin superbly spoofed his own he-man image in this laugh-a-minute western knockoff.

musical interludes are a reference to the ballad form of storytelling popularized in the western classic *High Noon* and add to the movie's merriment with witty lyrics and lively tunes.

Cat, the opening song informs us, is in jail and is about to be hanged. But for what? And is she a wicked woman or an innocent victim? We are about to find out, as a flashback takes us to the beginning of the walloping tale. When we meet Cat, she is a prim and proper teacher who has just completed her eastern education and is aboard a train back to her father's ranch in Wolf City, Wyoming. The matron who entrusts Cat to a man of the cloth has no idea she's just left her charge in the hands of a drunken cattle rustler, Jed (Dwayne Hickman), who is disguised as a preacher to spring his nephew Clay (Michael Callan) from the law. Cat becomes entangled in the getaway and finds herself attracted to Clay, a rogue and a Romeo. Both Jed and Clay are harmless rascals rather than dangerous outlaws, however, in a comedy where the good guys aren't so good and the bad guys aren't always so bad.

Back at the ranch, Cat is dismayed to find that her father (John Marley) is locked in a battle for his once prosperous property, which the city wants for its water rights to seal a large land deal. Aided only by his faithful Indian cowhand Jackson (Tom Nardini), the stubborn old man refuses to be driven off his land, so a hired gun is brought in to intimidate him. Tim Strawn (Lee Marvin) is a classic caricature of the gunslinger—he's so tough that he wears a steel nose because his own was bitten off in a fight. Clay and Jed pop up unexpectedly at a square dance, and Cat invites them to stay at the ranch to help protect her father. Unfortunately, neither desperado has ever shot a man, and Clay suggests she fight fire with fire by hiring her own sharpshooter.

Marvin reappears as Kid Shelleen, the fast-shooting hero of dimestore novels whom Cat recruits to take on Strawn. Cat has apparently wasted her money on Shelleen, who has spent it all on whiskey and arrives too soused to hit the broad side of a barn. A sorry sight, Shelleen is a mere shadow of his former self. Kid Shelleen does eventually pull himself together long enough to rise to the challenge of killing Strawn, who turns out to be his evil twin—but not before Cat's father is killed and she's driven out of town by the crooked sheriff.

Determined to seek revenge on the town, Cat, Clay, Jed, Jackson, and Kid Shelleen head for Hole in the Wall, where Cat plans a train robbery and convinces her reluctant companions to help her pull off the daring heist, outlined in one of Kid Shelleen's books. The robbery is a success, but Cat's thirst for revenge is not yet sated, and her next move almost costs her her life. She is, of course, saved from the gallows by the men who have all come to love her.

This being a film made in the 1960s, it is only fitting that the western hero is a woman, and a brave, smart, sexy woman at that. Fonda's first starring role in an acclaimed motion picture launched her to fame and led to her appearance in another popular comedy, *Barefoot in the Park.* Following 1968's futuristic comic book satire, *Barbarella,* Fonda appeared in a succession of serious films, including *They Shoot Horses, Don't They?, Klute, Julia, Coming Home* and *On Golden Pond.* Not known as a comedienne, Fonda's performance as Cat remains her finest comic turn.

The film's best comedy work, however, is done by Marvin, whose boisterously entertaining performance gave his career a big boost. Marvin finally became a recognized star after years of being typecast as villains and he-men in supporting roles. Marvin won the best actor Oscar, a Golden Globe Award, and the National Board of Review's citation for best actor for his dual roles in *Cat Ballou,* which demonstrated his talent for comedy and his ability to spoof his own macho image. Kid Shelleen's reeling incompetence is indeed marvelously played by Marvin in scenes such as the one in which Shelleen staggers into Cat's father's funeral, sees the candles, and begins singing "Happy Birthday." Shelleen is the classic lovable drunkard.

There have been many memorable movie drunks over the years in such diverse comedies as *City Lights, Arthur, Topper,* and *Tom Jones.* W. C. Fields mined much humor from his fondness for liquor—and was toted on a horse-drawn stretcher in *his* comic western, *My Little Chickadee,* just as Shelleen is in *Cat Ballou. The Thin Man's* comic couple, Nick and Nora Charles, made imbibing downright glamorous. Although in recent years the recognition of alcoholism as a tragic disease has put a damper on the fun, intoxication continues to be a source of humor. Marvin's Kid Shelleen can hold his own with any of the screen's celebrated boozers.

A hit with the public and the critics, the high-stepping *Cat Ballou* was directed with a steady hand by TV veteran and Yale Drama School grad Elliot Silverstein (*A Man Called Horse*). Critics noted that the comedy epitomized the sheer fun of moviemaking and appreciated its round trouncing of western conventions.

"As honest-to-gosh Westerns go, *Cat Ballou* is disgraceful," Bosley Crowther wrote in the *New York Times*. "As a shibboleth-shattering spoof, it dumps all the heroic traditions of horse opera into a gag bag, shakes thoroughly, and pulls out one of the year's jolliest surprises. What's good about the comedy is nigh irresistible. What's best about it is probably Lee Marvin."

Judith Crist, writing in the *New York Herald Tribune,* proclaimed it "a small package of enormous delight" and "a Western to end all Westerns," which of course it didn't. *Cat Ballou,* in fact, set off a stampede of western comedies. The comic western actually began to supplant the straight western in popularity until Clint Eastwood returned the form to respectability in 1991 with his antiwestern, *The Unforgiven.*

Some of the notable comic westerns that rode after *Cat Ballou* include *Support Your Local Sheriff* (1969), starring James Garner, and *The Frisco Kid* (1979), starring Gene Wilder as an immigrant rabbi who hooks up with an outlaw (Harrison Ford). Billy Crystal found an original way to update and transplant the western in *City Slickers* (1991). Jack Nicholson had a go at the genre with his tongue-in-cheek comedy *Goin' South* (1978). Paul Newman took to the comedy saddle in *The Life and Times of Judge Roy Bean* (1972). An offbeat western spoof, *Rancho Deluxe* (1975) featured Jeff Bridges and Sam Waterston as footloose and fancy-free cowpokes. Bridges also starred in 1975's *Hearts of the West,* which satirized the making of movie westerns. Dustin Hoffman debunked the heroics of the old West in *Little Big Man* (1970).

The influence of *Cat Ballou,* with an award-winning screenplay by Frank Pierson based on Roy Chanslor's novel, is most strongly felt in *Blazing Saddles,* not so much in style as in content. Both films run roughshod over the sacred myths of the old West, denouncing the small-mindedness, ignorance, prejudice, and corruption of the era. Perhaps coincidentally, both films equate Indians with Jews. While Mel Brooks has his Indians speak Yiddish, Cat's father is convinced that Jackson, a full-blooded Sioux, is a member of the lost tribe of Israel. The egalitarianism and liberal political subtext of *Cat Ballou* no doubt contributed to its success in 1965—if audiences could stop laughing long enough to notice.

43

Playtime

Spectra Films (1967)
CAST: Jacques Tati, Barbara Dennek, Jacqueline Lecomte,
Valerie Camille, Leon Doyen
DIRECTED BY: Jacques Tati
108 minutes [Not rated]

Playtime, widely regarded as a four-star comic masterpiece, has no plot, minimal dialogue, and no firmly established characters. The camera simply follows a group of people around an ultramodern Paris, first at an airport, then at a department store, then at an office building, and finally at a brand-new restaurant. The classic comedy offers a microcosm of modern life as it observes the comings and goings of the human specimens in their particular settings.

Anyone unfamiliar with the distinctive humor of the famed French comic actor, director, and writer Jacques Tati may have a hard time understanding how a plotless, wordless, characterless comedy could possibly be considered brilliant. Indeed, not everyone appreciates the parade of subtle sight gags in Tati's minimalist classics, which have no peer in film comedy. Although Tati's films rely on silent film tradition, they are utterly unique inventions that cannot truly be compared with any other films.

That has not kept critics from trying. It has been noted that Tati's work bears resemblance to the mechanical virtuosity of Keaton, to Chaplin's timing and resilience, and to Langdon's scrambled innocence. Generally, however, critics are content to heap superlatives on his comic artistry. Although he made only six films in a career spanning thirty years, they earned him a permanent place in the movie comedy pantheon. "*Playtime* is Jacques Tati's most brilliant film, a bracing reminder in this all-too-lazy era that films can occasionally achieve the status of art," Vincent Canby wrote of this "droll, elegant, meticulous and spare comedy."

Tati's films have only the barest outline of a story. In *Playtime* some of the action revolves around Tati's famed Mr. Hulot character attempting to keep a business appointment. The rest of the film concerns itself with the activities of a group of American tourists who never see the real sights of Paris, such as the Eiffel Tower, except reflected in the steel-and-glass structures that dominate the futuristic urban landscape. Tati is always fascinated by locale, and *Playtime* is another comedy of settings, a satire of contemporary architecture.

Tati may not rely on the standard staples of narrative film, but his comedies do have themes. In *Playtime* Tati offers a social commentary on the conditions of human life. *Playtime* is about dehumanization, mechanization, and routinization. He makes fun of the sterility and efficiency of the increasingly complicated and impersonal modern world. Technology proves a perilous adversary, presenting a series of obstacles for the individual to surmount. The serious subject of the playful *Playtime* is the uniformity and conformity of the bland new age in which we live. The comedy is a carefully choreographed ballet of ordinary movements, a dance that reveals the nature of mankind.

· *Playtime* opens inside an antiseptic building that we at first take to be a hospital waiting room. A man paces, a baby cries, a woman pushes what appears to be a patient in a wheelchair, nuns briskly click along the gleaming floor, and a couple sits speaking in hushed tones. Suddenly we realize that we have been deceived. The building is actually the Orly Airport. The woman with the wheelchair reappears, but now we see she is pushing her luggage, not a patient. Arrival information is broadcast on the intercom. A group of chattering American women disembark, among them a pretty woman (Barbara Dennek) who will eventually cross paths with Hulot and leave France the next morning with a memento of their brief encounter.

The point of the visual trick Tati plays on the audience is that all our public buildings look alike, that a deadening sameness afflicts our environment. We are prisoners of our architecture, a point best illustrated later in the film when Hulot is caught in a maze of office cubicles like a rat in some horrible experiment designed to test the subject's resilience in the face of frustration. Tati's disdain for modern architecture reaches its fullest comic fruition when the tourists go to a newly opened nightclub that begins to fall apart as it is put to use.

Tati had earlier ridiculed modern conveniences and taste in *Mon Oncle* (1958), in which Mr. Hulot's simple life in an old section of Paris is contrasted with the foolishly contemporary excesses of his sister and brother-in-law. Although his earlier hit and first great international success, *Mr. Hulot's Holiday* (1953), was set entirely at a seaside resort, it introduced the theme of man at odds with his environment through the introduction of his title character. Tati's trademark figure, Mr. Hulot, is a gangly, good-natured sort who continually grapples with gadgets and can never quite get into the swing of the fast-paced world around him. Implicit in the character is a sentimental longing for the values and simplicity of earlier times and a resentment of the encroachment on the gentle past by the harsh forces of modernity.

HOT TATI   Jacques Tati (in overcoat and argyle socks) in *Playtime* (1967). A comic perfectionist, Tati made only six films in thirty years, each one a masterpiece.

By the end of the 1950s Tati had become such a popular screen comedian that he was offered an American TV series, which he turned down in favor of continuing the painstaking process of constructing his elaborate films. *Playtime* featured his largest cast (which consisted mostly of amateurs) and crew and was shot in 70 millimeter with stereophonic sound to heighten the impact of the comic sound effects. The ambitious undertaking involved the construction of a huge set outside Paris that took five months to build. The set, which was dubbed Tativille, became a tourist attraction. The entire project took three years to complete.

Because Tati insisted that *Playtime* be presented only in 70-millimeter format, its distribution in France in 1967 was severely limited and its American premiere was delayed until 1973—after the release of his next film, *Traffic*. Despite these problems, Tati pronounced himself proud of the results and gratified by its critical reception. Tati considered *Playtime* his best film, the culmination of his work as an artist, and insisted that it be shown last in any retrospective screenings of his films.

Although Mr. Hulot appears repeatedly throughout *Playtime,* he could hardly be considered its central character. Tati had begun to diminish the importance of his comic persona since *Mr. Hulot's Holiday.* Although Mr. Hulot was always meant to be a representative of everyday society, in *Playtime* Tati chose to focus on the group rather than the individual. *Playtime* fulfilled Tati's stated desire to create a truly "democratic comedy."

The Mr. Hulot character, however, remains a curious comic creation. He is not a clown. In fact, he's rather serious and somber, with his pipe and hat and air of dignity. Hulot is the product of Tati's belief that it is funnier to see a dignified person engage in comic activity than it is to watch someone funny do the same thing. Unlike comedies that play on the humor of a relatively sane world decimated by the antics of one comic citizen, Tati's creations revolve around a world made more comic by Hulot's sobriety. We rarely see a close-up of Mr. Hulot and therefore cannot see his facial expressions. Viewed in long shot, he is swept along by circumstances beyond his control. He is but one figure on the broad canvas Tati paints in *Playtime.*

What makes *Playtime* so funny is its endless series of visual gags, which range from the slender to the absurd. When an office building's glass door is shattered, the doorman keeps up the charade of opening and closing the nonexistent door, using the remaining large round knob to maintain the illusion—the purpose of which is anyone's guess. That gag, in essence, sums up *Playtime*'s humorously expressed message. We are silly creatures obsessed with artifice, appearance, and order and invested in our meaningless rituals. The real beauty, romance, magic, and mystery of life we see only as fleeting reflections in our gleaming glass monuments to monotony.

44

The Bellboy

Paramount (1960)
CAST: Jerry Lewis, Alex Gerry, Bob Clayton
DIRECTED BY: Jerry Lewis
72 minutes [Not rated]

In 1960 Jerry Lewis was already one of the most consistently popular comedy stars in Hollywood history when he went out on a limb, making his directorial debut with *The Bellboy,* a comedy that had no plot. In a further act of daring, the innovative comic decided that the title character would not utter a word in this series of related comic vignettes focusing on an eager-beaver bellboy at the famed Fountainebleau Hotel in Miami Beach.

Bravely billed by Paramount as "a series of silly sequences," the comedy showcased Lewis's aptitude for physical comedy. This "visual diary of a few weeks in the life of a real nut"—as the phony film producer who introduces the comedy describes it—allowed Lewis to concentrate on the creation of burlesque routines and Borscht Belt–style comic set pieces rather than to waste time justifying them in the context of a ridiculous story.

Lewis, who was never known for his wit or clever dialogue, was hardly at a disadvantage when forced to rely on pantomime, which has always been his forte. He does speak in a secondary role he plays in the comedy, that of a famous movie star (billed under Lewis's real name, Joe Levitch) who arrives at the hotel with an entourage of fawning sycophants. With this autobiographical cameo, Lewis makes a comment about the price of fame that would later be echoed by his self-referential performance in *The King of Comedy*.

Hastily conceived and slapped together so it could be released before the already completed *Cinderfella, The Bellboy* was filmed on a limited budget in less than a month on location while Lewis was appearing at the Fountainebleau, where he wrote the script in eight days. Because he didn't have time to find a director, he decided to direct himself. Paramount was nervous about a black-and-white "silent" film, so Lewis—then the highest-paid performer in Hollywood, with a $100,000-a-year clothing budget—used his own money to finance the picture. *The Bellboy* cost less than $1 million and made ten times that amount.

JERRY-ON-THE-SPOT Critics were generally less than kind to Jerry Lewis, but the public adored him. In this scene from *The Bellboy* (1960), Lewis is confounded by the intricacies of a Volkswagen engine.

Although something of a fluke, *The Bellboy* has come to be regarded as one of Lewis's most original and inspired creations. As his biographer Shawn Levy concludes in *King of Comedy, The Bellboy* is as accomplished a first film as any comic director ever made. Almost avant-garde in its minimalism, it has moments of pure comic poetry, such as when Stanley conducts an imaginary orchestra.

Like many comedies more appreciated in hindsight, *The Bellboy* did not generate many rave reviews in its day. Although a few critics called *The Bellboy* a masterpiece, others dismissed it as "minor league screen comedy." Lewis was accused, among other things, of trying to emulate Chaplin. If he was, he certainly succeeded. Chaplin requested a print of the film, which was his favorite Jerry Lewis comedy, and sent Lewis a new print of *Modern Times* in return.

In point of fact, however, Lewis was directly inspired by another comic legend, Stan Laurel, whose work he imitated in spirit as well as substance in *The Bellboy*. A Stan Laurel impersonator appears in the comedy, acknowledging the homage. Lewis even borrowed his idol's name for the inept bellboy, Stanley.

Lewis, who once worked as a bellboy in the Catskills hotel where his father was master of ceremonies, plays one of "the unsung heroes of the hotel business." Like so many of the characters Lewis has played, Stanley is a good-natured jerk. He is an idiotic klutz of the highest order yet oddly able to accomplish amazing feats from time to time, like setting up a huge hall with chairs in a matter of minutes or piloting a blimp.

Above all, Stanley is an overgrown kid, innocent and immature, goofy and strange, always seeking approval but never really fitting into the grown-up world. Lewis is often criticized for being juvenile—if not infantile—which is indeed the hallmark of all his films. Critic Stuart Byron aptly described the arrested adolescence that pervades Lewis's work when he wrote in 1964 that the comic always portrays "the adult whose emotions have been frozen at the mental age of about 14 and who retains the desperate loneliness, the desperate sense of rejection, the desperate desire to please of the awkward and alone boy of that age."

Lewis indeed grew up under difficult circumstances that no doubt left scars on his adolescent psyche. An only child of show business parents who routinely shipped him off to friends or relatives or took him out of school to take him on the road with them, Lewis moved so often that he never had time to make friends. By the time he dropped out of school in the tenth grade, he had become the class clown.

Lewis honed his comedy skills performing in the Borscht Belt and in 1946 teamed with Dean Martin and became an instant hit on the nightclub circuit. They began appearing in films together in 1950 and made sixteen popular and profitable comedies in succession before Martin left the act in 1956 and Lewis began his solo career. Before fading from favor in the late 1960s, Lewis appeared in thirty-seven straight hits, which must be some kind of Hollywood record.

Although *The Bellboy* is often cited as the purest expression of Lewis's art, many critics consider *The Nutty Professor* (1963) to be his masterwork. In that more dated comedy, Lewis plays a variation of Dr. Jekyll and Mr. Hyde, a sweet but socially inept scientist who invents a formula that transforms him into an obnoxiously overconfident swinger, Buddy Love. The character is so intolerably abrasive, some viewers find him more annoying than amusing.

In truth, Lewis has always been an acquired taste. American critics have tended to dismiss him as a vulgar clown who performed the basest kind of slapstick, although he enjoyed greater critical acclaim in Europe, particularly in France, where he was revered.

There is no denying, however, that he wielded enormous influence over the succeeding generation of screen comedians, most notably Steve Martin (*The Jerk*) and Jim Carrey. Billy Crystal paid Lewis tribute by including him in *Mr. Saturday Night*. Martin Scorsese launched a reappreciation for his range by casting him as the somber talk show host in *The King of Comedy* (1983).

There is also no doubt that he was a pioneer. He was the first Jewish comedian to direct himself. He invented the video assist, which is widely used today, as a way of seeing on video what the camera was recording. He ran his own production company and exercised complete creative control over all aspects of his films, which he wrote, directed, produced, and starred in. He experimented with sound, editing, plotting, cinematography, and decor.

While the determinedly lowbrow comic may not have always earned critical respect, he is a renowned philanthropist who has dedicated much of his life to raising more than $1 billion for his favorite cause, muscular dystrophy. Because of his work on behalf of "Jerry's kids," he was nominated for a Nobel Peace Prize.

There are many sides to Lewis, who recently returned to Broadway in a revival of *Damn Yankees* (and, in the process, became the highest-paid stage performer to date). As the living embodiment of fifties comedy, he has become retro-chic and is not above satirizing his own image. It is only fitting, in the end, that Jerry Lewis gets the last laugh.

45

Harold and Maude

Paramount (1972)
CAST: Ruth Gordon, Bud Cort, Vivian Pickles
DIRECTED BY: Hal Ashby
90 minutes [Rated PG]

Harold is a deeply troubled young man who can find no meaning or pleasure in life. Maude is a profoundly eccentric old woman who has lived her life to the fullest. Harold is alienated, depressed, and morbid. Maude greets each day with joy and zest. Opposites in temperament as well as age, Harold and Maude are soulmates who share a mutually rewarding, albeit utterly unconventional, relationship.

The romance between twenty-year-old Harold (Bud Cort) and seventy-nine-year-old Maude (Ruth Gordon) shocked viewers in 1972 and continues to be provocative. But this ink black comedy is powerfully unsettling not just because *Harold and Maude* breaks a sexual taboo. Hal Ashby's disconcerting cult classic lays systematic assault on a number of sacred institutions, including the family, the church, the military, and modern medicine.

This intensely strange comedy was overlooked by the public and dismissed by the critics on its release but gained astounding popularity over the years and was successfully rereleased at the end of the seventies. Very much ahead of its time, the film is now regarded as a consummate black comedy that best exemplifies the genre's obsession with death and sex.

The madcap and macabre story of a rich kid who stages gruesomely realistic suicide scenes and a Holocaust survivor who has decided to end her eventful life on her eightieth birthday, *Harold and Maude* began its improbable life as a graduate thesis. Screenwriter Colin Higgins (*Silver Streak, Foul Play, Nine to Five*), then a twenty-eight-year-old student at UCLA, wrote a twenty-minute script and showed it to his landlady, who happened to be the wife of a producer. Thus did the offbeat idea wend its way to the screen.

Director Hal Ashby, whose father had committed suicide when he was twelve, had worked as an editor on *The Loved One,* Tony Richardson's hilariously offensive 1965 comedy set inside the funeral business. Ashby's impressive directing debut, *The Landlord,* focused on a disaffected rich kid (Beau

Bridges) who buys an apartment building and becomes fascinated by the tenants. Ashby has said he felt an immediate affinity for Higgins's disturbing yet oddly delightful story of the triumph of the life force, personified by Maude, over the deep attraction for oblivion by prematurely disillusioned Harold, a poster child for an apathetic generation.

Although Rex Reed dubbed the movie "obnoxious, sick and demented" and Roger Ebert deemed it as lifeless as a wax museum, *Harold and Maude* is now hailed as howlingly funny for the very same reasons. The highly stylized film flirts with the limits of good taste in its depiction of simulated violence. It also pushes the sexual limits—the sight of Harold and Maude in bed the morning after was simply too much for many viewers.

Today *Harold and Maude* is more often appreciated as high camp, a drolly macabre romp that goes gleefully over the grim top. Bud Cort's deadpan, dolorous performance is bitterly amusing. Gordon, a ham if there ever was one and the screen's reigning eccentric, plays the free-spirited swinger as a quaint caricature of peculiarity. Gordon almost seems to be parodying herself, much in the same way that Mae West and sometimes Marilyn Monroe played parodies of themselves.

The movie's "seize the day" message may not be original, but its style and attitude are audacious and fresh. It is the film's highly self-conscious sense of the absurd that makes us laugh even as we grimace.

We first meet Harold as he apparently prepares to meet his death. A well-dressed, somber young man, Harold solemnly hangs himself in the library of the family mansion he shares with his widowed socialite mother (Vivian Pickles). When his mother walks in and finds her son swinging from the rafters, she barely bats an eye and exhorts him to behave at the party she's throwing. "Do try to be a little more vivacious," she coolly commands the presumed cadaver, who is, in fact, faking his death for his own perverse reasons.

Harold's next simulated suicide, with fake blood graphically splattered around the bathroom, does elicit a distressed reaction from his cold, domineering mother. Fed up with his "amateur theatrics, even if they are psychologically purging," Harold's mother sends him into psychoanalysis. When the glibly detached analyst proves useless, she sends Harold to Uncle Victor, an army officer she claims was "MacArthur's right hand man." Ironically, Victor has no right arm at all, although a mechanical device in his sleeve allows him to salute, an obvious reference to Peter Sellers's mechanical arm rising of its own will into a "Heil Hitler!" salute in *Dr. Strangelove.*

Victor's advice that Harold find purpose in patriotism is as ridiculous as the analyst's. The priest Harold is sent to next is equally fatuous and ineffective. Undaunted, his mother determines that the solution to Harold's failure to

Rex Reed Hated It Bud Cort, left, and Ruth Gordon, center, in Hal Ashby's *Harold and Maude.* Mr. Reed described this 1972 black comedy as "obnoxious, sick and demented," which in this case is not necessarily a bad thing. Ignored at the time of its release, it has gained cult status over the years.

accept the responsibilities and duties of adulthood is marriage. Harold prefers funerals to weddings, however.

While engaging in his favorite pastime, Harold meets Maude, who also attends funerals for the fun of it. Afterward, just for kicks, she steals a car. When she steals Harold's hearse and offers him a ride home, a friendship is born. They picnic at demolition sites and junkyards. She asks him what flower he'd like to be. When he tells her she can't transplant a sickly tree from public property to the forest, she asks why not. She describes her history of social activism in her native Europe (never mind that she has no European accent) and shares her philosophy that life is full of opportunities and choices. They smoke pot in a hookah and dance.

"It's best not to be too moral," she tells him. "You cheat yourself of too much life. It's best to aim above morality." Later she sums up her advice: "Live! Otherwise you've got nothing to talk about in the locker room."

Slowly Harold's blank expression begins to change to one of amusement and even a hint of enjoyment. A smile begins to pull at the corners of his pouty lips. "You have a way with people," Harold tells her admiringly. "Well, they're my species," she responds gaily. When he gives her a gift, she tells him how much she loves it, then throws it into the lake. "So I'll always know where it is," she adds. And when he tells her he loves her she replies warmly, "That's wonderful. Now go and love some more." In the end, Harold does just that. He learns that we can't hold on to things, that life is to be lived in the moment. Maude has given Harold a great gift: the lust for life.

Although *Harold and Maude* is scathingly satirical in its view of traditional social institutions, its rebellious heart is sweet and light. Gloriously, garishly, wickedly extravagant, *Harold and Maude* endorses individuality and nonconformity. It acknowledges existential angst but argues for the possibility of human happiness.

Ashby, who went on to make more conventional and serious films (*The Last Detail, Shampoo, Coming Home,* and the slyly amusing *Being There*), struck a nerve with this infamously edgy comedy. The jarring juxtaposition of grisly, self-destructive violence and bleak pessimism with bubbly, giddy romance caused discomfort in many critics. But as Wes Gehring points out in *American Dark Comedy: Beyond Satire,* films that mixed genres tended to elicit to this reaction, from *The Great Dictator* to *To Be or Not to Be* to *Monsieur Verdoux.* Death had become a subject of comedy in earlier films such as *Arsenic and Old Lace, Kind Hearts and Coronets,* and *The Loved One,* but *Harold and Maude* went even farther in its morbid humor.

As black comedy became more accepted in the seventies, a cult following grew around *Harold and Maude.* By mixing screwball comedy with social satire, gallows humor with romantic comedy, *Harold and Maude* managed to be both bleak and upbeat. Aimed squarely at the youth culture, it also championed the perspective of wisdom and experience that comes with age. *Harold and Maude,* in fact, reversed the "don't trust anyone over thirty" counterculture cry. Films don't get more radical—or more comical—than this.

46

Local Hero

Enigma (1983)
CAST: Peter Riegert, Denis Lawson, Burt Lancaster, Fulton MacKay
DIRECTED BY: Bill Forsyth
112 minutes [Rated PG]

There are no belly laughs in *Local Hero,* no one-liners, gags, or pratfalls. But if this exquisitely pleasing comic treasure doesn't put a smile on your face, check your pulse to make sure you're still alive.

Comedy this graceful, gentle, and gratifying doesn't come along very often, and when it does audiences aren't always sure what to make of it. Beautifully observed, carefully paced, delicately acted, and ever so slightly daft, *Local Hero* defines a style of comedy that relies solely on charm. Written and directed by Bill Forsyth, this whimsical, wistful, slyly offbeat, and utterly delectable British comedy offers many small pleasures to be savored.

As refreshing as the ocean breeze that blows over the coastal Scottish town of Ferness, *Local Hero* is also a comedy *about* small pleasures, all the little things that make life worthwhile. It asks no less an important question than what life is all about. Is it about success, power, acquisitions? Or is it about tranquillity, natural beauty, and love? These are among the complicated questions that are not so easily answered in this wise and stimulating comedy.

When Houston oil executive Mac (Peter Riegert) is assigned to close a deal for an oil refinery to be built on an isolated bay in Scotland, he assumes the simple transaction can be done by telex. Much to his surprise, his eccentric boss, Felix Happer (Burt Lancaster), wants him to close the deal in person, reasoning that with the name MacIntire he'll be accepted by the Scots. Mac, who is actually of Hungarian ancestry (his grandfather chose the name MacIntire because he thought it sounded American), is reluctant to leave the city for a tiny village in the middle of nowhere.

When Mac arrives at the sleepy seaside village of Ferness with his corporate colleague from Edinburgh, Danny (Peter Capaldi), he's frustrated by the lack of modern conveniences. But he's optimistic that the site is suited to a refinery and encouraged by the locals' willingness to sell. Mac and Danny walk the beautiful beach, wearing suits and ties and carrying briefcases, plan-

FORSYTH SAGA Burt Lancaster, top row, left, and Peter Riegert, center row, middle, in Bill Forsyth's charming 1983 comedy, *Local Hero.*

ning their strategy, showing not an inkling of remorse over the natural beauty that is about to be spoiled or the bucolic lives that will be disrupted.

The locals, who work hard trying to scrape by, are keen to sell their property and are secretly planning to soak the rich oil company for all it's worth. Gordon Urquhart (Denis Lawson), who owns the local inn and is the town's unofficial mayor, lawyer, and accountant, is especially eager to get rich quick. Gordon enjoys his quiet life, however, and uses his plentiful free time to make love to his wife whenever he gets the notion. Gordon does have some reservations about selling the town. "We won't have a place to call home, but we'll be stinkin' rich," he observes ruefully.

As Mac allows Gordon to negotiate with the residents to arrive at a fair price, and Gordon stalls to drive up the price, a change gradually comes over Mac. He walks on the beach, now wearing a sweater, collecting shells in a tidal pool. He takes off his watch and sets it on a rock. Later we see the incoming tide washing over his beeping electronic symbol of fast-paced modern life. Mac has also been instructed to observe the night sky by his boss, an avid amateur astronomer, and he finds himself dazzled by meteor showers and the aurora borealis.

Mac begins to fall under the spell of the rustic village as he gets to know the quirky inhabitants. He's fascinated by the black minister from Africa who arrived as a student missionary and never left. He finds a kindred spirit in the boisterous Russian fisherman who comes to town to have a good time. Mac's partner, Danny, falls in love with a web-toed marine biologist. Mac also finds himself drawn to Gordon's sexy and sweet wife, Stella.

Mac slows down and falls sway to the sleepy rhythms of rural life. He finds himself seduced by the town's allure and begins to question the wisdom of replacing pristine beauty with an ugly refinery. One night after a town shindig—the lively Ceilidh—he drunkenly approaches Gordon with a proposition, offering to trade lives. Gordon can go to Houston, drive the Porsche, and pull down eighty grand a year. He'll stay here, run the inn, do bits of business and live with the lovely Stella. It's a joke with more truth than either man will admit.

The negotiations hit a snag when Gordon discovers that the beach itself is owned by the eccentric Ben (Fulton MacKay), who lives in a shack by the shore. Ben has no interest in selling the beach that has sustained him and that he regards as his sacred trust. Ben does not see how one can put a value on a beach that has been there since time immemorial. When asked what he thinks the entire bay is worth, Ben just laughs at the absurdity of the question.

Back in Houston, Happer is having a problem with the nutty psychiatrist he's hired to try an unconventional form of abuse therapy and who refuses to be fired. To escape the out-of-control shrink and intrigued by Mac's descriptions of the activity in the Scottish sky, Happer flies in to close the deal with Ben himself. The skygazer and the beachcomber prove to be soulmates, and together they devise a much more appropriate use for the bay. Mac is sent back to Houston, where the skyline from his balcony no longer holds the glamour it held before his transformative trip.

Much of the film's subtle humor stems from the low-key performances. Riegert's laconic attitude allows us to see the gradual changes taking place in him. It's an unhurried, unforced performance that seems to just happen, which is precisely the desired effect. Riegert again used this seeming passivity and stillness to great advantage in the engaging romantic comedy *Crossing Delancey.*

Fresh from the success of *Atlantic City,* Lancaster also refrains from hamming it up in the flashy role of a capricious millionaire with his head in the clouds. The comedy is filled with understated comic characterizations, played with casual, affable ease.

In style, *Local Hero* is a throwback to the chipper, brisk, civilized British comedies of the forties and fifties, particularly the Ealing comedies of Alexander Mackendrick such as *Whisky Galore/Tight Little Island.* But Forsyth's quirky vision is more affectionate and warmer. His singular style is modest and self-effacing, and he instructs his cast to throw away the best jokes. He takes a standard setup—corporate America seeks to despoil nature—and moves the story in unexpected directions, steering clear of clichés and avoiding the obvious.

As Sheila Benson observed in the *Los Angeles Times,* the comic fable "works delicately against every one of our preconceived notions for pictures of this sort." *Local Hero* earned similarly rapturous reviews from the vast majority of American and British critics who succumbed to its serene appeal. The *Village Voice* applauded its "artistry, charm, finesse, amiability and deadpan hilarity." The *Christian Science Monitor* found it "a magical film . . . from the wry beginning to the bittersweet finale." *New York* magazine's David Denby declared Forsyth "a director with a comic vision of his own, a way of seeing the world that is funny or odd down to its roots. This director is beginning to create a world that operates according to laws that he alone could give it." Roger Ebert gave the comedy four stars and praised it as "loving, funny and understated." Only Rex Reed of the *New York Post* cast a dissenting vote: "The acting is terrible . . . the pace is slow enough to make a snail impatient."

Forsyth was named best director by the British Academy Awards, and his screenplay was honored by the National Society of Film Critics and the New York Film Critics. Although Forysth had earned minor acclaim for *That Sinking Feeling* and *Gregory's Girl, Local Hero* was his first major hit, produced by *Chariots of Fire's* David Putnam. Forsyth went on to make the amusing British comedy about a popular Scottish disc jockey, *Comfort and Joy,* followed by his first American film, *Housekeeping,* a comic drama starring Christine Lahti as an eccentric aunt. Working from a John Sayles script, Forsyth cast Burt Reynolds in his first quirky character role in the curious and only sporadically successful comedy *Breaking In.* Forsyth again proved his originality in *Being Human,* an uneven comedy starring Robin Williams as five men at five different historical periods.

Local Hero remains Forsyth's masterpiece, a film whose plot has been emulated in recent years by 1997's *The Matchmaker,* in which an aggressive American urbanite (Janeane Garofalo) travels to a remote Irish village on business and, in spite of herself, falls for a local hero. But a movie as slippery and strange as *Local Hero* can never be imitated, nor can its enticing enchantment be duplicated.

47

Airplane!

Paramount (1980)
CAST: Peter Graves, Robert Hays, Julie Hagerty, Robert Stack,
Lloyd Bridges, Leslie Nielsen, Kareem Abdul-Jabbar
DIRECTED BY: Jim Abrahams, David Zucker, and Jerry Zucker
86 minutes [Rated PG]

There is no doubt that *Airplane!* revolutionized film comedy, although not everyone would agree that the trend it instigated elevated the American cinema. Although *Airplane!* was not the screen's first parody, its success not only propelled its makers to stardom, but produced an onslaught of gag-laden comedies lampooning every conceivable film genre, style, or hit.

Parodies of popular movies have existed since the days of silent film, when Buster Keaton, Ben Turpin, and Will Rogers were among several film artists to parody current films. Mack Sennett especially delighted in spoofing D. W. Griffith's melodramas. Parody, which had fallen from favor, made a comeback in the contemporary cinema with Woody Allen's Japanese monster travesty *What's Up, Tiger Lily?* (1966) and the popular western spoofs *Cat Ballou* (1965) and Mel Brooks's *Blazing Saddles* (1974), which really got the ball rolling. *Blazing Saddles* was followed by Brooks's brilliant horror spoof, *Young Frankenstein* (1974), and his inventive Hitchcock rip-off, *High Anxiety* (1977).

Airplane!, however, created a potent new formula for parody. Instead of casting comedians, parody pioneers Jim Abrahams and Jerry and David Zucker—a writing-directing-producing team collectively known as ZAZ—peopled their spoof of aviation disaster movies with has-beens and newcomers. TV veterans from earlier decades—Lloyd Bridges, Robert Stack, Peter Graves, and Leslie Nielsen—were paired with the fresh faces of Robert Hays and Julie Hagerty, who both made their screen debuts in *Airplane!*.

All of the actors essentially play it straight, somberly delivering the most ridiculous lines and earnestly indulging in outrageous sight gags. Credited with raising the art of deadpan humor to its comical zenith, *Airplane!* is a gleefully goofy gag fest made funnier by the performers' gravity.

The jokes keep flying in *Airplane!,* a loony compendium of outrageous, ridiculous clichés. The humor ranges from subtle to sledgehammer, from sexual innuendo to gross-out jokes, from sophomoric to almost sophisticated. Fast-paced, short, and cheesy looking, *Airplane!* was greeted with surprising acclaim by the critics, who called the film "a remedy for bloated self-importance," "clever, confident and furiously energetic," and "firmly disciplined." The Writers Guild of America bestowed its award for best adapted screenplay on this inspired send-up of earlier movies.

The plot of the satirical disaster film is loosely based on 1957's *Zero Hour,* in which a plane's pilots are felled by ptomaine poisoning. *Zero Hour* was adapted from a short story written by Arthur Hailey, whose best-seller *Airport* was turned into the ultimate aviation disaster thriller and spawned several sequels. *Airport* (1970), a heavy-handed, simple-minded, slick entertainment that featured an all-star cast, also became an object of ridicule in *Airplane!*

Airplane!, which does not restrict itself to parodying the aviation genre, begins with a credit sequence set to music from *Jaws,* with a plane's back "fin" ominously emerging and disappearing into the clouds. At the airport all the familiar elements from life as well as movies are assembled, from Hare Krishnas to a little girl en route to the Mayo Clinic (where jars of "mayo" sit on the desk) for a kidney transplant (a plot device neatly pilfered from *Airport 1975*).

The satirical romantic drama centers on Ted Striker (Hays), a former flier so traumatized by his wartime experience that he is mortally afraid of flying. He boards the plane only in a last-ditch effort to win back his lady love, the sweet stewardess Elaine (Hagerty). Naturally, when the time comes, he will be forced to land the troubled airliner.

In the cockpit, Captain Clarence Oveur (Peter Graves) solemnly talks to ground control, confusing his navigator, Roger (Kareem Abdul-Jabbar), every time he says "roger." Oblivious of his words, the straight-faced, straitlaced captain keeps saying things like "What's our vector, Victor?" And when a little boy comes to visit, the captain shows his prurient interest by asking the lad sexually provocative questions such as "Do you like gladiator movies?"

In the cabin, a nun reads *Boy's Life* while a boy reads *Nun's Life.* The multilingual sign flashes "Putana da Seatbeltz." Two black men talk in jive so incomprehensible, it is subtitled. When a passenger asks for some light reading material, she's handed a tiny pamphlet, "Great Jewish Sports Legends." Ted tells his tale of woe to anyone who will listen, and flashbacks detail his experience in the Peace Corps, where he sold Tupperware to African natives and introduced them to basketball. The flashbacks also include a spectacular send-up of the disco scene from *Saturday Night Fever.*

Soon everyone who had fish for dinner is ill, and the call for a doctor on board is answered by Dr. Rumack, played by Leslie Nielsen, who has a small

FROM HERE TO INSANITY Julie Hagerty and Robert Hays, covered in kelp, in 1980's *Airplane!,* which set the tone for cinematic spoofs that continues to this day. It also jump-started the career of Leslie Nielsen. Howard Thompson, film critic for the *New York Times,* found *Airplane!* ". . . a howl. Truly."

role but some of the best lines. "Surely you can't be serious," the captain says. "I am serious, and don't call me Shirley," replies Nielsen, whose career was jump-started by this comedic role, which led to his casting in a successful series of follow-up parodies.

The script features one wonderful play on words after another. The following exchange is typical ZAZ fun: "There's a problem in the cockpit!" "What is it?" "It's a little room in the front of the plane." The problem in the cockpit is that there's no one left to fly the plane, and the automatic pilot is an inflatable doll that keeps deflating. Luckily Ted is one of the only passengers who did not eat the fish and is able to manage the lousiest landing in aviation history, thus concluding the frivolous foolishness.

Airplane! was the directorial debut of ZAZ, who also wrote and produced the high-flying comedy. The ZAZ team met while students at the University of Wisconsin at Madison and formed a comedy troupe called the Kentucky Fried Theater, which combined improvised skits with filmed satirical sketches. The

Zucker brothers and Abrahams moved the company to Los Angeles and wrote *Kentucky Fried Movie* in 1977. An underground hit, the independently produced comedy is a series of sketches lampooning American culture, particularly TV shows and commercials. *Kentucky Fried Movie* was also the directorial debut of John Landis, who went on to direct the revolutionary youth-oriented comedy classic *Animal House* and made the hugely popular comedies *The Blues Brothers* and *Trading Places*.

Following the astounding success of their own directorial debut, *Airplane!*, ZAZ released *Top Secret* (1984), a very clever spoof of espionage movies. They deviated from parody in their next film, *Ruthless People* (1986), a first-rate farce based on a story by O. Henry. They then cowrote and coproduced *The Naked Gun: From the Files of the Police Squad*, starring Nielsen and directed by David Zucker, who then wrote and directed *Naked Gun 2½: The Smell of Fear*, which was coproduced by ZAZ. The partnership dissolved as each team member began to pursue solo careers.

Jerry Zucker scored a smash hit with his blend of comedy, romance, and suspense, *Ghost* (1990). Abrahams went solo with *Big Business* in 1988 and *Welcome Home, Roxy Carmichael*. He returned to parody with *Hot Shots!* (1991), a spoof of *Top Gun*, followed by *Hot Shots! Part Deux*, a parody of *Rambo*, and 1998's *Mafia*. David Zucker spoofed sports movies in the flagrantly sophomoric 1998 comedy, *BASEketball*.

But while members of the ZAZ team continued to mine gold from film genre parody, which became a genre of its own, they were not alone. *Airplane II: The Sequel* (1982) reunited the cast but was directed by Ken Finkleman. John Landis went the parody route with *¡Three Amigos!* in 1986. Nielsen starred in *Spy Hard* (1997), a *Die Hard* meets James Bond spoof directed by Rick Friedberg.

Carl Reiner directed *Fatal Instinct*, his spoof of *Basic Instinct*, in 1993, the same year National Lampoon got into the parody act spoofing *Lethal Weapon* in *Loaded Weapon*. Mel Brooks has continued to perform his own brand of parody in movies such as his *Star Wars* spoof, *Spaceballs*, (1987) and the swashbuckling send-up *Robin Hood: Men in Tights* (1993).

There's no end in sight to parody, a form of cinematic cannibalism that feeds off itself. At its best, however, parody reminds us of how much we love movies, with all their silly conventions, predictable plots, and absurdly unrealistic situations. *Airplane!* still soars smoothly high above the rest in the comic clouds, untroubled by the turbulence that has affected so many of its competitors flying the funny skies.

48

Beverly Hills Cop

Paramount (1984)
CAST: Eddie Murphy, Judge Reinhold, John Ashton,
James Russo, Bronson Pinchot
DIRECTED BY: Martin Brest
105 minutes [Rated R]

Dirty Harry with a sense of humor, Eddie Murphy's Axel Foley is a renegade cop who breaks all the rules to get the job done. While Clint Eastwood never so much as cracks a smile, Murphy makes us laugh as he resorts to brazen charades and outrageous scams to solve the case in *Beverly Hills Cop.*

Although the role of Axel Foley was originally intended for Mickey Rourke and was offered to Sylvester Stallone before Murphy was considered, the part of the maverick cop appears tailor-made for the rising comedy star, then only twenty-three. Murphy, known to *Saturday Night Live* audiences for his mimicry and quick comic character sketches, masterfully assumes a series of disguises as Axel crashes the gates of swanky society, armed with bluster, bravado, and comic banter. Riding high on attitude, Murphy is at his irreverent, indomitable best in this culture-clash comedy, which remains his funniest film and his best role.

One of Hollywood's biggest blockbusters, *Beverly Hills Cop* remains a prime example of the increasingly popular action comedy hybrid. The action comedy combination had frequently been seen in the silent era, particularly in Buster Keaton's films. And although *The Thin Man* series of the thirties, starring witty sleuths Nick and Nora Charles, were short on violence and special effects by today's standards, they were suspenseful whodunits that smoothly blended screwball comedy into the typically mirthless murder mystery genre.

Beverly Hills Cop was not only a trendsetting contemporary comedy action film, but also the first to feature a comic cop. Although comedians had been cast in a few action films before *Beverly Hills Cop,* in these previous ventures they tended to be featured as either criminals or hapless bystanders who get drawn into criminal activity. In fact, two years before being cast as the street-smart Detroit cop who takes a working vacation in Beverly Hills, Murphy had

L.A. LAW Judge Reinhold, left, and Eddie Murphy in *Beverly Hills Cop* (1984). Back-to-back hits *Trading Places* and *48 Hrs.* put Murphy squarely on the movie map; *Beverly Hills Cop* propelled him to superstar status and spawned two sequels.

made his debut in *48 Hrs.*, playing a street-smart crook who is sprung from jail for forty-eight hours to help burnt-out cop Nick Nolte solve a crime.

Although *48 Hrs.* became a monster hit and helped generate a series of buddy-buddy action comedies, it was not the first film of the modern era to merge violence with humor. The modern mania for car crashes coupled with chuckles was ushered in with the James Bond films, beginning with 1962's *Dr. No,* which infused the thrill-a-minute action formula with tongue-in-cheek humor. But the wildly successful action comedy formula so popular today was first employed in 1976's *Silver Streak,* a Hitchcock-style thriller starring comic Gene Wilder as a mild-mannered book editor who becomes embroiled in a deadly murder mystery aboard the Amtrak train from Los Angeles to Chicago. Director Arthur Hiller's experimental amalgam of mayhem and humor was a smash hit that, perhaps not coincidentally, starred another black comedian as a crook who helps the white guy to solve the crime, as Murphy was to do four years later in *48 Hrs.*

Richard Pryor, who was Murphy's mentor, appears late in *Silver Streak* but was so richly funny in the role that he was again paired with Wilder in 1980's *Stir Crazy,* a very funny action comedy about two buddies who accidentally land in jail and manage a daring escape. Wilder and Pryor were less felicitously reteamed in *See No Evil, Hear No Evil* (1989) and *Another You* (1991). The reigning black comic actor of the seventies and early eighties, Pryor did some of his best work in his two concert films, *Richard Pryor—Live in Concert* (1979) and *Richard Pryor Live on the Sunset Strip* (1982). The brilliant, volatile comedian was struggling to regain his health and revive his career following his drug-related, near death accident when Eddie Murphy burst on the scene and supplanted him in popularity with back-to-back performances in *48 Hrs.* and *Trading Places.*

Murphy is all moxie, less vulnerable than Pryor, flaunting his sexuality and projecting a machismo appeal tinged with arrogance. Just as profane and foul-mouthed as Pryor, but with less of an underpinning of anger and pain, Murphy became known as a sassy, swaggering punk who wasn't about to let anyone push him around.

In his third film Murphy found the perfect role and his first positive black role model in Axel Foley, a cocky, scruffy brother from the inner city who is able to show up all the lily white and lily-livered gentry living in Lala Land. Axel, who can't be intimidated or outsmarted, is sharper, tougher, and a lot more fun to be around than anyone on the screen with him. The entire supporting cast serves as his collective straight man, with the sole exception of Bronson Pinchot, who does a hilarious satire of affectation playing Serge, who works in a posh art gallery and speaks with an incomprehensible and unidentifiable accent. (The film pokes more fun at arty pretensions when Axel takes one look at the paintings and bursts out laughing.)

Serge is the only character allowed to be funnier than Axel, a wiseguy who hasn't lost touch with his wild side while engaged in law enforcement. A gifted prankster—the banana in the tailpipe trick is an all-time classic—Axel is also not one to carry a grudge. Once he outwits the real Beverly Hills cops, he extends his hand to them and forms a professional partnership, although he is always clearly in charge. An ultimately amiable guy, Axel is a winning character, cheeky and defiant yet likable.

Director Martin Brest, working from Daniel Petrie Jr.'s Oscar-nominated script, puts the emphasis on humor in this hip and raucous "fish out of water" comedy. The gunplay, fistfights, car chases, explosions, and assorted high-tech stunts that typically occupy a central place in action comedies such as the *Lethal Weapon* series and many of Arnold Schwarzenegger's films are kept to a minimum in *Beverly Hills Cop.* Axel relies less on physical prowess or ammunition than on his ability to bamboozle, bluff, and bully.

The film's warmth also lies in the way it treats the button-down, by-the-book members of the Beverly Hills police force. Although they initially regard Axel—dressed in cutoff sweat shirt, jeans, and sneakers—with suspicion, they gradually begin to appreciate his unconventional methods and his ability to operate on his instincts. Sweet-faced Billy Rosewood (Judge Reinhold) is the first to succumb to Axel's brash style, but his gruff partner, Taggart (John Ashton), also eventually recognizes the method in Axel's blatant disregard for departmental procedure. Even their genteel boss, Lieutenant Bogomil (Ronny Cox), finally backs Axel after he has single-handedly blown the case wide open by bringing down the smarmy art dealer–cum–drug smuggler who murdered Axel's old friend.

Beverly Hills Cop, which ends with Axel being "escorted" out of town by his new buddies, brought a smile to the faces of most of the nation's critics. The *Christian Science Monitor* proclaimed Axel to be "one of the most engaging characters in recent memory . . . a people's hero all the way." The *Los Angeles Times* declared that "the movie sparkles with intelligence. Crackling with energy, it races, skitters and leaps along, dragging you unresisting in its wake." *Newsweek* observed that "the movie is as brazen, charming and mercurial as Murphy himself, which is to say it is unimaginable without him."

Murphy went on to make the disappointing sequels *Beverly Hills Cop II* (1987), which he cowrote, *Beverly Hills Cop III,* and *Another 48 Hrs.* (1990). He has been sporadically funny in his subsequent films, most recently turning to the family film market with his loose adaptation of Jerry Lewis's *The Nutty Professor* and his even looser remake of *Dr. Dolittle.* He has never lived up to his early promise, however, or topped his freewheeling performance in *Beverly Hills Cop.*

The practice of casting comics in action films escalated following the huge commercial success of *Beverly Hills Cop.* Director Martin Brest returned to the genre in 1988 with another of the best action comedies, *Midnight Run,* featuring Charles Grodin as an accountant who has stolen Mob money and donated it to charity, and Robert De Niro as the bounty hunter and former cop charged with bringing him in. Brest recruited *Beverly Hills Cop* costar John Ashton to play De Niro's bounty-hunting rival.

Comic Billy Crystal teamed with Gregory Hines as unorthodox Chicago cops out to crack one last case in the amusing *Running Scared* (1986). In 1987 Richard Dreyfuss and Emilio Estevez played detectives in the above average comedy thriller *Stakeout.* In that same year Mel Gibson and Danny Glover were paired as wisecracking cops for the first of four *Lethal Weapon* films, with Joe Pesci providing additional comic relief in all but the first one.

All of these comic cop dramas owe a debt to *Beverly Hills Cop,* which influenced virtually all future action films. Ever since Axel Foley set the trend, it has become imperative for all movie cops to utter funny lines in between the business of busting bad guys.

49

Bull Durham

Orion (1988)
CAST: Kevin Costner, Susan Sarandon, Tim Robbins, Trey Wilson, Robert Wuhl
DIRECTED BY: Ron Shelton
108 minutes [Rated R]

Sunny, strange, sexy *Bull Durham* is a comedy about love, baseball, and the love of baseball. In other words, it's a comic fusion of America's two favorite pastimes.

One of the most amusing and erotic romantic comedies of recent memory, *Bull Durham* also ranks among the wittiest sports movies ever made. Director Ron Shelton's deliciously literate and deliriously jocular script exudes a brazen affection for its wonderfully curious characters and bursts with awe and admiration for the Zen of baseball. Shelton expresses uncommon insight into human nature in all its follies and peculiar passions while he evokes the world of minor league baseball with rare accuracy, summoning the sounds and smells and sights that make the game so irresistible.

Susan Sarandon stars in this out-of-the-park hit comedy about a devout fan who has tried many religions but has come to find that the only one that satisfies the soul, day after day, is "the church of baseball." Annie, who prefers metaphysics to theology, worships not only the sport, but the men who spend their adult lives playing a kids' game. Every season she picks one promising player from the minor league team in her hometown of Durham, North Carolina, and takes him under her wing and into her bed.

"There's never been a player who slept with me who didn't have the best season of their career," she rightfully boasts. Annie gives these boys of summer confidence, imparting both sound advice and her own life wisdom, maturing them through her amorous private mentoring program. She doesn't get much in return from the 142-game affair, but bad trades are a part of baseball, she observes philosophically.

As the Durham Bulls begin a new season, Annie sizes up the two most auspicious candidates for her personal spring training. Ebby Calhoon LaLoosh (Sarandon's real-life partner, Tim Robbins) is a wild young thing, a pitcher with a million-dollar arm and a five-cent head. A loose cannon, Ebby has loads of natural talent but no control. On his first day on the mound he sets a new league record for walks as well as strikes. He hits the mascot twice and the sports announcer once. Annie is not the only one to realize Ebby could use some seasoning—as well as a nickname. The Bulls' manager (Trey Wilson) brings in a veteran catcher to mature the hotheaded kid, whom Annie dubs "Nuke," presumably for his explosive potential and tendency to melt down.

"I'm the player to be named later," catcher Crash Davis (Kevin Costner) announces as he shows up to play for the Durham Bulls. Crash is none too pleased to be baby-sitting a player headed for the major leagues while he winds down his respectable career in the minors.

Annie is impressed with Crash's impromptu speech about his beliefs—he believes in "the soul, high fiber, good Scotch, that Lee Harvey Jr. acted alone, that the novels of Susan Sontag are self-indulgent trash, and in long, slow, wet kisses that last three days," among other things. Crash is also taken with Annie, a very sensual and frank woman who, like him, is a seasoned veteran who is unusually perceptive about the inner and outer game of baseball. But Crash is too old to audition and doesn't like competing with an immature boy for Annie's affection, which makes Annie's decision easier.

By default Annie settles on Nuke, who is badly in need of some guidance. Annie helps Nuke focus his erratic energy and helps him appreciate the finer points of baseball. Crash also teaches him to respect himself and the sport. Like Annie, he passes on his own oddball theories. "Fast balls are boring and fascist," he tells Nuke, teaching him to throw the "more democratic" ground ball. In one of the film's many hilarious scenes, Crash also teaches him the right lyrics to "Try a Little Tenderness." "Young girls do not get woolly," he bellows. "They get weary!" Later he tells Nuke that baseball should be played with a combination of fear and arrogance. "Right, fear and ignorance," Nuke replies, this time deliberately testing Crash's patience.

Under the tutelage of Annie and Crash, Nuke does start to live up to his potential. The Durham Bulls start to play with poetry, precision, and joy. Nuke and Crash begin to form a friendship. On a road trip Crash answers the team's prayers for a rain-out by turning the sprinklers on the field at night. Crash, who takes baseball as seriously as Annie, also knows that the essential appeal of the game is that it is fun. We see the fun-loving side of Crash when he leads his teammates through a midnight mud spree on the soaking field.

Annie is thrilled to see her beloved team finally winning but is more than a little miffed when Nuke superstitiously decides that having sex with her will jinx the winning streak. She also begins to suspect that she's picked the wrong guy.

The sweetly nostalgic yet utterly contemporary and hip comedy comes

CURVEBALL   Kevin Costner and Susan Sarandon in Ron Shelton's 1988 *Bull Durham,* a rare foray into comedy for both. Sarandon and costar Tim Robbins became lovers off screen following the film's release.

sliding into home plate when Nuke is called up to "the show" and Crash is let go so a promising young catcher can take his place. With nowhere left to go, Crash shows up at Annie's place. In one of the cinema's most arousing vignettes, Annie and Crash spend a memorable night together. They make love, eat ice cream, dance, and take a bath by candlelight, and Crash paints Annie's toenails. It's your basic dream date.

Crash moves on to complete his "dubious distinction" of hitting the most home runs in the minors but returns to Annie at the film's touching fade-out. Nuke carries on their dream of big-time baseball glory, proving, "The world is made for people who aren't cursed with self-awareness."

There's a rueful undercurrent in Shelton's dazzlingly droll screenplay, which teeters on the edge of farce but never steps over the line. Certainly the characters are incredibly colorful and often speak with an eloquence and wit that tests the limits of audience belief. Still, the magnetic performances are so assured and brimming with life that we accept and embrace the extraordinary creatures simply because we enjoy their company so much.

Shelton, who played second base in the Baltimore Orioles' farm system for five years and made it to triple-A ball before writing *Under Fire* and the football movie *The Best of Times* for director Roger Spottiswoode, has said he left the game because he didn't want to become a Crash Davis. The story is based on the first screenplay he wrote, in 1979, titled *The Player to Be Named Later*. For his highly atmospheric directing debut, Shelton shrewdly chose to return to a subject he knew firsthand.

Shelton and Costner collaborated again in the sex-and-sports romantic comedy *Tin Cup,* about a has-been golfer who gets a second chance at the big time. Although the milieu is rendered authentically and the screenplay brims with wit, *Tin Cup* is a not as winning a comedy as *Bull Durham*.

A grand slam hit with audiences, *Bull Durham* scored with critics as well. "What's this? A movie with dirt under its nails, lust in its heart and a sense of humor that comes from the marrow of the funny bone? Could it be a summer movie that's actually for grown-ups?" David Ansen wondered in *Newsweek*. The *Los Angeles Times* applauded Shelton for "showing off a rowdy knowledgeability in the fiercely funny baseball scenes" and for the movie's poignancy and sensuality. David Denby, who adored Sarandon's "lustrous and flamboyant" performance, observed, "Genuine writing in American movies is now so rare that some of us may enjoy hearing a line of exuberantly composed dialogue even if it isn't all that good."

Shelton wisely cast sensitive actors in his robust and ribald comedy, giving the comedy much needed emotional grounding. *Bull Durham* gave a huge boost to the careers of its three stars, all of whom quickly became major Hollywood hitters following the come-from-behind victory of the low-budget comedy by a first-time director. Costner's association with baseball continued in his next film, the wildly popular fable *Field of Dreams* (1989). Although he displayed fine comic sensibilities playing the cynical but smolderingly sexy catcher in *Bull Durham*—and was very funny in Lawrence Kasdan's *Silverado*—Costner has made only rare forays into comedy in the ensuing years.

Sarandon has also preferred flexing her dramatic muscles in films such as

Thelma and Louise, Lorenzo's Oil, and *Dead Man Walking,* although she often brings lusty vivaciousness to her roles. Much of the credit for the success of *Bull Durham* lies with Sarandon's ability to take a male sexual fantasy figure and turn her into a flesh-and-blood woman.

Robbins, an intelligent actor with the rare ability to play dumb, has gone on to do fine work in dark comedies such as Robert Altman's *The Player* and *Short Cuts, Bob Roberts* (which Robbins also directed), and the Coen brothers' *The Hudsucker Proxy.* He also appeared opposite Meg Ryan and Walter Matthau (as Einstein) in the bright and cheery romantic comedy *I.Q.* His performance as the goofy, dim-bulb pitcher with lightning in his arm in *Bull Durham* remains one of the best in his comic canon, however. Even his pitch is funny.

Shelton relishes details such as the pitch but avoids the usual clichés of the game. There are no "the bases are loaded at the bottom of the ninth" scenes. There is, however, a hilarious encounter on the pitcher's mound, when the irate manager sends out his upbeat, motor-mouthed coach (Robert Wuhl) to see why half the team is gathered in conference. Crash explains the dilemma, which centers on how to remove a curse that has been placed on a player's bat and the forthcoming marriage of the team's devout Christian (William O'Leary) to an adorably amoral groupie (Jenny Robertson). As this wacky scene reveals, *Bull Durham* does not play by the usual rules for sports movies.

The movies have been making sport with sports since the dawn of cinema. Harold Lloyd had fun with football in his silent classic *The Freshman,* and the Marx Brothers ran with the ball in *Horse Feathers.* The list of sports comedies is almost as long as the list of sports dramas, with earlier baseball comedies *The Bad News Bears, It Happens Every Spring, The Bingo Long Traveling All-Stars & Motor Kings, Woman of the Year,* and *Damn Yankees* at the top. Although recent comedies have tackled every sport, from bobsledding (*Cool Runnings*) to basketball (*White Men Can't Jump*), for some reason sports comedies have focused more often on baseball than any other sport. Perhaps it's because there's something inherently lighthearted and silly and engaging about the game.

Bull Durham, which came out of left field, revitalized the baseball movie, which has not had a particularly good batting average in Hollywood. Recent years, however, have seen the popular success of *Major League* and *Major League II, Little Big League; A League of Their Own, Angels in the Outfield,* and *The Scout. Bull Durham,* however, is still the most brilliantly executed and craziest curveball yet to be thrown on the Hollywood diamond.

50

Smiles of a Summer Night

Svensk Film (1955)
Cast: Gunnar Bjornstrand, Ulla Jacobsson, Bjorn Bjelvenstam,
Eva Dahlbeck, Harriet Andersson, Jarl Kulle
Directed by: Ingmar Bergman
108 minutes [Not rated]

Although Ingmar Bergman is largely known for his brooding cinematic expressions of psychic angst and human torment, the acclaimed Swedish director was catapulted to international stardom by a comedy. *Smiles of a Summer Night,* a work of great gaiety and mirth, not only established Bergman as a leading light of the world cinema, but remains one of his most perfectly realized films.

Without a doubt, Bergman's formidable reputation as a film artist rests on such probing, unsparing dramas as *The Seventh Seal, Wild Strawberries, Persona, Through a Glass Darkly, Cries and Whispers,* and *Scenes from a Marriage.* Known for his bleak worldview, his propensity for despair, his morbid fascination with death, his existential questioning, and his earnest use of symbolism, Bergman has cut a towering figure in the European art cinema and is credited with ushering in the age of the auteur.

Smiles of a Summer Night, the best known of Bergman's rare comedies, is also widely regarded as one of the finest romantic comedies ever made, proving that genius knows no genre boundaries. A sparkling comedy that owes much to the French cinema of Ophüls and Renoir as well as to French stage comedy, *Smiles of a Summer Night* details the amorous adventures of eight aristocrats over the course of a long weekend. Bergman, who has divided his time between the theater and film, has said he admires classical French farce but mourns their lack of meaning. *Smiles of a Summer Night* is the fulfillment of his desire to create a meaningful sex farce. Indeed, beneath the frivolity and foolishness of this spirited tale of tangled passions lies a layer of anguish. *Smiles of a Summer Night* is proof that human suffering is a fitting subject for comedy.

Set in 1901, the story begins in the home of the well-heeled lawyer Frederick Egerman (Gunnar Bjornstrand) and his child bride, Anne (Ulla Jacobs-

SWEDISH MEATBALLS   We generally don't think of Ingmar Bergman movies as big yuk fests. It was for that reason that Bergman made *Smiles of a Summer Night*—to prove to the world that he did, in fact, have a sense of humor.

son), who is still a virgin after two years of marriage. Frederick has a sullen and lovesick son, Henrik (Bjorn Bjelvenstam), who is the same age as Anne, whom he married following the death of his first wife. He also has a former mistress, the popular stage actress Desiree Armfeldt (Eva Dahlbeck).

Clearly frustrated with his unconsummated marriage, Frederick arrives home with tickets for the theater. He suggests a nap before leaving, and while sleeping fully clothed next to his chaste wife, he begins to caress her, murmuring the name Desiree. At the theater Anne gets a glimpse of her rival and leaves the theater in tears. Frederick takes his wife home and returns to the theater, presumably to seek Desiree's advice. Desiree, who clearly still loves Frederick, invites him home with her. On the way to her home, Frederick slips in a puddle and ends up wearing a robe and nightshirt belonging to Desiree's current married lover, Count Carl-Magnus Malcolm (Jarl Kulle), who appears unexpectedly and throws Frederick from the house in his nightshirt.

The next day Desiree visits her rich, eccentric mother (wonderfully played by Naima Wifstrand) and asks her to invite both her current lover and her former lover and their wives to her estate for the weekend. Desiree, operating on the assumption that "men never know what's best for them," hatches a plan to win back Frederick and enlists her lover's wife, Charlotte, in her scheme.

The invariable complications arise in the ensuing romantic roundelay, which ends with Henrik and Anne running off together, Frederick and Carl-Magnus engaged in a game of Russian roulette, and the maid Petra (Harriet Andersson) engaged to the lusty coachman.

Smiles of a Summer Night delights in deflating the pomposity of its male characters. Decorum, propriety, and the utter emotional incompetence of men are subjected to vicious satire in this merciless exposé of vanity in all its forms. Frederick is a mincing, stuffy, supercilious professor whose dignity is routinely trammeled by humiliations and embarrassments. Carl-Magnus is an officious, jealous military man whose arrogant self-importance is the source of much humor. Henrik, a theology student, is also self-absorbed, morose, and confused.

Bergman may make brutal fun of the men in his comedy, but he obviously identifies with their follies, hence the film's sympathy for its silly characters. The film reflects Bergman's own troubled relations with his wives, children, and parents. His feelings of failure as a father are most overtly manifested in Frederick, who is cuckolded by his own son. Like Henrik, whom Frederick regularly ridicules, Bergman is a famously depressed personality. The product of an unhappy childhood, Bergman reports that from an early age he was considered "sullen and sensitive," while his brother delighted in making people laugh.

In his autobiography Bergman acknowledges that he turned to comedy in part to prove that despite his dolorous personality he did have a sense of humor. He also admits he made *Smiles of a Summer Night* to make money. "This does not embarrass me in the least," he writes. "Most projects in the world of film come into being for that very reason."

Bergman began working on the script during a vacation at a Swiss resort that he found unbearably depressing. He was seriously contemplating suicide when he was called back to Sweden to work on the script for *Last Couple Out*. When he returned to work on *Smiles of a Summer Night*, his spirits were much improved and he was able to invest the story with comic warmth and wit. Still, the film's underpinning of sorrow and sarcasm gives it depth and bite.

"This comedy may have been a tragedy but the gods were kind," Bergman had written of his earlier comedy, *A Lesson in Love,* a statement that also applies to *Smiles of a Summer Night.* The precarious relationship between tragedy and comedy is best illustrated in one of the film's funniest scenes, in which Henrik becomes so despondent over his unrequited love for his father's wife that he attempts to hang himself. He falls against a secret device—installed by a king to arrange for trysts with his lover—that causes Anne's bed to be delivered into his room through a hidden door. Thus does suffering lead, however accidentally, to fulfilled desire in this heady mixture of sentimentality and ridicule.

"An incredible confection of lyricism, farce, fantasy, satire and naturalism," is how the *New Statesman* aptly described the comedy. Although the film opened without much fanfare in Sweden, it won the Special Jury Prize at the Cannes Film Festival and soon enjoyed enormous acclaim on the American and European arthouse circuit.

Smiles of a Summer Night, Bergman's international breakthrough, has also proved a seminal comedy. It inspired Steven Sondheim's Broadway musical *A Little Night Music* and served as the basis of Woody Allen's *A Midsummer Night's Sex Comedy.* Allen, a filmmaker also given to gloomy introspection, had paid tribute to Bergman in 1978's *Interiors,* a humorless and unpleasant drama that failed to find favor with audiences or critics. He was far more successful in his homage to *Smiles of a Summer Night. A Midsummer Night's Sex Comedy,* which also borrows from Shakespeare, Chekhov, and Renoir, features Jose Ferrer as a pompous professor—modeled on Frederick—whose young bride-to-be (Mia Farrow, in her first film with Allen) is the object of lust for two younger and more appropriate suitors, played by Woody Allen and Tony Roberts. The action unfolds over the course of a weekend at the country home of an inventor (Allen) and his lovely but sexually repressed wife (Mary Steenburgen). All six of the characters get caught in a web of romantic entanglements as they find themselves attracted to different partners.

Like *Smiles of a Summer Night, A Midsummer Night's Sex Comedy* is an enchanting period piece and a triumph of ensemble acting. Allen's comedy does not, however, achieve the precision of tone that distinguishes *Smiles of a Summer Night,* a comedy that delightfully encapsulates the human dilemma. "Shall we go or scream or stay or laugh?" Desiree asks as the action draws to its climax. In *Smiles of a Summer Night,* Bergman chose to laugh at human desire and "the pangs of the heart." His affection for "the clowns, the fools, and the unredeemable" is poetic, palpable, and profoundly amusing.

Bibliography

Adamson, Joe. *Groucho, Harpo, Chico and Sometimes Zeppo*. New York: Simon & Schuster, 1973.

Bergman, Ingmar. *Images: My Life in Film*. New York: Arcade Publishing, 1990.

Byron, Stuart, and Elisabeth Weis, eds. *The National Society of Film Critics on Movie Comedy*. New York: Grossman Publishers, 1977.

Carey, Gary. *Judy Holliday: An Intimate Life Story*. New York: Seaview Books, 1982.

Coe, Jonathan. *Jimmy Stewart: A Wonderful Life*. New York: Arcade Publishers, 1994.

Cohen, Hubert. *Ingmar Bergman: The Art of Confession*. New York: Twayne, 1993.

Curtis, James. *Between Flops: A Biography of Preston Sturges*. New York and London: Harcourt Brace Jovanovich, 1982.

Dardis, Tom. *Harold Lloyd: The Man on the Clock*. New York: Viking Press, 1983.

Dickens, Homer. *The Films of Katharine Hepburn*. Secaucus, N.J.: Citadel Press, 1990.

Edwards, Larry. *Buster: A Legend in Laughter*. Bradenton, Fla.: McGuinn & McGuire, 1995.

Evans, Peter. *Peter Sellers: The Mask Behind the Mask*. Englewood Cliffs, N.J.: Prentice-Hall, 1968.

Everson, William. *American Silent Film*. New York: Oxford University Press, 1978.

_____. *The Art of W. C. Fields*. Indianapolis/Kansas City/New York: Bobbs-Merrill Company, 1967.

Eyles, Allen. *The Complete Films of the Marx Brothers*. Secaucus, N.J.: Citadel Press, 1992.

Gehring, Wes D. *American Dark Comedy: Beyond Satire*. Westport, Conn.: Greenwood Press, 1996.

_____. *The Marx Brothers: A Bio-Bibliography*. New York: Greenwood Press, 1987.

_____. *Personality Comedians as Genre*. Westport, Conn.: Greenwood Press, 1997.

_____. *Screwball Comedy: A Genre of Madcap Romance*. New York: Greenwood Press, 1986.

Goldblatt, Burt, and Paul Zimmerman. *The Marx Brothers at the Movies*. New York: G. P. Putnam's Sons, 1968.

Gottfried, Martin. *Nobody's Fool: The Lives of Danny Kaye*. New York: Simon & Schuster, 1994.

Harris, Thomas. *Bogdanovich's Picture Shows*. Metuchen, N.J.: The Scarecrow Press, 1990.

Harvey, James. *Romantic Comedy in Hollywood, from Lubitsch to Sturges*. New York: Alfred A. Knopf, 1987.

Jacobs, Diane. *Christmas in July: The Life and Art of Preston Sturges*. Berkeley: University of California Press, 1992.

Jenkins, Henry, and Kristine Brunovska Karnick. *Classical Hollywood Comedy*. New York: Routledge, 1995.

Kagan, Norman. *American Skeptic: Robert Altman's Genre-Commentary Films*. Ann Arbor, Mich.: Pierian Press, 1982.

Kamin, Dan. *Charlie Chaplin's One Man Show*. Metuchen, N.J.: The Scarecrow Press, 1984.

Karp, Alan. *The Films of Robert Altman*. Metuchen, N.J.: The Scarecrow Press, 1981.

Kendall, Elizabeth. *Hollywood Romantic Comedy of the 1930s*. New York: Alfred A. Knopf, 1990.

Kerr, Walter. *The Silent Clowns*. New York: Knopf, 1975.

Kline, Jim. *The Complete Films of Buster Keaton*. Secaucus, N.J.: Citadel Press, 1993.

Konas, Gary, ed. *Neil Simon: A Casebook*. New York: Garland Publishing, 1997.

Kramer, Stanley, with Thomas M. Coffey. *A Mad, Mad, Mad, Mad World: A Life in Hollywood*. New York: Harcourt Brace & Co., 1997.

Krutnik, Frank, and Steve Neale. *Popular Film and Television Comedy*. New York: Routledge, 1990.

Lally, Kevin. *Wilder Times: The Life of Billy Wilder*. New York: Henry Holt & Company, 1996.

Levy, Emanuel. *George Cukor: Master of Elegance*. New York: William Morrow & Company, 1994.

Levy, Shawn. *King of Comedy: The Life and Art of Jerry Lewis*. New York: St. Martin's Press, 1996.

Long, Robert Emmet. *Ingmar Bergman: Film and Stage*. New York: Harry N. Abrams, Inc., 1994.

Maddock, Brent. *The Films of Jacques Tati*. Metuchen, N.J.: The Scarecrow Press, 1977.

Madsen, Axel. *Stanwyck*. New York: HarperCollins, 1994.

Maland, Charles. *Frank Capra*. Boston: Twayne Publishers, 1980.

Mast, Gerald. *The Comic Mind: Comedy and the Movies*. Chicago and London: University of Chicago Press, 1973.

McBride, Joseph. *Frank Capra: The Catastrophe of Success*. New York: Simon & Schuster, 1992.

McCafferty, Donald. *Assault on Society: Satirical Literature to Film*. Metuchen, N.J.: Scarecrow Press, 1992.

McCarthy, Todd. *Howard Hawks: The Grey Fox of Hollywood*. New York: Grove Press, 1997.

McGilligan, Patrick. *George Cukor: A Double Life*. New York: St. Martin's Press, 1991.

McGovern, Edythe. *Neil Simon: A Critical Study*. New York: Frederick Ungar Publishing, 1978.

Meade, Marion. *Buster Keaton: Cut to the Chase*. New York: HarperCollins, 1995.

Nelson, Thomas Allen. *Kubrick: Inside a Film Artist's Maze*. Bloomington: Indiana University Press, 1982.

Paul, William. *Ernst Lubitsch's American Comedy*. New York: Columbia University Press, 1983.

Phillips, Gene. *George Cukor*. Boston: Twayne Publishers, 1982.

Plecki, Gerard. *Robert Altman*. Boston: Twayne Publishers,1985.

Radovich, Don. *Tony Richardson: A Bio-Bibliography*. Westport, Conn.: Greenwood Press, 1995.

Richardson, Tony. *The Long-Distance Runner: An Autobiography*. New York: William Morrow, 1993.

Robinson, David. *Chaplin: His Life and Art*. New York: Da Capo Press, 1994.

Rozgonyi, Jay. *Preston Sturges's Vision of America*. Jefferson, N.C.: McFarland & Co., 1960.

Scagnetti, Jack. *The Laurel & Hardy Scrapbook*. Middle Village, N.Y.: Jonathan David Publishers, 1976.

Schickel, Richard. *Cary Grant: A Celebration*. Boston: Little, Brown and Company, 1983.

_____. *Harold Lloyd: The Shape of Laughter*. Boston: New York Graphic Society, 1974.

Sennett, Ted. *Laughing in the Dark: Movie Comedy from Groucho to Woody*. New York: St. Martin's Press, 1992.

_____. *Lunatics and Lovers: A Tribute to the Giddy and Glittering Era of the Screen's Screwball and Romantic Comedies*. New York: Limelight Editions, 1985.

Siegel, Scott and Barbara. *American Film Comedy*. New York: Prentice-Hall, 1994.

Sikov, Ed. *Laughing Hysterically: American Screen Comedy of the 1950s*. New York: Columbia University Press, 1994.

Simon, Neil. *Rewrites: A Memoir*. New York: Simon & Schuster, 1996.

Skretvedt, Randy. *Laurel and Hardy: The Magic Behind the Movies*. Beverly Hills, Calif.: Moonstone Press, 1987.

Smith, Julian. *Chaplin*. Boston: Twayne Publishers, 1984.

Starr, Michael. *Peter Sellers: A Film History*. Jefferson, N.C.: McFarland & Co., 1991.

Sturges, Preston. *Preston Sturges*. New York: Simon & Schuster, 1990.

Taylor, Robert Lewis. *W. C. Fields: His Follies and Fortunes*. New York: St. Martin's Press, 1967.

Trescott, Pamela. *Cary Grant: His Movies and Life*. Washington, D.C.: Acropolis Books, 1987.

Walker, Alexander. *Stanley Kubrick Directs*. New York: Harcourt Brace Jovanovich, 1971.

Weales, Charles. *Canned Goods as Caviar: American Film Comedy of the 1930s*. Chicago and London: University of Chicago Press, 1985.

Winokur, Mark. *American Laughter: Immigrants, Ethnicity and 1930s Hollywood Film Comedy*. New York: St. Martin's Press, 1996.

Index